HOW NOT TO BE A
MESSIE

The Ultimate Guide for the Neatness-Challenged

Two Bestselling Books
Complete in One Volume

The Messies Manual · The Messie Motivator

SANDRA FELTON

GALAHAD BOOKS
NEW YORK

CONTENTS

THE MESSIES MANUAL

The Procrastinator's Guide To Good Housekeeping

To my mother, Seco Haley, whose example kept me striving for a better way of life when it was difficult to remember that another way of life existed.

Contents

I just love the story of Cinderella, don't you? One day Cinderella is living by an unpleasant fireplace dressed in tatters, getting dirty, working hard, never getting out for fun, and receiving no reward for all her effort. She was sad and frustrated. (Does it sound a little like your life?)

But the next day she is found by the prince, whisked off to the palace, and lives as a princess in a beautiful castle, never needing to turn her hand to clean house. And she lives happily ever after.

And who brings about this wonderful transformation? Why, it is her fairy godmother, of course!

For years I waited for my fairy godmother to come and wave her magic wand over me and magically change my hovel into a castle—and my frustration into joy.

But she never came.

There *is* magic to be found, but I was looking in the wrong place for it. The program you are about to begin will work its magic on you. You are about to enter the world of the Messie and the Cleanie. You will learn about the Mount Vernon Method, the Flipper System, and other secrets of housekeeping. Each chapter contains a little magic dust, and when you are finished you will be prepared to become that princess you dream of becoming.

But *you* must wave the wand. *You* must sprinkle the magic dust. And I know you will, because I know you won't settle for that stool in the cinders once you know that there is a castle waiting for you and that there is hope of finding it.

I want your home to be a castle, full of beauty and dignity. I want you to be a princess in your own home.

"Oh, no," you protest, "I'm not reading this book to get some kind of magic. I just want to be able to find my shoes, get the piles off the tables, and get my kids off to school with matching socks. I live a practical, mundane life. I just want to survive. I have no time or patience for fairy tales or dreams."

Maybe so. I know you would be satisfied if the house were just under control. This is a very practical book. You will be able to find that order you want.

But maybe, just maybe, after things begin to clear, somewhere in your house you'll find the corner of the castle.

God bless you, Princess.

Introducing
(AS IF YOU NEED IT!)
The Messie

We all know them. They are the people who never seem to get control of their housework and their time, the type who need all day to accomplish nothing. They live in dread of opening a closet door, for fear they will be buried under an avalanche of canned goods, flashlight batteries, tissue boxes, and stockings with only one run that might come in handy someday for something. (Well, you never know.)

A casual visitor to the home of such a person would be in constant danger of tripping over roller skates, knocking piles of paper to the floor, and stepping on a ten-year-old's pet frog.

But a casual visitor is not likely to get into this person's home. She won't even invite her best friend — not with the house in such a mess.

This type of housekeeper—if that is not too strong a term for a person whose house appears to keep her—has a name. She is known as a "Messie."

If you are reading this book, chances are you know her very well indeed, because she is you. Furthermore, you are tired of it. You are ready to take command of your house and your life—if only you can figure out how.

11

Perhaps, until now, you have felt yourself to be alone. You thought no other person could possibly have a house that looks as if a tornado has just struck it. And you have not wanted to talk about it, not wanted to do anything that might reveal your secret shame to the world.

Intelligence is the quickness in seeing things as they are.

GEORGE SANTAYANA

Well, take heart, because you are very far from being in a class by yourself. Millions of women—men, too—share your problem. And it's curable, or at least controllable.

I know. For many years I went through the same agonies you face, always searching for the answer to this terrible embarrassment. Finally, by studying my friends whose houses seemed always to be in order, I discovered some principles that I was able to apply to my own life and home.

The results were gratifying—so gratifying that I began to believe these principles might be of use to other struggling housekeepers. So I established the "Messies Anonymous" seminars to teach others what I had learned. To date, hundreds of housekeepers have attended these classes. Many have reported that what they learned has changed their lives for the better.

Literally dozens of these people have asked whether I would write a book that set forth the Messies Anonymous principles in greater detail. To help these people, as well as to reach others who may not be able to get to the seminars, I have written just such a book, and this is it.

May it be the beginning of a new, happier way of life for you.

Help!
House Out Of Control!

PART ONE

What's Your M.Q.*?
*(MESSIES QUOTIENT)

To cure anything—a disease, a stutter, an ingrown toenail—you first have to *classify* it. Try this short test:

YES NO

☐ ☐ Are all the spoons in your kitchen drawer neatly nested up to one another, while all the pots in the house sit in the sink and sulk? *See* The Perfectionist Messie.

☐ ☐ Did your mother have a "thing" about emptying bathroom wastebaskets? Is yours overflowing into the shower stall? *See* The Rebellious Messie.

☐ ☐ Would you love to come home and read the evening paper? Are there six papers currently residing by your favorite chair? *See* The Relaxed Messie.

☐ ☐ Are you still finding your teenager's baby teeth in the corners of the drawer in your bedside table? *See* The Sentimental Messie.

☐ ☐ How long ago did you toss out your ironing board? *See* The Spartan Messie.

☐ ☐ After your dress comes back from the cleaner's, how long does it hang on the back of the kitchen door? *See* The Clean Messie.

☐ ☐ Is it true that a gritty bathtub is less slippery than a sparkling one? *See* The Safe Messie.

☐ ☐ Do you truly believe there is something sinful in serving children a pie from the supermarket? *See* The Old-Fashioned Messie.

☐ ☐ Have you figured out a simple solution to worldwide hunger, while your six-year-old learned to make toast in self-defense? *See* The Idealistic Messie.

1

Messies Classified

The
Perfectionist
A. Messie

The
Rebellious
B. Messie

The
Relaxed
C. Messie

The
Sentimental
D. Messie

The
Spartan
E. Messie

The
Clean
F. Messie

The
Safe
G. Messie

The Old-
Fashioned
H. Messie

The
Idealistic
I. Messie

Messies have one thing in common: On a scale of 0 to 10, on which 0 is disaster and 10 is perfection, their housekeeping falls into the 1–3 range.

This, of course, makes them the opposites of the housekeepers we know as "Cleanies," whose efforts are rewarded with a rating in the 7–10 range. It also sets them apart from average housekeepers — those whose homes fall into disarray on occasion, but not often and not for long, and who therefore merit a 4–6 rating.

Aside from their abysmally low housekeeping rating, Messies have little in common. They got to be where they are by different roads, and they have different styles of messiness.

Let us, therefore, take a look at different types of Messies. If you can recognize yourself in one of these word portraits, you will be well on the way to finding a solution to your problem.

The Perfectionist Messie

This person has very high standards for individual jobs. The house may be a wreck, but she decides to begin by cleaning the oven. And it is well done, *very* well done.

If you say, "No one sees the inside of the oven," she takes pride in saying, "But *I* know it is clean." In the meantime, the whole picture deteriorates.

Here, indecisiveness is cloaked in the guise of perfectionism. Generally this housekeeper cannot decide which approach to putting the house in order would be best. So she decides not to decide. This is a bad decision.

The Rebellious Messie

This Messie has psychological hang-ups from childhood. Mom insisted on cleanliness and order, and now that she is grown, she is going to show independence by defiance.

The tragedy, of course, is that we are adults now and it is a shame to let infantile reactions ruin our own lives and those of our families.

I heard a middle-aged woman say she had procrastinated for years about hanging a mirror even though it was in her way on the floor. The reason she didn't hang it was because the sight of the unhung mirror annoyed her mother, and she derived pleasure from the annoyance it caused. I guess she is showing Mom that Mom can't make her do it. But she is paying a high price for trying to show how grown-up she is.

The Relaxed Messie

This person rationalizes that the world outside is hostile and home is the place to relax. Why work at home, too?

So things are let go. The result is that when the rationalizer comes home from that high-pressure job, she faces a hostile house. Things assault the eye and clutter life.

How nice it would be to come home to a beautiful, inviting home that says, "Welcome," and invites us to relax! The truth, as any Messie can tell you, is that messiness is not relaxing. It causes strain, pressure, and jangled nerves.

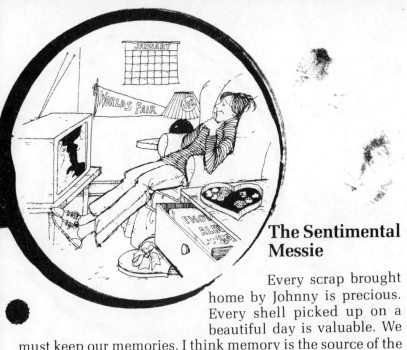

The Sentimental Messie

Every scrap brought home by Johnny is precious. Every shell picked up on a beautiful day is valuable. We must keep our memories. I think memory is the source of the problem here. Some of us Messies have poor memories, so these things are the only way we can remember. When we throw them out, our memories actually *are* gone. In such cases, I suggest a memory journal. Write down the day's activities, especially the nice ones. These pages will be invaluable not only to you, but to your children and grandchildren.

Token remembrances also can be kept, of course, in easy-to-store, labeled plastic shoe boxes. But remember, keep only *token* items—not everything!

The sentimental Messie is also a picture-taking Messie. Pictures are another aid to a poor memory. Sometimes we don't even have to have them developed. We just like to know they are available for some time when we might get them developed.

So in virtually every drawer in the house, undeveloped film can be found. One woman said she had her film developed so late that she did not recognize the people standing with her in the picture.

The Spartan Messie

This is a special approach to the difficulties of house-keeping. The ancient Spartans lived with only the necessities of life. Similarly, it may occur to a Messie that if there were less to care for, or if it were somehow shut up or nailed down and not used, it would be possible to handle it.

The next step is to see what can be eliminated: "Let's see, I could always have one-pot dinners so I would have just one pot to wash. I could have one set of sheets so I'd just have to wash them and put them back on the bed, which would eliminate folding them or having them lie around in a basket. Or better still, I could make up the bed and sleep on top of the spread. That would eliminate washing sheets *and* bed making. I could clean up some of the other rooms and not use them anymore, just put a velvet rope across each door."

And so, to some degree or another, they cut out the things they have to handle. As a rule they don't actually get rid of them, they just exclude them from their care.

The Clean Messie

As long as things are clean, such Messies reason, they can be left out. This is the reason clean clothes are left in the basket and not folded. (After all, they *are* clean, and that's the main thing.) The dishes are washed and left out on the counter. But they *are* clean. Isn't that what counts?

The Safe Messie

This Messie leaves the bed unmade, "because it can air out better, and that kills more germs." The floors are not waxed, "because they might be slippery and danger-ous." The dishes are not dried by hand, "because the germs from the dishcloth might get on the dishes. Air drying is more sanitary."

And finally, "I can't have a maid, because she might have a boyfriend who is a thief, and I'll be robbed." One cannot be too careful, after all.

The trouble with all these ways of thinking is that they tie us up and reduce our options for keeping the house the way we want it.

The Old-Fashioned Messie

For some reason, there are people who just enjoy doing things the old-fashioned way. For them, the only good way is the old way. This is a definite matter of principle—though it is hard to know what the reason is.

This might mean our Old-Fashioned Messie will have as a principle that the only way to do the floor is on her hands and knees with a brush. Now actually, the floor never gets done that way because it is too much work. But believe me, if it ever did get done, it would be done *right*. Their motto is "Do it right—or not at all." A lot of time it turns out "not at all."

Some other ideas the Old-Fashioned Messie may have are to bake pies and cakes from scratch instead of using a mix, to wax and buff the wooden floor with a cloth instead of a buffer, to beat the rug instead of vacuuming, or use cloth instead of disposable diapers. It's not that some of these things aren't appropriate sometimes, but to do things the hard way just because it is an old-fashioned way is a hindrance to progress in housekeeping.

The Idealistic Messie

This person's head is in the clouds. Great thoughts and ideas are what interest this Messie.

But the results are disastrous to an idealist. The beauty and charm, the satisfying family life, all melt under the heat of the messy home. The idealist, attuned to greater things, seldom notices the relationship between the messy house and the fading dreams.

In short, no matter what type of Messie you are, it's an unsatisfying life.

2

Confessions of a Reformed Messie

Compared to what we ought to be and can be, we are only half awake.
WILLIAM JAMES

My mother was a Cleanie. What a marvelous thing it was in those days of my youth always to have a clean, beautiful house to come home to!

Keeping house seemed to come naturally to her. My drawers were always neat, my room in order. I functioned in the order she created. And she did try to train me, her only daughter. What a discouragement it must have been for her! I took to housekeeping like a cat to water.

We had spells when she did her best to get me in the groove and other spells when she gave up and found it was easier to do it herself. In the meantime, I had other things of greater consequence to do.

In high school there was school work. To me, studying was heady stuff. I worked on developing writing skills by turning out short stories and poetry. I took art lessons after school and was tutored privately in French.

Who in the world cared if there was dust on the table legs with art and philosophy hovering so excitingly close? Then came college, a career as a junior high school math teacher, and marriage to a minister. Then I was on my own with a house to keep.

That's when I first noticed something seriously amiss. I found that the well-kept look, which had seemed to come effortlessly to my mother, didn't come to me at all.

At first I blamed the houses. The first one was too little. The next one was too big. I was sure there was just some small adjustment I needed to make in my situation and things would be all right. I was still busy with other, more important things. My husband was pastoring churches, and I was involved in his work. The children came, and I reacted to the housework. But I never controlled it.

Newton's second law of thermodynamics states that anything, left to itself, tends toward disorganization. This is especially true with houses. Felton's law is that "Any house left to keep itself tends to disaster." Murphy's law applied to housekeeping is, "Any mess that *can* happen, will."

It's tough being a Messie and a minister's wife. People like to drop around, especially if you are living in the parsonage right next door to the church.

Ivan's first church was in the northern Indiana farm region. Of Southern stock, I had grown up in Tennessee with its real or imagined tradition of frail womanhood.

These Indiana women were heartier than I was. They never even considered the concept of a "lady of leisure."

I once heard a parishioner talk about having done her spring cleaning. I was amazed that as part of it she had varnished the window sills with marine varnish. Most of our parishioners sewed, canned, had gardens, ran tractors, did church work, and kept neat homes, while I just wandered around trying to keep my head above water wondering what was wrong.

These women were gracious and never mentioned the gap between my abilities and theirs, which I felt so keenly. The worst part was that I could not figure out why they were succeeding and I was not.

In those days, as a young mother, I was able to tell myself that there was a *reason* for my poor housekeeping. More babies came, giving me further reasons. I was feeling better about my messiness now that I had collected so many good reasons. A really good excuse is a valuable thing. Several good excuses are a treasure.

The excuses satisfied my mind somewhat, but the soul is not so easily quieted. The frustration of not being able to find things, the embarrassment of having company drop in without warning, the hard work that never gets anywhere—there is no way to make these things somehow all right. They sap the joy from life.

It's really tough being a Messie.

excuse ik-'skyüs n. A perfectly reasonable explanation for the fact that your husband can't find the monthly bills ... or the checkbook ... or one pen that hasn't gone dry because someone left the top off for two weeks.

FELTON'S LAW: "Any Mess That Can Happen, *Will.*"

3

There Is a Reason— It Is Not Laziness

There is occasions and causes why and wherefore in all things.
WILLIAM SHAKESPEARE

Messies are generally wonderful people. Just between you and me, I think they are a cut above the average. They are creative, intelligent, nice people. My mother once answered a hundred calls making reservations for a class I was giving. She said it seemed to her that Messies were the nicest people in the world. One of the pleasures of having the class is meeting such interesting folks.

Messies are optimistic. Not many people could keep on going in the face of such discouragement and still hold on to such good humor. Fatigue and frustration take their toll at times, but somehow Messies keep going, looking for a better day.

If Messies are so wonderful, why, then, do they live "that way"? The reason is that housekeeping, though it seems to be a natural skill, is really a complex grouping of small, learned skills. If we are weak in one or several of these skills, we can run into all kinds of trouble in housecleaning and never know why. It is like someone who is color blind but not aware of it trying to make a career as an interior decorator: he or she would be gravely handicapped.

31

"Why are you late for dinner? I left you behind at the supermarket—again?"

Poor Memory

"What petrified meatloaf in the oven?"

Distractibility

"Your briefcase? I put it in a safe place. Well, I must have *thought* the laundry hamper was safe!"

Disorganized Thinking

"What do you mean, you need a guide dog to navigate this room?"

Visual Tune-out

"Socks? I'd have them sorted, but do you realize everyone in this family wears the same white socks?"

Slow Movement

Most Messies are "handicapped" by several factors. One characteristic common to Messies is absentmindedness. We seem to have difficulty remembering the simplest things.

Poor Memory

I have a terrible memory, but it used to be worse! I frequently locked myself out of my car. Sometimes I would arrive at an appointment, only to discover that I had left an important piece of material behind. Worse, sometimes I forget the *appointment* itself! Once I left my purse with our entire life savings in it on a park bench. Another time I left my son at the junior high school where I teach math. I simply went home without him!

But if my memory was bad away from our house, it was equally so at home. It failed me so often that I used to be afraid to put anything in a drawer for fear I would forget where it was, or even that I had ever had it. Bills would pile up as I thought, *I'll get to them as soon as I can. I'll keep them out here so I won't forget.*

Then another item which I was afraid to put away would go on top of them, and then.... Soon there would be another "special" pile with who-knows-what in it beside the other piles of things too important to put away. The bill would be gone for good, or at least removed from the area of my influence.

Sometimes we Messies come to grips with some big cleaning project, organize the thing elaborately and well, and then forget what our organizational plan was. "Where *did* I plan to put these papers?"

"Out of sight, out of mind," is a statement of real truth where I am concerned. I cannot tell you how many times I have let the tub run over because I turned on the water, went off to do something else while it filled, and forgot the whole thing. Fortunately, we don't have wall-to-wall carpeting, wooden floors, or an apartment below us.

Forgetting where I am going, losing my keys, letting the bathtub overflow — are these patterns peculiar only to me? While absentmindedness is not limited to Messies, my guess is that it is more common among us. But why do we tend to be absentminded?

Distractibility

One reason for our absentmindedness may be that Messies tend to be easily distracted. If something grabs our attention, it is as difficult for us to ignore it as it is for a cat to ignore a mouse.

We notice a good book and begin reading it while cleaning the bookshelf. We take an item from the drawer or closet we are cleaning to put in a better storage place, but first we have to clear a place for it. Messes spring up like ant hills because of our big housecleaning project. Cleaning this way is tiring and messy, too.

If a person flits from one job to another—straightening this, clearing that—that's distractibility. Often a job is begun, the phone rings or a child interrupts, and the task is left, or worse, forgotten. An absentminded person usually cannot do two things at one time. Distractibility is akin to absent-mindedness.

One of the stories I like best is of the absentminded professor who met a student as he crossed the campus. The two stopped to talk. When they finished conversing, the professor asked the student which way he had been heading. When the student told him he had been heading toward his office he replied, "Good, then I have eaten," and continued happily on his way. Now that's absentminded!

Disorganized Thinking

Another reason Messies tend to be absentminded is that clutter muddles our minds. A messy house stimulates further distractibility in us, which results in absentmindedness, which results in more clutter. It's a downward spiral. Consider the words of a Cleanie wife who lived with a Messie husband:

"I need order like an alcoholic needs a drink or a smoker needs a cigarette. I become irritable and disconsolate without it, unable to work or even to think straight. I am miserable."

But why are some people more organized than others? Some people are born organized, and some are not...or so it seems to me. It may be due to something in the nervous system.

Studies have been done relating right- or left-handedness to organizational ability. The theory is that people who are ambidextrous (who can use either the right or the left hand) tend to be disorganized because the brain gets signals from different sources and has difficulties in establishing organizational patterns. A person who is strongly right- or left-handed keeps using the same routes in the nervous system and therefore finds it easier to do the tasks that require organization.

After I graduated from college I did a survey on how people knew their right hands from their left. The typical reply was, "You just know." This was not too useful to me because I didn't "just know." If, therefore, you are not quick to tell one hand from another, you might be consoled—a little—to know that your inability to organize is not so much your fault as your nervous system's. It is good for batters in baseball and for sculptors to be ambidextrous—but it is bad for organizers.

Visual Tune-out

This has nothing to do with being unable to see. It does have to do with having what you see register. Some of us are not very quick on the visual uptake. When my family passes an accident scene, my husband and children see many more details than I do: "Did you notice the woman in the front seat of the blue car and the woman and little boy beside the station wagon?"

I am doing well if I notice the cars. Given enough time, I would pick out the details, but it doesn't come quickly or easily as we drive by.

Now apply this idea of visual sensitivity to housekeeping. Cleanies are visually alert. They want to see clear, clean, uncluttered lines. If they finish a cup of coffee and don't want another one, the cup is gone, swooped up to the kitchen and sometimes washed, rinsed, and put away in order to maintain the clean lines of orderliness. A Cleanie friend once told me she wished she *could* tune-out a fluff of thread on the carpet—but she *had* to pick it up, no matter how tired she was.

A Messie, on the other hand, can tolerate a great deal of clutter simply because she is not sensitive to visual things. An educator would say the difficulty is a lack of response to visual stimuli due to a figure-ground problem. No matter what others call it, when company comes to the door unexpectedly, we call it embarrassed.

35

Slow Movement

This usually isn't because of slow muscle movement. Some jobs take a long time to figure out.

Sorting laundry is the worst for me. There are five people in my family. After my eyes send a message to my brain telling me what they see, my brain has to figure out two things: whose piece of clothing it is and which of the piles in front of me belongs to each respective person.

Every piece of clothing requires this process. All that thinking can wear a person out, especially if the piles to be sorted become too large. I've discovered that I can save energy by sorting the laundry while the piles are small and manageable. I also put the piles in the order of the ages of family members. Then I don't have to figure where each pile is.

That speeds things up a lot. However, I have seen folks sort laundry zip, zip, zip—and they don't even seem to be thinking. The point is that if a person processes information slowly he is not going to be able to work as fast as others who do not have the same difficulty, and this can make house-keeping slow and fatiguing.

Sometimes, too, the idea of doing a job perfectly slows a person down. The job has to be so good that as a result, one little corner of the house is clean while the rest is still cluttered.

If you have one of these problems, or all of them, can you still hope to take charge of your house and your time? Yes, you can! I know, because I have done it.

To get some clues as to how this is possible, let's take a look at some Cleanies I have known and what we can learn from them.

4

Cleanies
I Have Known

These I have loved: white plates and cups, clean—gleaming.

RUPERT BROOKE

Unlike Messies, Cleanies have mental schedules they themselves are not aware of. Their minds are like computers going down their list of things to do.

The power that activates the computer is in the eyes. Again and again they say, "When I see..." or "If it looks dirty, I...."

Their goals are visual, and they become uncomfortable if something is out of place. Cleanies are not afraid to use shortcuts because they are confident in their own cleaning ability and don't feel it necessary to prove anything by doing things the hard way.

They tend to get up with a bang and get going with purpose. They frequently have a time goal in mind and work fast to meet it. You might think they are uptight people. They don't seem to be. In fact, they often are gracious, warm, and creative. They can afford to be because they have enough time to do whatever they want to do!

These are general statements, of course. Let's meet some of these paragons individually, to see if we can learn to do as they do.

One thing my Cleanie friends have in common is that they don't understand. They don't understand at all. I can always tell true Cleanies by the way they react when they hear that I teach a class on housekeeping. They look blank—very blank.

"Oh, it is a class on cooking."

"No, housekeeping."

"Oh, I see, a class on interior decorating."

"No, actually it's *housekeeping.*"

"Oh."

Silence. How can you continue discussing the inconceivable? Why would anybody need a class on housekeeping?

One blank-faced woman told me soberly that if I did have a class on housekeeping nobody would come. Since I had been having well-attended classes, I asked her why she thought nobody would come.

"Obviously if people have messy houses it is because they want them that way. And, if they want them that way, why would they attend the class? So nobody will come."

If Cleanies only knew how we struggle! But housekeeping comes so naturally to them that they don't understand at all.

It follows that the best way to learn from Cleanies is to meet some of them and watch them in action. And that is precisely what we are going to do now.

Carmen

Carmen works full-time in the import-export business. She is a widow and has a daughter eleven years old.

Going to her small condominium is refreshing. It is beige in color for warmth, but shining and cool to the touch. She has a floor of Italian tile and a lot of glass on tables and shelves. Vertical blinds regulate the light.

She herself radiates style. Most of her wardrobe is beige and black so that she can mix and match freely. Accent colors bring variety to her look.

Carmen has developed several tricks to keep her house beautiful without working at it. She freely admits that she dislikes housework and has better things to do. So she plans not to do it.

When her husband was alive he used to put the white pillows from the couch on the floor to watch TV. When she bought a new couch she bought one with attached pillows so that she would not even have to say anything to him about not putting the pillows on the floor.

Carmen also had a counter top that stuck out beyond the wall which divided the living room and kitchen. It fairly begged people to stick something on it as they passed. So they obliged.

Carmen didn't want to have to hassle people about this, so she had her husband extend the wall so the counter was not exposed and tempting. When she bought shelves for her living room, she bought the kind with glass in front so she would not have to dust as frequently.

Since Carmen's condominium is small, she does not have a dirty clothes hamper. Instead, she folds dirty clothes and puts them in a decorative chest at the foot of her bed.

Carmen uses "little minutes." She never cleans cabinets. When the cabinets are nearly empty, she wipes them out. When the refrigerator is nearly empty, she gives it a quick cleaning. When she puts her clean, folded laundry into the drawer, she gives the drawer a quick straightening. So there is no need for a cleaning marathon. She used to have a dog, but deliberately hasn't replaced it since it died. She is finished and ready to go at 9:00 or 9:30—A.M. that is!

Joyce

Joyce is a former 10. She used to pull her refrigerator out from the wall weekly and clean behind it. Now she is more relaxed and cruises at a comfortable 8 or 9. Joyce, an artist, is also a collector of trinkets. I do not recommend the trinkets. They are nothing but trouble when it comes to cleaning.

Joyce is married and has an eight-year-old boy, a long-haired dog, and two cats. She works at home full-time as a wife and mother.

If you ask Joyce whether she has a schedule she will say, "No," and then add, "but of course, I do the kitchen floor on Mondays. I don't have to, but I usually do. And I change sheets on Friday." And on and on it goes.

Joyce keeps a more casual schedule than Carmen and is finished about noon. When I say finished, I mean finished!

Then she is ready for painting. So she paints for a while, watches television, puts away the paints, cooks dinner, and welcomes her family home. It sounds so easy, doesn't it? But I remember days of full-time homemaking when I had the same amount of time and *never* finished.

How does she do it? The key can be found if we listen to what Joyce says: "When I *see* dog hairs, I go over the floor with a dust mop." "I put the paints away because I don't like to *see* them left out. It looks cluttered." "I think it *looks* nicer when the clothes are all put away." Cleanies are very visually oriented and want the house to look pleasant.

Joyce also uses little minutes shining the bathroom mirror with a dry bath towel each day after she brushes her teeth.

Marcella

Marcella had a lot of trouble telling what schedule she kept. One thing she did know, she was usually finished by 9:00 or 9:30 A.M.

Marcella is married, has two children, aged six years and five months, and baby-sits for a one-year-old. She also has a short-haired dog.

Her main principle is to keep her house in order so that she never has to do a big cleaning job. She gets up at 5:30 or 6:00 A.M. to feed the baby. She gets her six-year-old, Ginny, up at 7:00 A.M. to leave for school at 8:00.

Ginny is ready by 7:30 and plays with the baby until 8:00. Then the baby is ready for a nap, and Ginny is ready to go to school. From 7:30 to 9:00 or 9:30, Marcella does all of her cleaning.

At 7:30 she cleans the kitchen, does the dishes (no dishwasher), vacuums and mops the kitchen floor, and wipes the counter. Then she makes the two beds (five minutes), wipes down the bathroom (ten minutes), and does a few other chores.

Tuesday and Thursday are her free days when she is finished by 8:00 or 8:30. Monday and Friday are heavy days, on which Marcella works until 9:30, because they are at the beginning and end of the week. Wednesday is a moderate day when she does a little catching up for the middle of the week.

What does she do on the heavy days? She vacuums two bedrooms, one bath, and the den, then dusts the furniture and goes over it with window cleaner. Every day while she does the cleaning, she puts in two loads of laundry to wash, dry, and fold so that everything is done at the same time, and she doesn't have to worry about housecleaning for the rest of the day. She wants to be free for whatever comes up that day, whether it be business or pleasure.

How does she maintain the house during the day? She puts things away at once.

What does she do the rest of the day? She visits with friends who have children so the children can play together, goes to a painting class, and cares for personal needs such as nails and hair washing.

Of course, Cleanies' tricks of organization don't come naturally to us Messies — that's our problem. Nevertheless, with some thought, we can develop devices that will help us keep our homes as orderly as those of our Cleanie friends. (Well, nearly!)

First of all, though, let's take a look at some of the attitudes that get in our way.

Once upon a midnight
        dreary,
There I stood, my eyes all
        bleary.
'Mid coffee cup and Twinkie
        wrapper—
How I yearned to be a
        midnight napper!

But once upon a morning
        bright,
I'd vowed to clean before the
        night.
Though ambition fled before
        the noon,
I still refused to change my
        tune.

Once upon a dawn less
        dreary,
My whole house shone,
        spotless and cheery.
And though no one would
        know but I,
I claimed a victory with my
        sigh...

...and woke the kids for
        breakfast.

5 | Outlooks That Hinder

We has met the enemy, und he is us.
WALT KELLY (Pogo)

The mind is the key to what we do. Sometimes we slip into a pattern of thinking that hinders us from making progress, and we never realize that while our wills are saying, *Go, go,* our minds are saying, *No, no.* So we end up failing because we are harboring pet ideas that keep us from going forward. We have to be willing to make some changes in the way we think if we are ever going to make permanent changes in our houses. In this chapter are attitudes that need to be dealt with if we are going to succeed. These may include some of the outlooks you, personally, will need to change.

Task-Orientation

People who say, "I've got all day to vacuum the rug," are indicating that they are going through the motions of housekeeping and doing the job just to get it done, not because it is an important part of a larger picture. As long as we look at housekeeping as a group of isolated tasks lined up in order to be done, we can put them off because there is no reason to do them except to get them off the list.

The solution is goal-orientation rather than task-orientation. We

43

should never lose sight of our overall goal, which in this case is an orderly house. When we see our work in terms of this goal, individual tasks become a means to an end.

Let's look at it this way: Suppose two people are given two different jigsaw puzzles. The puzzles are identical except that one has a beautiful picture on it that cannot be seen or enjoyed until it is assembled, while the other one has no picture, only gray pieces. If you ask the first person what he is doing he will say, "I am making a beautiful picture." If you ask the second person he will say, "I am fitting together one piece after another. After a while I will have each piece fitted in." The first person is goal-oriented, the second is task-oriented.

A person who is task-oriented can wait all day to vacuum the rug, as long as it does get vacuumed that day. A person who is goal-oriented, however, won't wait all day since his goal is to maintain a nice-looking house at all times, and a dirty rug will short-circuit that goal.

Practicality

Why put the toothpaste away if you are going to get it out again in a few hours? Why make the bed just to unmake it that evening? Is it practical to wash a few dishes? Why not wait till you have a whole sink full and do them all at once? These ideas *are* practical, but they delay your reaching your goal—a beautiful house.

The Myth of Creative Disorganization

Everybody knows creative and intelligent people can be very disorganized. Some creative people are deliberately disorganized. Have you ever seen the sign on a desk that says, "A neat desk is a sign of a sick mind"? This is some disorganized creative person taking the offensive.

Frequently, however, this clutter interferes with the fullest use of the creative gift. Imagine the writer who can't find his paper or research material, or the artist who misplaces supplies. Looking for things saps the creative process.

Losing things is a sign of disorganization. A book called *The Borrowers* attempts to explain how items just "disappear." This book tells of little people who live under the floorboards and behind the baseboards of houses and "borrow" things. *That's* why they disappear.

A lot of these little people used to live at my house. However, they must not like living in organized houses, because since I organized mine they seem to have moved out.

Idea-Orientation

Messies are intelligent people on the whole. We have high ideals and a worldwide perspective.

World hunger, dedication to the children and youth of our nation, art, music, literature, careers — these are areas that deserve our time. Dusting, moving a dish from one place to another—how can such things be important in the light of such weighty pursuits? They seem insignificant by comparison.

The trouble is that if we are disorganized at home we can lose our chance to do something about the problems we consider more important. How can we finish our book if we can't find the first six chapters of it? How can we organize a drive to ease world hunger if we can't locate the addresses of the people and organizations we need to help us?

Psychological Hang-ups

Because Messies are born with a problem when it comes to organization, housekeeping has frequently been a problem from childhood. If Mother is a Cleanie, the situation can be frustrating for both Mother and child. Mother can't understand why the job she gives her child is so poorly done or only half-completed.

The child, on the other hand, may think she has done it well, or she may have been distracted by something else and forgotten that the job was not completed.

Mom becomes frustrated and sees this as evidence of an uncooperative spirit. The child may be surprised to learn that the job is poorly done; she cannot understand why Mom is so upset. She becomes resentful at what seems to her to be unjust criticism.

So housekeeping becomes associated with unpleasantness early in life. It is only a short step from here to the idea that housekeeping causes frustration and should be avoided. After all, if you don't try it, you can't fail.

Depression or Emotional Upset

One of my worst periods of housekeeping was at a time when I was going through a trying emotional experience in another part of my life. I felt as if I were walking in molasses; things just didn't get done. Whatever a person's weakness is, it gets worse during such times. My bad housekeeping became my terrible housekeeping.

I don't believe I would have been able to respond to help in organizing my house during that time, even if help had been given. I had to wait until the psychological problem righted itself before my housekeeping returned to merely "bad."

Frequently, however, the housekeeping actually causes the depression. The feeling of being out of control and the problems caused by poor housekeeping can lead to such despondency that housework is further neglected, and a destructive downward spiral begins.

Sometimes this is accelerated if some overwhelming event occurs. A flood, hurricane, earthquake, or some natural disaster which further messes up the house can easily destroy all hope of ever getting control.

A less traumatic event, such as your mother moving, with her furniture, into your already crowded house; the moving of furnishings from an office which has been closed into your place for storage because there is no other place to keep them; the starting of a home business requiring storage of some items—any of these may bring about the breaking point.

If housekeeping is causing you depression, the only way I know to overcome it is to start to reverse the downward spiral by taking control of things. It is not easy to begin; but one success, however small, will lead to another, and slowly a pattern of success will emerge. Remember, it took you a long time to get into this situation, and it will take a while to get out. The important thing is to be heading in the right direction. You are allowed to get discouraged occasionally, but not to give up.

Always remember, too—you don't have to aim for perfection. In fact, as you will see in the next chapter, a too perfect house can be as bad as one that is chaotic.

6

You Don't *Really* Want to Be a 10

Extremes are always bad. Once in a while you hear about people who have been found dead in their homes because some trash has fallen on them as they walked through the passageways left by their walls of junk. Such a person is a 0 on the Cleanie scale. No 0's would come to a Messies Anonymous seminar or read this book.

Once, when Messies Anonymous had just begun, we had a ½ come to the seminar. He had disposed of his kitchen appliances so he would have room for more items. He had shelves lining his walls and set up in the middle of his rooms, library style. They held all of his many collections.

He subscribed to thirty-eight magazines a month and kept them all, envisioning the value of a complete collection. He was now starting to store some things outside.

The reason he came to the seminar was to see if we knew of any way to store more things in his, by now, decidedly limited area. Coming to our seminar for this reason is like going to Weight Watchers to inquire if anybody knows where bigger clothing can be bought.

> *Nothing in excess.*
> EURIPIDES

48

The odd thing was that I felt upset that evening, not because of John — he could live however he wanted — but because his story stirred up in me the desire to have thirty-eight magazine subscriptions and a room full of shelves. That is a scary and uncomfortable feeling. I know how much harm indiscriminate gathering can cause.

The feeling went away by the next day. I wonder if I would feel the same discomfort now that I have broken the gathering habit.

But if a 0 (or ½) is an extreme, so is a 10. When I was a child, we lived in Memphis, Tennessee, where it gets very cold in the winter. From time to time I would hear the children of a neighbor begging to come in out of the cold, but their mother wouldn't let them in. When I asked my mother why, she told me the neighbor didn't want her children messing up the house. When we went over to her house I was warned not to touch anything or move around much. This woman was an example of a 10.

We also lived next door to a woman who used to hose down her house after it rained because the rain had splattered dirt on the outside wall. I went into her house. It looked like a model home. I commented that she must have just had her kitchen cabinets painted. "About seven years ago," was her reply.

Don't ask me how she did it. Her husband spent a lot of time down the street in a bar and took his shoes off at the front door when he did come in. That's a 10 for you—hard to live with.

We don't want to be either a ½ or a 10. Those who rate from 4–6 are average housekeepers. Their houses are satisfactory most of the time, varying with the circumstances. A 4–6 would not be likely to come to a Messies Anonymous class unless she was dissatisfied with being average and wanted to be a more efficient housekeeper. Some have come and found the class helpful.

The 7–9 group are Cleanies. This is a generally wonderful group, and I admire its members a great deal. As I have already suggested, if we Messies want to get our own houses in order, Cleanies are the people we must emulate. But where do we begin?

HOUSEKEEPING LEVEL	TELL-TALE SIGN
☐ 0	No one cares to enter your house.
☐ 1	Fools rush in where angels fear to tread.
☐ 2	If you *had* to, you could find at least one clean towel.
☐ 3	The dishes are clean, but stay out of the upstairs bath!
☐ 4	At least once a week, everything's spotless—for a day.
☐ 5	You can read a book without overwhelming guilt.
☐ 6	The minister's wife can call without panicking you.
☐ 7	You can hold elaborate luncheons twice a week and have everything neat by 3:30 P.M.
☐ 8	You gave away the dog and made the kids understand.
☐ 9	Your children aren't allowed downstairs, except to eat (neatly).
☐ 10	No one dares to enter your home.

PART TWO

Turning Things Around

7

Goal-Setting: He Who Aims at Nothing Is Likely To Hit It

You got to have a dream,
If you don't have a dream,
How you gonna have a dream come true?
OSCAR HAMMERSTEIN (*SOUTH PACIFIC*)

If you don't know where you are going, there is no need to start. Perhaps those of us who had Cleanie mothers have one advantage over those who did not—we know how nice a clean house can be. How lovely it is to have one's drawers neat and tidy. How lovely it is to bring friends home and be proud of the decor and the order.

If your mother did not leave you this legacy, then you can pick it up now from friends whose homes you admire. In our church we have frequent get-togethers in homes of various members of the congregation. At first I thought they had just fixed things up for the church get-together, but when I went into the back bathroom or the garage, or chanced to look in an open closet door, and saw the same neatness there that I saw in the more public areas, I was sure this was the way they always lived.

Halloween was also a revelation. At that time, when mothers walked their little tots around trick-or-treating, I would move the clutter which was around the living room door out of sight and down the hall.

Then I would close the curtains that revealed the other parts of the house. From the vantage point of the front door, things were passable.

But I would see that my neighbors didn't have their homes curtained off. Their windows were open for viewing and, perhaps more startling to me, their homes were lovely. I didn't have time for beauty. I was just surviving. I began to dream that *my* house could be that way. I envied the well-placed figurine, the uncluttered space. It was a good envy. It made me want to change.

Daydreaming can be an excellent thing. Studies have shown that people who are high achievers are frequently daydreamers. They use daydreaming as a method of goal-setting. You can do that, too. Use creative daydreaming to work for you. My daydream is something like this:

I see clean, shining tabletops warmly reflecting the lamp and the well-chosen items on the tables. I see sunlight and leafy shadows playing across the vacuumed rug. I see my favorite colors artfully used, affirming that this is a place for me to be happy and comfortable.

I see my family moving happily in their home, clothes and food easily provided. I see myself full of energy because I am in control.

I see myself developing and growing stronger in spiritual ways, because I have time and energy for the Spirit. I thank the Lord for the opportunity to live up to my unique potential for my own pleasure and that of those around me.

Get out a piece of paper and write out your own daydream. How do you want your house to look? Once you have written it down, you are on your way to achieving that goal.

It is valuable to state your goal specifically. When I set out to gain control of my house I had only a general, foggy idea that things had to be "better." But as I gave it further thought, I hit upon a goal statement that says it all: "I want my house to be like Marcella's."

You have already met Marcella, one of my Cleanie friends. I want my house to be like hers because hers is consistently neat, shining, and pretty. I was just there today, around ten in the morning. Marcella was caring for her six-year-old, home from kindergarten, her five-month-old baby, and a friend's year-old baby. What an invitation to chaos! But as usual, the house was spotless and even prettier than I remembered it. Obviously it isn't because she keeps people out; she is always willing to share her home with children and adults alike.

On the same piece of paper on which you wrote your creative daydream, write a sentence or two stating your goal. If you write it, your muscles will already be in the act and you will be starting to change. Set a five-year goal and a life goal, too.

Vaslav Nijinsky, one of the great ballet stars of all time, is legendary even today though he lived in a time when there were no moving pictures of his dancing. It is said that he could leap higher than any other dancer, five feet into the air, and hover there a second or two. Now, on the surface, this would seem to be an impossible task. When people asked him how he could do this, he replied, "It's easy! I just made up my mind to do it." He could not do it the day after he decided to, of course, but once a determined individual sets a goal, he finds a way to reach it. And he did.

In athletics, successful goal-setters abound. Tom Dempsey, who holds the record for kicking the longest field goal in NFL history, hobbled onto the field because he has only half a foot and wears special shoes. But he did the job. Boy, did he do the job! Obstacles are insignificant to a determined goal-setter. They do not disappear, they are just overcome.

I was watching the televised Olympics. A young American runner who had come in second was being interviewed. He told an interviewer that he would continue to train for four more years for the next Olympics when he hoped to win the first-place gold medal. "When you put yourself under the strain of training for four years for one race, what is likely to give out first? The legs?" "No," was the reply, "the mind."

55

"The secret of success," said Benjamin Disraeli, "is constancy to purpose." Winston Churchill said it another way: "Never give in, never give in, never, never, never, never—in nothing, great or small, large or petty—never give in except to convictions of honor and good sense."

The hardest part is keeping one's goal in view when the going gets rough and the end is not in sight.

That's why it is so important to write it down. If it is written, you have made a stronger commitment. If you have not written your goal yet, you can write it in the margin of this book. If you have written it on paper, store it in this book so you'll know where to locate it.

In order to reach this goal, you will need to welcome the three C's into your life. They are:

Change — There have got to be changes if things are going to improve. But change is hard to bring about. The way things are is at least familiar and somewhat comfortable, however unsatisfactory.

Perhaps the hardest changes to make are in the mind. The ideas that "creative people are messy," or that "a person with three preschool children cannot keep a neat house," or worst of all, "I am hopeless," must be changed or no improvement will come.

The truth is that we are all made in the image of God. God is not a God of disorder. This means two things. First, we are not happy living in disorder because it is against our natures. Second, we do have the power to control and order our lives.

When God first put Adam in the world, He told him to have dominion. We need to take that position in our homes— we are going to have dominion. I believe it is God's will that we take control of that portion of our lives which is our responsibilty and rule it competently and well.

Commitment — Commitment involves dedication to a project. If your house is really important, dedicate yourself to the task of cleaning it up. Put it at the top of your list of priorities.

56

Control — I have already told you what nice people Messies are. Some of us are too nice for our own good, and for the good of our families. We are the Room Mothers, the Cub Scout leaders, and the Sunday School teachers.

But we need to use good *judgment*. It is hard to suggest cutting back on such obviously worthwhile activities. Nevertheless, I am going to suggest that you do cut back. The good is enemy of the best.

Our first responsibility is our home, not for the sake of the house, but for the sake of ourselves and our families. The home is the base from which we reach out into the world. When our base is in order and we have a schedule of maintenance, then we can begin to add a little at a time until we see how much we can handle.

Here's where control takes over. If you have been known as a community worker, people will continue to ask you to do jobs. You must take control of your life. Make your decision in the light of your priorities and if necessary, say, "No, I'm sorry I won't be able to help you on that."

Sometimes you can suggest an alternative. If you are asked to bake cookies for a class party, ask if you can buy them. If requested to take part in a money-raising event, make a donation instead.

The hardest person to say no to is yourself. Your hobbies of ceramics, gardening, writing, painting, and friendships vie so pleasantly for control. If your top priority for right now is organizing the house, promise yourself and your friends that later, when things are different, you will return to your old acquaintances and activities refreshed and happy.

You have only a limited amount of time and energy. Spend it where it will help accomplish your goals.

THE DIAMOND OF SUCCESS

In housekeeping as in any other job we set out to do, there are factors that set the successful achiever apart from the frustrated wheel spinner.

What sets Cleanies apart from Messies? They have a formula for success whether they are consciously aware of it or not. This can be diagrammed by the diamond of success given below.

Meaningful
Evaluation
4

1 Definite
Goal

Planned
Action 3

2
Sufficient
Motivation

Let's apply them one at a time to our plan of house-keeping.

1. Goals—A goal must be specific in order to be meaningful or useful. Just to say, "I don't want to live this way anymore," is not enough.

How do you want to live? Make it clear by deciding something like this: "I see myself being able to have friends over anytime without three days work."

"I see myself waking up in the morning with the house under control and I see myself with a plan to keep it under control."

Emerson has said, "Thoughts rule the world."

Make your thoughts concrete. Even if you have done it before, write on this line your statement of your goal for yourself.

MY GOAL FOR MY HOUSE IS _____

_____

Remember: "He who aims at nothing will likely hit it."

2. Motivation—Athletes know that 90 percent of preparation is mental and 10 percent is physical. They know that many times they lose because they beat themselves, they psych themselves out. The main thing is to have a winning attitude. In order to win in athletics you must expect to win.

Use what is called the movie technique to get yourself going in the morning. See yourself doing the jobs you have planned, leaving the house with it in order, returning to a supportive house.

Now mix what you see with emotion while you are seeing it. Feel determined as you see yourself working, feel happy when you see your job completed.

3. Planned Action—Halfhearted doing will doom us to failure.

There is a verse in the Bible which says, "And whatever you do, do it heartily, as to the Lord," but you and I know that the big part of our problem is lack of knowing what to do and when to do it. That's why the Mount Vernon Method and the Flipper Method, described in Part Three, are so important. They give us a plan for getting the house organized and keeping it that way.

We can wear ourselves out just deciding what to do if we don't have a predetermined plan.

And once you decide what to do, do it heartily.

Remember the older woman who was asked for the secret of her lifelong success. She replied: "When I works, I works hard; and when I sits, I sits loose."

Work hard; **then** sit loose.

One word of warning. Don't plan to do so much in the beginning that you wear yourself out and quit. Pace yourself and take a day off each week.

4. Meaningful Evaluation—One temptation is to put a plan into motion and just keep on keeping on with it simply because it is our plan and not because it works. We need to stop and evaluate whether it works or not.

Mayor Koch of New York City is known for asking frequently, "How am I doing?" Stop and ask yourself, "How am I doing?"

Now that you have your goal set firmly in your mind, and have written it down as well, let's take a look at the five problem areas which often afflict the Messie housekeeper. Afterward, you will be given a test to help you determine which of these areas is causing you the most difficulty.

8

Five Pitfalls for the Wanderer in Messieland

If you want a golden rule that will fit everybody, this is it: Have nothing in your houses that you do not know to be useful or believe to be beautiful.
WALTER KITTEREDGE

As noted, problems with housekeeping seem to fall into five main categories. Some of them overlap a bit, but I am sure you can recognize them easily and pick out the ones that relate to you most strongly.

The usual problem areas are:

1. Storage or Organization. This includes maintaining orderly drawers and closets and the storage of seldom-used items such as Christmas things and light bulbs. Storage is the basis for what is to follow in other areas of cleaning. If you don't have a place for everything, how can you put it away?

Few people see whether or not we have messy closets, but they do see the results of it. If you have to look and look for the phone book, or keys, or whatever, this area needs work.

2. Neatness. Some people tell me they are disorganized in their closets and drawers but have neat-looking rooms. This is difficult for me to understand since the same things that made me messy inside the closets, made me messy outside them, too.

61

A neatness problem is best identified by our feelings when people drop in on us unexpectedly. Much visiting has been done on the front porch because we aren't ready for unexpected callers. Many invitations have not been issued because it would take too much work to clean and organize. This is unfortunate because Messies are frequently warm, sociable people who would enjoy sharing their homes with others and entertaining friends. But the house won't allow it!

3. Paper. Where do all the papers come from? Children bring them home from school. Newsboys deliver them. The mailman brings his stack. Magazines come. We pick them up in stores. And occasionally people stick them under our windshields when we are at the store.

But we don't mind, do we? Papers have such fascinating stuff on them. Some of them have ideas, and Messies are very practical. Papers can also be very important. They can have to do with taxes, children's school activities, and so forth. We are especially infatuated with papers. And we love to keep them.

4. Bills and Banking. This is an area of life that requires organization or it falls apart. A bill makes no demands for a while, so it is easy to set aside and forget until it has gone into oblivion. Banking is the same way. The statement comes so quietly and so neatly packaged that the tendency is to let it stay closed up in its little envelope. At least that way the canceled checks will all be together in a pile somewhere. So long as they are there somewhere we are comfortable.

But that doesn't quite solve the checking problem. Some people attending my seminars have told me they keep two accounts and switch back and forth as the need arises in order to keep current with the balance in an account. One woman told me she has even changed banks, letting one account stand long enough to get it under control and to let all the checks come in. That was the only way she could know how much money she had in the account.

I understand this. For me the detail and tedium of the checking process is very difficult. Since I am distractible, I do not find it an automatic process to record every deduction and every withdrawal. Failure to do so, though, can cause havoc in a checking account.

5. Collecting. The word *collecting* is not the best word to describe this problem. *Collecting* indicates some order or design which in this case is lacking.

What I have in mind is the keen desire to gather lots of things because they "might come in handy someday." Or to keep them for the sake of the past.

Why do we love to collect so many things and have such a hard time throwing them out? Either we do it for the past or for the future. Certainly it isn't for the present, since the present is suffering because of all this stuff we are trying to live with.

We feel we have to hold on to things from the past because we are trying to preserve some beautiful memory. The things we keep are attached in our minds to some important person or event in our lives, and we keep them out of respect. This is a particular problem when the person whose things we are keeping has died. One of my seminar students felt compelled to keep several houses full of furniture because they were from the estates of deceased loved ones. The same woman had four closets full of clothes four sizes too big from her admired, deceased mother-in-law, whose memory she wished to preserve. A widow I knew felt that if she threw away anything that had belonged to her husband she would be throwing away part of him. My guess is that anyone who loved us would be the first to urge us to live our lives in the present and not try to hang on to the past.

We also try to keep things for the future—just in case we ever need them. We save for possible needs or emergencies that might come. Don't sacrifice the present for the future. That's no healthier than living in the past.

We also keep things because they are valuable. Everything has some value, no matter how small. I had occasion to take metal bones out of several bras. Do you know that I was reluctant to throw them away? *There must be something they would be good for*, I thought. *Maybe I ought to save them. Perhaps I could glue them together to make Christmas ornaments.*

It's true, there *might* be some use for them, but no one has appointed me keeper of everything which might have some

63

value. That is too big a burden to bear — "keeper for the world." I threw them away happily when I realized I didn't have to think that way anymore.

My mother who, as you already know, is a Cleanie, told me yesterday of her latest garage sale. "It's so nice in the house now. I got rid of all the things I didn't use. Now the closet floors are empty and only what I need is in the drawers. It's wonderful, wonderful, wonderful!" From staying with her on visits I can tell you that living that way is wonderful. There is freedom in having no more than you need, no more than you can control.

But the collecting impulse is hard to control because on the surface it seems so logical. Why *not* keep that yarn? Someday you may learn to knit, and it will be wonderful to have your own supply already! (*If* you can find it.) Why not keep all prescription medicines? Someday your child may be very ill in the middle of the night and the doctor may say that only one medicine will help him. You'll look in the cabinet and find that you have that very medicine, even if it is ten years old. The doctor will say that it is better to have ten-year-old medicine than none at all, and you will give it to your child and he will be saved. So, you see, it is dangerous to throw anything away.

The problem with this thinking is that it just doesn't work. We gather and gather and gather good things, and some things that are not so good. Soon the pile gets out of control, and we can't find what we want when we need it.

Things control us and our lives. We begin to make adjustments in our way of life to accommodate all the "stuff" we have. We tell ourselves that we *can't* throw anything out. We end up with so much that it *is* a monumental task to clean or organize.

I am not saying that everything must go. But the collecting mania has to be taken in hand and controlled if we are ever going to get off the un-merry merry-go-round.

Not everyone wants to break the collecting cycle, but there's a good chance you do. You bought this book because you want to change and because you know there is more to life than amassing great globs of junk. You can avoid all of the pitfalls and problems that are part of the habit of hoarding.

One way to start is to identify which of the five pitfalls is your greatest problem. In the following chapter you can evaluate just exactly where you are in the vicious cycle of messiedom.

Where is it written...
• that a closet with no door is not a closet?
• that Collector's collections grow to fill all available space?
• that anything unused for six months automatically migrates to the smallest room in the house?
• that no paper is vital until it's lost?
• that a Saver always marries a Thrower? And always wins!

9

A Personal Evaluation

The best way to escape from a problem is to solve it.

BRENDAN FRANCIS

Now that you know the five major pitfalls that cause Messies their greatest difficulties, you will want to know which is your most significant problem area. The following evaluation exercise will help you get a handle on your strengths as well as your weaknesses.

Respond to each statement with the answer that best reflects your situation today. Resist the temptation to give what you think is the "proper" reply. Then, using the answer key, interpret your evaluation so you can see which of these problems needs the most attention in overcoming your "Messie" status.

Answer each of the following "true" or "false."

____ 1. It is hard for me to throw away newspapers because I might have missed something good in them.

____ 2. I am successful in using coupons.

_____ 3. I have to work all day to have dinner guests that night.

_____ 4. I follow a plan for bill paying and have a place to keep the receipts.

_____ 5. I still have my high school dance program (or the equivalent) somewhere in the house.

_____ 6. I have medicine over five years old in my medicine cabinet.

_____ 7. I know how much I have in my checking account.

_____ 8. I keep my bedroom door closed when I have guests.

_____ 9. Having houseguests is next to impossible.

_____10. I know what I would do with an extra shoelace or light bulb.

_____11. I keep magazine issues that have good articles in them.

_____12. I clip newspaper articles, but don't have any special plan for keeping and finding them.

_____13. My trading stamps are under control.

_____14. My matching sheets and pillowcases are together.

_____15. My least favorite thing is for unexpected visitors to drop in.

_____16. I decide what to have for meals as I shop.

_____17. My cleaning materials are close to where I use them.

_____18. Cleaning the stove is part of my regular cleaning.

_____19. There are pieces of jewelry I can't find.

_____20. I buy things I don't need just in case I might need them someday.

Answers

1. F (C)	6. F (C)	11. F (C)	16. F (O)
2. T (P)	7. T (B)	12. F (P)	17. T (O)
3. F (N)	8. F (N)	13. T (P)	18. T (O)
4. T (B)	9. F (N)	14. T (O)	19. F (O)
5. F (C)	10. F (O)	15. F (N)	20. F (C)

Evaluations

C = Collecting, P = Paper, O = Organization, B = Banking, and N = Neatness. Count up the number missed for each letter.

Multiply each C missed by 4. My score is _____.
Multiply each P missed by 6. My score is _____.
Multiply each O missed by 3. My score is _____.
Multiply each B missed by 10. My score is _____.
Multiply each N missed by 5. My score is _____.

The problem area in which you made the highest score is likely to be the one you most need to work on. Still, this is not always the case. You may feel some other area causes you more difficulty. In that case, go with your own intuition about the matter.

Now list your problem areas from the biggest to the smallest. As you go about implementing your new housekeeping system, you will be aware of which areas require the most concentration on your part.

BIGGEST PROBLEM 1 _____
         2 _____
         3 _____
         4 _____
SMALLEST PROBLEM 5 _____

Once you have isolated your specific problem areas, it will be easier for you to take command of them. Now you are ready to get started on the road to good housekeeping. In the next section of this book I am going to share with you exactly how I took command of my house, the system that helped me get organized, and the tools that help me stay in control.

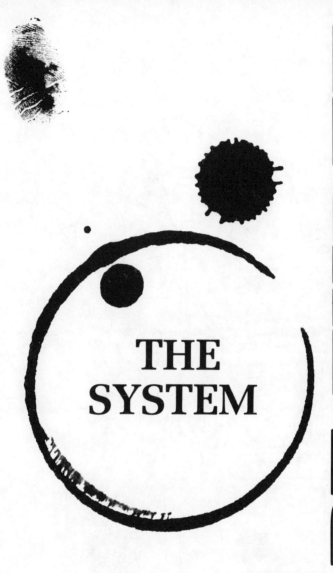

THE
SYSTEM

PART THREE

The Mount Vernon Method: How I Took Command

The first thing you need to know about in order to organize your home is the Mount Vernon Method. Some years ago during my desperate search for help, a Cleanie friend told me about the Mount Vernon Method. While touring George Washington's estate, my friend had been so impressed with the maintenance that she made a point of asking the woman who was in charge of housekeeping about the method they used.

The housekeeper explained that she directs her cleaners to start at the front door and work their way around the outside periphery of the room. When one room is finished, they proceed to the next, doing everything that needs to be done in each room so the rooms are left clean and organized. They dust and wax from the time they come to work early in the day until it is time for the public to arrive. A few minutes before opening time the workers collect their boxes of cleaning supplies and leave. Each day they begin where they left off the day before and keep going from room to room until it is quitting time.

But it is easy to clean Mount Vernon. George is not there to mess it up! I decided not to use the method for dusting and polishing, for cleaning walls, drapes, upholstery, or carpets. First I needed to get organized. I started at the front door.

The first item of furniture beside my front door was a lamp table with one small drawer. After I had cleaned that little drawer, throwing away several very old school calendars, old classified ads, and a lot of junk, I felt I could do anything.

Next, I came to a piece of living room furniture that had six drawers, two of which literally had not been opened for years. I was actually afraid to open them. Why afraid? I think I believed I would not be able to handle what I found—that my decision-making apparatus would be sprung and broken.

But after a good night's rest, I did open the drawers. The challenge turned out to be a paper tiger. I could easily handle the things I found there. There were no terrible decisions to make. I am still surprised at the unreasonable fear I felt about those drawers.

As I continued around the house I threw out twelve-year-old medicine from my medicine cabinet. In my clothes closet I came across my wedding shoes. They were twenty-three years old, were missing a decorative buckle, and had never fit. However, I thought perhaps someday I might locate the buckle and they might come back in style. (You never can tell, you know. Miracles do happen!)

I threw them out. I wasn't going to let the past with its lovely memories muddle today. Messies are hopelessly sentimental.

You have to think about your total house organization. We think because we are capable in other ways we can handle anything. Yet even the most capable person can't work when things are disorganized. So think organization.

The most important thing about the Mount Vernon Method is that you pace yourself and not overdo. The temptation is to work like a crazy woman because of the frustration you feel. Don't start out too fast. You will not be able to accomplish the Method in a single day (it took me three and a half months to "Mount Vernonize" my home).

Think of this as a marathon as opposed to a sprint. Since a sprint is a short-term race, you start out giving it all you've got. For a marathon, however, you have to conserve at the beginning of the race because you know you have the end to think about. Housekeeping is a marathon, not a sprint. Go slow and steady. Don't start a whole closet if it is too much. Plan to do two shelves at a time if you can handle this better.

When you have done enough for one day, stop. Wait until tomorrow. Take one day off each week so you can look forward to a break. I also advise that you leave the kitchen until last. Kitchens aren't for rookies!

During my stint with the Mount Vernon Method, I sometimes came to a place I felt I just couldn't tackle. To get around this obstacle, I did two things: (1) I took an extra day off, and (2) I decided to reward myself with something extra special when I finished the "big bad job."

That kept me going!

When you are ready to start, make a list of several items —three to seven—that you plan to do each day before you start Mount Vernoning. Remember that the Method is for organizing, not for heavy cleaning.

Begin at the front door and start with the first piece of furniture you come to that has a nook, cranny, drawer, etc. As you move from one spot to another, take with you three boxes: a give-away box, a throw-away box, and a storage box. Open the first drawer.

Throw away every piece of junk that has accumulated there. Be serious about it. Don't keep the pen that only works half the time; toss the pretty calendar that's already a year old. Your freedom from clutter is more important than they are.

When you find things that are too good to throw out, put them in the give-away box. And give them away soon! You'll be glad you shared. Two cautions are in order:

1. Don't take anything out of the give-away box once you've put it in.

2. Don't wait for the perfect time or the perfect person to

73

give it to. Get rid of it right away. Don't save a matchbook for Mary's son who saves matchbooks. Don't even save it for a garage sale unless you have a specific date set for a sale. After that date, give it to the Salvation Army or Goodwill.

Be willing to take a risk that you may later want what you discarded. One Messie who is succeeding at becoming a good housekeeper wrote to tell me that the risk is worth it:

> I can honestly say that we have never missed any- thing that we got rid of. We did replace one ancient single bed which we sold and later needed. Cost was seventy-five dollars—a small price for the use of a room for three years. (The bedroom had been so stuffed with junk, it was unused until then!)

Remember that although it may cause temporary pain to throw something out, it also causes definite pain to keep it. Tossing it out is mild pain compared with the pain that comes from having to live helplessly with all that clutter. There is an exhilarating feeling of freedom that comes once the decision is made to take control of the house.

The storage box is there to keep the things that don't need to be discarded but are in the wrong place. Do not hop up and put them in another place while you are cleaning, because this will break your concentration. You may never return to your job there. Just put them into the box to be put away when you finally reach the place where each belongs.

It does not matter how quickly you complete the Mount Vernon phase. What matters is that you are consistent in your efforts and determination to complete the task. This does not mean that all I had to do to put my house in order was to apply some willpower. Not so! Over the years the willpower method had not worked any better than anything else for me. No, it required a *system*—and some very special tools.

11 Four Friends In Deed

Any Messie can tell you that the real problem of housekeeping is not getting the house in order; it's *keeping* it that way! There are four devices which together will keep your whole life organized. They are the *Flipper*, the *Box*, the *Notebook*, and the *File*. Here's how they work.

The Flipper: Magic Key to Maintenance

Doesn't that sound quaint — *Magic Key to Maintenance*? But there really is something magic about the Flipper: It works, and lists don't!

The Flipper is the heart of the Messies Anonymous organizational program. Many books on housekeeping say, "Make a schedule of daily activities for the house." Sometimes they then give a sample list so that you can get the idea.

Well, I used to make lists—usually at the insistence of my frazzled husband, who kept repeating in a comatose way, "Something has to be done."

Then I either put the list in a pile where it would be safe and lost, or I attached it to the refrigerator where I got so used to seeing it I no longer "saw" it and didn't miss it when it slid down between the refrigerator and the counters.

One reason I didn't use these lists is because I didn't really trust that they were good lists. I didn't respect them. Maybe they were poor lists. Maybe I didn't have every job listed and at the right intervals.

Then, too, the lists looked sloppy. They were handwritten and irregular, like everything I tend to do is. Who could respect a flimsy, messy, handwritten piece of paper that purported to tell me how to live? I resented that stupid list forced on me by grimy necessity!

But a system is necessary. One day when I was in the bathtub deep in thought, the idea of the Flipper dawned. Simply put, the Flipper is a three-ring notebook containing a series of twenty-four cards covered with plastic. The cards are arranged in a staggered series and attached to a larger heavier sheet of card stock. It is the type of system sometimes used to store and show snapshots.

You can flip each card up to see the one below. That's why it is called a Flipper. On these cards I decided to list information that would help me with my housework and menu planning. I stored three weeks of permanent menu plans on three cards and three weeks of daily household jobs like "make bed," "wash dishes" on three other cards. The rest are used to spread out all of the other household jobs that are not done daily (like mopping the kitchen floor) over a three-week period. Some are done weekly, some twice weekly, some every three weeks, and so on, depending upon the job.

After the cards are filled out to meet your needs, they are slipped into the plastic sleeves where they are kept in proper sequence and protected.

The net result is that you have, contained in your Flipper, a predecided plan of cleaning for each day and a menu plan for three weeks. Let me explain the highlights of the Flipper System to help you understand it a little better.

The Flipper System puts you on an easy-to-keep daily maintenance schedule. The house will not always be perfect, but with the Flipper it will always be maintained at an acceptable level. After I started using the Mount Vernon Method in conjunction with a few daily jobs from my own Flipper System, my house showed a remarkable change in only three weeks' time. It is important to realize, however, that you cannot use the Flipper successfully until you have "Mount Vernonized" your home.

Another nice use of the Flipper is the menu-planning system. It is designed to save time. I originally came up with the idea from something I read about Ethel Kennedy. She makes up two weeks of menus, goes through them, then starts again at the beginning for the next two weeks. That's what we do. But we outdo Ethel and plan *three* weeks of menus!

You might say, "Won't that get monotonous?" Not really. Studies show that, without planning, 80 percent of the time the same ten dishes are used over and over again. It is not easy to think of twenty-one different dishes—seven dinners a week for three weeks. You may wish to repeat a dish — spaghetti, hamburgers, or whatever your family favorites are — more than once during the three-week period. One day a week can be left open to take advantage of whims, gourmet recipes, or seasonal specials.

You can also change your menus every few months if you wish. Each week's menu is put on a separate card and stored in the Flipper. Now you have a permanent menu. From this permanent menu you can make a permanent shopping list—one for each week's menu. I don't know about you, but I hate to make shopping lists! Now we don't have to. Simply store the shopping list in the plastic sleeve on the back of the menu card and slip it out to take to the grocery store when you go shopping. Or, if you wish, you can put a duplicate page in your Notebook so you can have it if you decide to stop at the store unexpectedly (the Notebook is described later in this chapter).

One other convenience is possible with the menu plan. Let us assume you have some dishes that require a recipe. Instead of looking up the recipe each time, copy it and store it in the plastic sleeve above the day it is used. It will not only be readily available but protected from splatters, too.

For more information about how you can obtain a Flipper, see page 157.

The Box

Next to the Flipper, the Box is the most important tool in the organizational program. It would be easy to underestimate the value of the Box. Be sure to include it as part of your program. It will streamline your life and take a lot of pressure off the piles in the house. It is basically used for keeping records and storing information.

The Box is a wooden, metal, or plastic container that holds index cards. Such "recipe" boxes are sold in drug stores, grocery stores, and department stores; they can also be purchased in stationery stores, where they are called index boxes.

Although you may prefer to use 4 x 6 cards, I've found that 3 x 5 file cards work best for me. Along with your Box you will need to purchase one or two packages of file cards, a 3 x 5 scratch pad, some 3 x 5 dividers labeled *A* to *Z*, some dividers that are labeled with the months of the year, and some dividers that you can label yourself. These dividers will separate the contents of the Box into several main sections.

Address Book. The A-Z part of the Box will become your telephone and address file. Any number you call or address you use should be put into the file in the Box. Address books are hard to maintain. They get full; they need changing, so we cross out one address and put another over it. This looks messy. They become obsolete because of the changes. The Box file solves that problem because if a change needs to be made, the original card can be thrown away and a new card put in.

The Box is also better than an address book because there is room to make notes. Let us say you have a friend from college whom you never see but with whom you correspond at Christmas. You get a birth announcement from her. Write down on the card the name of the new baby and the date of birth. Then when you send your card you can write, "How is little Helen? She must be so cute at two." You can also make notes about friends' likes and dislikes in food, how their coffee is taken, and so on. They will be pleased you remembered.

Business Records. If it is a business call you make, you can make notes for that, too. I called Disney World and made a card for my file. I wrote down the prices they quoted to me and dated it. I will know where the price information is stored for use this year and will also have a record of how the prices change from year to year. It is filed under *D* for Disney.

If you have a plumber come, make a note about what he did and the date. Then if the same thing breaks down again, you can tell him when he was there previously and what he did. Keep records of car repairs and expenses under *C* for car.

Making notes in the Box is valuable for keeping track of orders you place. If you buy something by mail, write down the name and address of the company and the date you ordered it. If it does not come within a reasonable length of time, you can write, telling them how long it has been since your order. Put down the date of the inquiry letter on your card as well. In this way we can keep our lives under control by having necessary information readily available.

By the way, when you order by mail, put the address of the company on the back of the check to make it easier to write them if there's a problem. This has nothing to do with the Box, I just wanted you to know.

Newspaper Clippings. The A–Z file can also take the place of a newspaper clippings pile. Suppose you have an interest in restaurants and your local paper carries regular reviews of restaurants. Instead of cutting out the article, transfer the information to a card and file it under *R* for restaurants (see sample).

Restaurant
Le Flambeau
East Lang St.
Mon.–Fri. 11–10
Sat. & Sun. 5–11
#821-4620
Morn News: 8-5-81

79

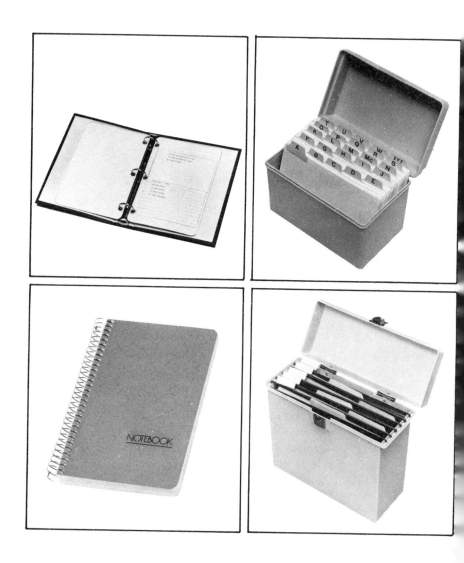

If someone recommends a book to you, write it on a card and file it under *B* for book. You'll have all the information summarized and at hand when you want it.

Monthly Activities. The monthly activities part of the Box is used to store reminders of activities that are done only seasonally or yearly. Check your monthly card at the beginning of each month. Let us say that you wish to turn your mattress four times a year. Behind January, April, July, and October put "Turn mattress in master bedroom." You can put notices to remind you to clean the gutter, store seasonal clothes, wash living room drapes, and other seasonal or annual things on the list of activities which you used for the Flipper.

You will also wish to list birthdays and anniversaries behind the month in which they occur so you can send a card or make a call for the special occasion. If the event is on November 1, put the notice in October.

Once you start using the Box you'll think of lots and lots of wonderful uses for it. If you have some short-term information you want to put in the file, put it on a piece of scrap paper and file it. Throw the paper away when you have finished with it.

Special Interests. The special interests part of the Box is for keeping information that is unique to your home and family. There are four or five blank dividers for that purpose. I use mine for storage information, like where I stored the Christmas, Halloween, or seasonal things. I use it for notes on a real estate course I took. I use it for records of special days, things like who came to the house on Christmas last year, what we had for dinner, and what gifts were received. I am sentimental, I guess. It makes me feel good to know one card per holiday has those memories safely preserved.

One person I know has a divider labeled *Health*. In that section she has a separate card for each member of her family. She records the dates of immunizations, surgeries, and so on, and details information about allergies.

In a section on *Finances* she keeps cards that contain all the insurance policy numbers for life, health, car, and fire insurance. She also records checking and savings account numbers and credit card information. Because her savings passbooks are exactly 3 x 5, she files them in this section. In the event of an emergency she has all her vital information at her fingertips.

The Notebook

The Notebook is the tool that will keep your *life*, as opposed to your house, organized on a day-to-day basis. If you try to organize everything in your mind, you'll become distracted and spill the details.

Mine is a small Notebook that fits into my purse easily and contains loose-leaf, lined paper separated by several dividers. Those calendars with little boxes for each day are too small for my busy life. I need a whole page for my daily "to do" list alone.

Here's how my Notebook works. Each divider is labeled, and I put information and reminders into the appropriate section. The divider labels are:

Goals. In this section I write my life goal, ten-year goal, five-year goal, and yearly goal. Your immediate goal for a special project, such as your house, may also be written here. Recently I put my goals in the Box. Because my goals were so personal, I didn't want to risk losing my Notebook, and I was reluctant to have anyone else see them. I feel more secure about keeping them in the Box, but the Notebook is also a logical place for them.

To Buy. Sometimes a special need comes to mind. While you are cleaning house you may see that you need batteries, light bulbs, rubber bands, and paper clips. I write these things here as a reminder. Whenever I'm in a store—even if I'm only window shopping—I flip my Notebook open to the "Buy" section to see if I need anything. This ensures that my house remains stocked with those little necessities that are easy to overlook.

To Do. I make a different page for each day as the need arises. Then I make a list of necessary activities for the day.

Make sure your Notebook isn't cumbersome. If you make it difficult to use, you'll ignore it.

Now comes the important part: EVALUATE EACH AC-
TIVITY AND ASSIGN IT A PRIORITY. The really important
activity or activities will be *AA*. The important ones are *A*.
Next are *B*'s and *C*'s.

Now you can tell at a glance which tasks of a day are
crucial. Our tendency is to do the easy tasks, not the important ones, first. Assigning priorities solves the problem and
gives direction to our activities.

Any special interest dividers may be added to meet your
needs. I have a *Prayers* section in which I write prayers, and
Bible Study in which I write notes from the Bible reading I
do. If you have these interests or others you may wish to
include them in your Notebook.

A companion to the Notebook is a yearly calendar book
of the kind necessary for appointments and so forth. A few
frequently used phone numbers can be kept here for use on
the road. The full phone and address information is kept in
the Box, however.

File—Don't Pile

The word *file* conjures up visions of a large, steel gray,
office-looking thing which we don't have room for in our
houses and might not want there if we did have room. This
kind of file is costly, unsightly, and bulky.

But there are other kinds of files that are cheaper to buy
and easier to find room for. I suggest a Pendaflex-type of
hanging file for home use. It is made of heavy rods which are
fastened together, and it can be put anywhere. These are sold
at many variety stores, discount stores, department stores,
and office supply stores. I bought mine at Sears and was
happy to find one so short. They can be cut down to fit if you
find one too big for your available area.

Where will you keep it? A hanging file can be slipped
into any file drawer, either in a file cabinet or in the file
drawer of a desk. But the beauty of this kind of file is that it
can be kept in out-of-the-way places. Carmen, my Cleanie
friend, keeps hers in the living room in a decorative carved
wooden box brought to her by a friend who visited Ecuador. I

keep mine in an alcove in my coffee table where it is hidden by a door. You can buy one-drawer home files which take up little space and can be set on a counter without looking out of place.

The File should be used for storing larger pieces of paper or information that do not fit into the Box. Receipts, bills, clippings—these go into the File. Addresses and short notes to yourself go into the Box.

A File is a necessity for handling the papers that come into our houses. I suggest you take all your mail and either file it or throw it away at once. Even if you don't file it immediately, you can file it under "To Be Filed."

My mother has a ritual. She gets the mail from the box and walks directly to the trash can, sorting as she goes. In go the things that don't interest her. The problem with many of us is that we have trouble making up our minds what to throw away. If you walk right to the trash can, you will soon get the hang of it. It's a good idea to tear up any of the papers with your address or any credit card numbers on them so that no one will pick up the information out of the trash.

An excellent book that deals with files, among other topics, is *Getting Organized* by Stephanie Winston. The reading may seem tedious but it is worth making the effort to get the File working properly.

A word of warning is in order: Messies *love* files. From my seminars and conversations, I find that Messies frequently have not just one four-drawer File, but three or four! It is the one big attempt at organization they have made. These are storage files. These files are frequently kept in some out-of-the-way place and seldom visited. In business, a study has shown that 80 percent of the items filed never see the light of day again. My guess is that 90 percent of things put in a home storage file are never used again.

But isn't it satisfying to know they are there somewhere in case we should ever want to see them again? In a way, yes; in another way, no. Frequently these large collections in our Files are unorganized and difficult to use. In addition, the drive to squirrel things away puts pressure on us. As long as we have a File with folders, we feel an obligation to look in magazines and newspapers for articles to feed the empty spot. This means we have to read lots of magazines, we have to clip things out, we have to put them into the File. In the end *we* are working for the File; the File is not working for us.

If you have grown and cultivated one or more of these Files and it is sitting fat and full at your house, what are you going to do with it now?

I suggest you leave it until last in your Mount Vernon organizing. Could you, would you, maybe, in some wild dream, consider throwing out some of that unused stuff — *and* its manila folder, so you won't be tempted to refill it? And might it be possible by some strange and wonderful miracle to sell or give away the whole four-drawer storage File and get a little one- or two-drawer working File?

How do you keep a working File working? By virtue of its size, the small File forces you to keep only the essential items and to choose which items must be discarded. A smaller File can be kept close to where you do paperwork, and that makes it more available. Availability helps you to overcome the temptation to "leave it until later."

"But what will I do with the things I want to keep?" you ask, a little angry at my lack of understanding in this important area. Ask a friend whose home and papers are under control. Be sure this person is not a collector. The best way to see how to live without all this filing is to find someone who lives successfully without a collection file.

The more you discard unnecessary items, the closer you will be to having an orderly home—and keeping it that way. The four tools—the Flipper, the Box, the Notebook, and the File are indispensible, and I encourage you to use them or to develop your own version of them.

Meanwhile, it's time to tackle the hidden nemesis of every Messie. It's time to figure out what to do about those closets!

12

Closets

Order is a lonely nymph.

SAMUEL JOHNSON

Don't you think it's wonderful when you go to see a Cleanie and she says, "Have you seen my house? Would you like a tour?" Then she parades you all through, even into the bedroom *and* opens the closet door! "This is my closet," she says. Wow! She even takes pride in her closets. And the closets reflect it.

Let me digress to say that the reason Cleanies show you around the house is because they consider the house an art form and they work at each part of their homes in the same way in which an artist paints different areas of canvas. As you work on the house, think that there might be a time when you will want to show people around your house with pride or at least take them to the bedroom closet to show them a new dress you have bought with the confidence that you will be proud of your closet.

Clothes Closets

What is the closet problem? Most closets are too small. However, if you look at your closet you will see a lot of wasted space, usually below the clothes and above the clothes rod.

86

The logical solution is to put two bars one above the other, thus making better use of more space in the closet. To put in two bars, the top bar needs to be raised. Carmen, my Cleanie friend, did this by taking out all the wood shelves and bars and replacing them with plastic-coated, ventilated wire shelving. There are three advantages to this type of shelving. One is that you can see what is on the high shelf more easily through the spaces between the wire. Another is that it requires less dusting since there is no solid shelf. A third is that if you wish to buy shelving without a bar, the shelf holds the clothes hangers apart evenly. The Sears catalog has a whole section on this type of closet.

There are closet companies that will do this for you if you cross their palms with silver. Look under *closet* in the yellow pages.

Now suppose you say, "That's too big a job for right now. What can I do with my closet the way it is?" Let me tell you my situation. If it requires a hammer and nails and takes more than five minutes to do, I don't do it. Neither my husband nor I are handy with building things and the few occasions when I have had someone do it for me have been unsatisfactory. So I look for easy-to-install ready-builts. In this case, add another shelf to the top of the closet with boxes and a board in order to make use of the empty space up there. Of course, that shelf will be pretty much out of reach so you should use it to store only seldom-used things. The unused space at the bottom of the closet can be utilized as a basket storage system. Look in department stores for suitable baskets.

An easy-to-install lower bar can be hung from the one above by two chains. Look in catalogs for this. A low bar in the closet helps the children get in the hanging-up habit, too.

Now comes what I think is the most chronic problem of the clothes closet—shoes. If they are left on the floor, even if they are on a wire floor rack with a hump for each shoe, they are unsightly, gather dust, and make it impossible to dust easily. There are several solutions. The one I am using now is the one Carmen suggested. I keep the boxes the shoes come in and stack them with the shoes in the bottom of the closet. I write in large letters on the outside of the box a description of the shoes. When I get my shoes out I leave the top ajar and the box pulled out a little so I will know where to put them back. It works well for me.

There are other good methods. The point is, don't let the shoes make your closet a mess. The back of the closet door is invaluable for storage of shoes, belts, ties, and some jewelry. If you make your closet a project (after you have finished the Mount Vernon Method, of course), you might get *How to Organize Your Closet* by Crislynne Evatt.

An important element of clothing storage that is often overlooked is the clothes hanger. Get rid of the wire hangers; buy plastic tubular ones instead. And have enough hangers. One reason people don't hang up their clothes is because it is so hard. Sometimes there aren't enough hangers. The wire coat hangers hook over each other, making them hard to take out. Frequently the wire hangers with the round cardboard tube given out by cleaners are broken in the middle of the tube when we get them out, which discourages hanging up pants. And then of course, there is the problem of too many clothes in the closet, which makes getting something in or out a tug-of-war.

Let me mention that you can pick up the plastic tubular hangers at many dollar-day sales, or buy a few each time you go to the store. Don't wait too long to get them, though. I suggest you paint your closet white and keep it that way so you won't have to repaint it each time you paint the bedroom. Buy one color of hangers; brown is good because it is stylish and somewhat neutral. Can you envision that beautiful neat closet with the white walls and brown hangers? Looks good, doesn't it?

The best color-coding application I have ever made is with my clothing. I divided my clothes into four groups: slacks, blouses, two-piece outfits, and dresses. In each group I arranged the clothes from light to dark like an artist's palette. This did wonders. Previously, I could not tell whether the pair of slacks I was looking for was out of the closet or in the closet, lost under something. Now I know that if my black slacks are not right at the end of the slacks section, they are not in the closet. This trick also helps me to see what clothes I have and how I can mix and match them. I highly recommend it to you.

Perhaps in no other area are we more tempted to keep unused things than with clothes. We have things too big or too small in case we gain or lose weight. We have things that are good but which we never wear because we don't like them. But they are *good*, that is, they fit and the buttons are on. So we *have* to keep them—especially if we paid a lot for them. We keep out-of-style things we used to love, just in case the style returns. It seldom does, and never in the same way. Sometimes we keep a dress which is out of style because the skirt could be made into something nice. We never get to that project; but if we ever do, we will have that wonderful dress to work with.

The worst reason to keep clothes cluttering up our closets is that we are keeping them in case someone else would like them. Sometimes we don't have a specific person in mind, so we keep them until we locate somebody who would profit by our generosity. Being perfectionists, we have to make sure it is just the perfect person. So we put the clothes aside until we get around to sending them to cousin Mary's boy. He'll probably have a son of his own before we get them in the mail!

Listen, let's quit dreaming. We are not going to do the alterations. We are not going to gain or lose weight while the style is still in. If we do, we can reward ourselves with new clothes. Don't wait for the perfect person to wear the outfit you are saving. Give it to the Salvation Army. Let *them* find the perfect person.

Utility Closet

Tangled extension cords, light bulbs, picture-hanging kits, these are the things that go into a utility closet. I have a super idea for solving that problem and I want to share it with you: Use clear plastic shoe boxes. I have about thirty in my closet. They are wonderful. When I first cleaned out the utility closet I found that the items to be put away were falling into categories. So I bought plastic shoe boxes (also frequently on sale at dollar days in variety and drug stores).

90

On the outside I wrote the various categories and put the groups of items in them. My boxes include:

- Shoe things (polishes, laces, brushes)
- Repair stuff (light switch plates, wall plugs, etc.)
- Curtain hardware (hooks for curtains, plastic balls for the pull cords, curtain rod brackets)
- Tape, ribbons, and strings
- Light bulbs
- Soap, toothpaste, and emery boards

Remember, the boxes must be clear plastic and the category must be put on the front either with plastic tape and a labeling gun or with tabs used for labeling in a filing system.

If you store mops or brooms in the utility closet, buy clamps and attach them to the wall. Awkward things like irons and ironing boards can be stored with special holders designed to keep them off the floor. Try to keep the floor as bare as possible. It's easier to keep clean that way and looks much neater.

It's a little-known fact, but true,
One I gladly pass on to you:
Paper clips—scarce in any home—
Have an inborn tendency to roam.

But coat hangers hang till the end,
Like crowded but genial friends.
They tangle and trip, and ofttimes fall,
But a coat hanger will always give you his all.

While you slumber deep in the night,
A paper clip starts on his flight.
As he moves, a wonderous change takes place:
He begins to grow a coat hanger's face!

And he hops into your closet with glee,
And crowds up by a coat hanger's knee,
For every paper clip has always known,
He'll be a coat hanger, when he's grown!

13 | The Kitchen

The general organization of the kitchen is very important. Things frequently used should be stored in an easy-to-reach place and near the point where they are needed. I found that my canned goods were near the dishwasher and my dishes were by the stove. I was amazed that I had violated the logical rule of keeping things near where they were used. I had to put the dishes closer to the dishwasher and the canned goods closer to the stove. I wonder if the most obvious rules aren't the most violated because we assume we will observe them automatically?

When I moved my canned goods I decided that color coding would be a good organizational trick. I put all my white and yellow canned goods first on the shelf with no regard to whether they are fruits or vegetables. I put my green foods next. Then come the red and orange foods and finally the brown ones. This saves me lots of time when I am looking for things.

I also color code my drinking glasses. Each person in the family has a different color. That way each person can use just one glass all day, and we can avoid the sink-full-of-glasses way of life. If people have a difficult time remembering which color is theirs, you can attach some meaning to the color. "Mary, your color is green because you are growing so fast." "June, you have the gold glass because you are so valuable and precious to us," and so forth.

But even with color coding my canned goods and my glasses, I came to the unhappy conclusion that most kitchens do not have enough storage space. One reason is that kitchens tend to collect too many unused items. Another reason is that there is a lot of unused space since the shelves are too far apart and several inches of space are wasted. Sometimes another shelf can be inserted to give more storage space. Wire rack shelves or wire hanging shelves can also be used to do the same thing.

The place under the sink is full of wasted space. It can be made useful by putting in shelves that avoid the pipe.

Hang-up Tips

I am becoming more and more convinced that Cleanies do a lot of hanging up of things without even realizing it. They do it to keep surfaces clean — but it also helps when there are storage problems. Here are some quick hang-up tips for the kitchen:

- Use cup hooks or an accordion coatrack to hang up cups.

- Use hanging baskets to hang up fruits and veggies. We had limes, avocados, and oranges that took up valuable counter space until I bought a hanging basket.

- Hang knives on a knife rack. It frees drawer space and keeps them from nicking and dulling each other in the drawer.

- Hang up brooms and mops. This gets them off the floor where they tend to fall over and clutter things. It takes the pressure off the bristles which can bend the broom and ruin it. You can buy holders for this purpose at the hardware store, or you can use a screw with an eye in the top of a wooden handle to hook on to a cup hook mounted on the wall.

The backs of doors are also very important for storage in the kitchen. You can put small wire shelves or racks for spices on the backs of doors. Racks made by Rubbermaid or other manufacturers for holding aluminum foil, bags, plastic wrap, soap and steel wool pads, and so on clear a lot of shelf space.

Cooking utensils can also be hung up, thus eliminating the clutter they cause in drawers. It is a good idea to hang measuring spoons on the back of a kitchen door on cup hooks. Hang pots on the wall, but be sure not to have so many things hanging around in the kitchen that it begins to look cluttered. Since shelf and drawer space are at a premium, hang or stand up anything that can be hung or stood up.

Shelves, Cabinets, and Counter Tops

However you arrange your shelves, you'll want to line them with an easy-to-clean liner. Use linoleum! You can buy it in smaller pieces at places like K-Mart. Less expensive than linoleum is Con-Tact paper. It is self-adhesive and lasts years. Drawers and cupboards are a pleasure to wipe out with a damp cloth.

If you've never used Con-Tact paper, you may find it a little difficult to handle at first. Cut to size first, leaving backing on. Tear off backing in one corner about three or four inches in diameter. Being careful that the corner is turned up so it does not adhere, fit the sheet exactly. Then place that corner down. Now the paper won't slip.

Start at opposite side and carefully peel off backing. Be sure sticky sides do not touch each other. Slowly slide your hand around so the paper spreads out and in place. Now lift the other end up—including the stuck corner—and remove the rest of the backing. Smooth paper into place. Many people have difficulty with their first attempts at laying Con-Tact paper, but with practice you can become adept.

If you have a kitchen cabinet with an open space above it, be sure to cover it. It will become really dirty and greasy, but the linoleum or Con-Tact will clean more easily than wood surfaces.

Kitchen cabinets do get grimy. You can clean painted ones with one cup of ammonia, a half cup of vinegar, and a fourth of a cup of baking soda in a large bucket. Clean greasy wood-finished cabinets by rubbing them with fine steel wool and paint thinner. Work in one area at a time, using long strokes.

Butcher block counters should be wiped with a cloth that has been wrung out with soapy water. Then dry the butcher block. Every two weeks, oil the top with mineral oil. Do not use vegetable oil, or it will become rancid. If your counter is made of formica, it will require very special treatment. Use baking soda to get stains off formica counter tops, and never use bleach or powdered cleansers.

Appliances

Refrigerator Helps. Use plastic grids made for holding fruits and veggies up off the bottom of the crisper. They save the vegetables from spoiling and they save on cleaning. Another good use for them is in the bottom of a self-defrosting freezer. The grids keep the food from defrosting while the refrigerator does.

Inside the refrigerator you can keep mildew at bay by wiping with vinegar. Don't forget to vacuum the refrigerator coils regularly. Some are under the refrigerator and some are in the back of it. Keeping the coils dust free helps the refrigerator work with less effort, giving you better service and longer life for the appliance. This kind of job should be recorded on your calendar or in the seasonally divided section of the Box. Remember also to clean the drip pan under the refrigerator regularly. Running it under hot water with a disinfectant, then spraying it with a mildew resistant spray will cut down on kitchen odors.

The Dishwasher. Automatic dishwashing powders can cause problems by stopping up the dishwasher with "gook." You can do several things about this. If it has been a problem to you, you might wish to try one of the dishwashing powders sold by private dealers such as Amway or Shaklee. These products have no fillers and therefore rinse away without scum.

In addition, set your water temperature to 140 degrees. (This setting will also prevent your clothes from becoming grayish.) It is also a good idea to turn on your hot water faucet for a little while to bring hot water into the pipes toward the dishwasher. Very hot water is needed to dissolve dishwashing powder and to keep scum from forming. Another trick is to run a half cup to a full cup of white vinegar through the wash cycle periodically to keep scum and lime deposits from forming.

Sneaking Up on the Oven

Nobody seems to know how long it takes to clean the oven, but most Messies seem to think it is a very long job indeed. Actually, it is not. Then why does it seem so long? It's because it is distasteful. The fumes, the goo, having to bend over in an awkward way. It's a messy job, so we think it is a long job.

Frequently, the more distasteful a job is, the longer we *think* it will take. This may or may not be the case. The only way to tell how long a job really takes is to time it.

What is the result of this kind of thinking? It causes us to procrastinate. We dread doing jobs we perceive as too long. We need to face the fact that sometimes we are just kidding ourselves. Some jobs are *not* as long as we build them up to be in our minds.

Some jobs, however, *are* long and hard, and we just don't get to them because they overwhelm us. They sort of hover in the back of our minds, draining off energy as they hover there.

In these cases, we have to manage a breakthrough to get started. The best method is to approach the job from its blind side. Don't let the job know you are really going to tackle it.

Let's take oven cleaning as a for-instance. First—make a commitment to do the job. In some place away from the kitchen where the oven can't hear, tell somebody that you are going to clean the oven or write it down as a commitment.

Second — get all the supplies in order. Buy an oven cleaner if you are out (I like Mr. Muscle), rubber gloves, and sponges. Read the instructions on the oven cleaner spray can. Keep the materials close to the oven but out of sight, so the oven doesn't see them.

Fortunately, oven cleaning is generally done in two parts, so your approach is already planned. You are ready for the attack. Now that you have made the commitment and actually begun, your mind knows that you are serious about what you are doing and it will begin gearing up for the job. Don't let too much time pass from this point on. Look for the first opportunity to do the deed. If you have a job outside the home, spray the oven and let it sit while you are away. If you stay at home all day, let it sit overnight. Don't plan to use the oven for the next meal because you probably won't have time to finish the oven before the next meal.

Now that the oven is sprayed, you *have* to finish it up. But by now your mind has adjusted to it. Besides, now the oven can't be used until it is finished so there is no turning back. So jump in there, wipe up all the goo, *put down aluminum foil*, and you're done!

In two isolated cases, people have told me they have no trouble keeping their ovens clean. When I asked, in surprise, why not, both told me they use lots of aluminum foil—to line the oven and to enclose food when it's cooking so it won't spatter onto the sides and bottom of the oven.

Three easy steps to a cleaner kitchen:

1. Outlaw snacking unless you're present. Then be absent from the kitchen as often as possible.

2. Feed all animals in the garage. Unfortunately, children don't classify as animals, for this purpose.

3. Eat out.

Helping The System Help You

PART FOUR

14

On Procrastination

An ounce of morning is worth a pound of afternoon.

What is that mysterious thing called *procrastination*? Why this chronic putting off of doing things when we know for sure that it is going to cause trouble later on? Why do we drop packages on the nearest chair instead of putting them away where they belong, put off paying the bills till they're late, toss clippings and mail in a pile, and leave the ice tray empty?

Like all things that have to do with human behavior, there probably are several reasons for this weakness which apply in some combination to each of us.

Probably the main reason we put off doing things is because we are not organized to do a job. Either we don't have a place set up for what needs doing, or we don't have a plan for handling it.

Akin to this problem is having a place or plan which is so hard to use that we just don't get to it. If our File is out in the garage we aren't going to use it; we're going to put our papers in a pile until we go out. That setup is asking for trouble. If we don't have enough coat hangers or if the clothes rod is jammed so close to the shelf above it that it is hard to get the coat hangers in, you've got a ready-made setup for procrastination.

We may put off the writing of checks to pay our bills because we really don't know how much money is in the bank. These are all organizational problems.

The more out of control a house becomes, the more there is to do, and the more impotent we become. On more than one occasion when my house has been in a total shambles, I have walked past a basket of clothes that needed folding and said to myself, *I really must get to that*, and then walked on.

The same is true of many other jobs, such as picking up a rubber band off the floor or filling the ice trays. In my case I was forever passing things by. It is because my housekeeping fuse was blown. Just as an electric circuit carries more and more electricity until it finally overloads and shuts down completely, so we keep going with more and more to do until our minds finally shut out what there is to do. It is almost impossible to get going again.

Thus procrastination is no mystery. It would be a miracle if a person did *not* put off doing things under these circumstances. Make it easy to do a job and you'll be much more likely to do it quickly.

Sometimes we procrastinate because we have let the job get so big that it has become very, very hard to do. One of the reasons Cleanies don't procrastinate is because they hate to do big jobs. They don't let big jobs develop because they know they won't want to do them and might procrastinate. In the case of some big job that can't be avoided, such as moving, plan to pack or unpack a few boxes at a time. Even though the job is big, we can set smaller, short-range goals and then we won't be so tempted to put off doing it.

I find that sometimes I put off doing something because I want the immediate gratification of some need. After a shopping trip, I am tired. I want to rest as soon as I get home. So I want to drop my packages, kick off my shoes, and lie down. I have reached the point now where the need to have an orderly, supportive home is more important than rest, so I am more likely to put away the things I bring in before I rest than to lie down and put them away later.

One of the most peculiar reasons for procrastination was one I noticed in myself after the change in my way of thinking took place. Somehow I had a vague feeling that someone else would do the job. Who,I do not know, but I definitely felt housework was not *my* job. Did I think I was an undiscovered princess, and the servants would do it? My favorite fairy tale was the one about the shoemaker who would awaken each morning to find that little elves had done all of his work during the night while he slept. Did I think little elves were frantically searching for my house and any day now, they would find it and surprise me? I don't know why I felt this way, but it certainly made me procrastinate.

There are other reasons for procrastination, such as lack of the clear-cut goal of having an orderly house. If this goal is lacking, it doesn't matter much whether a thing is done or not. Having such a pressured time schedule that we don't have time to do all that needs doing also encourages us to put off the harder jobs.

But there are other factors that influence our tendency to avoid the matter at hand. We find other things to do that are more appealing to us. Consider the following:

Reading: For bookworms, this is quite a temptation—a wonderful way of escape into another world which enables us to blot out the responsibilities around us. The piles around us grow dim as we lower our eyes to the book.

Daydreaming: Daydreaming, like reading, is a form of escape which takes time without showing results in the house. Sometimes we can use daydreaming about our house as an opportunity to set goals for it, but if we use up too much time daydreaming, what we daydream about never gets done.

Television: How easy it is to flip a switch and step into another world. Once I got hooked on a soap opera which became a problem because I felt I had to sit at home at a certain time for "my program." Housework faltered. Messies are particularly tempted by the TV Syndrome because it gives a certain order to the day. The coming and going of the programs helps us to pace our time. In addition, if we plan to watch a program and then do it, we feel we have accomplished one goal no matter how small.

Visiting: The desire to talk to friends is strong. We tell ourselves that friends are more important than the house. Hours of escape time can be spent on the phone, at a friend's house over coffee, and so on — and our time for doing the housework is gone even when we vowed we were going to "get to it" that very day.

Turning the phone off, leaving it off the hook, or just not answering it unless it is a special ring from someone you have a prearrangement with, are ways of cutting out this unplanned use of time. However it is done, cut down on talking time if it is a problem for you.

Leaving Home: One definite way of escaping housework is to be absent from home. Frequently too many social engagements, clubs, volunteer obligations, or shopping trips can effectively cut out the housekeeping chores. "I'm just so busy, I don't have time for housework." Sometimes extra reasons for leaving home such as making daily trips to the grocery store and ferrying children to too many functions cut up large blocks of time. Each one seems very reasonable in itself, until you add up the wasted time which you could have used more productively.

Perfectionism and High Ideals: Spending the whole morning cleaning the oven, ironing wash-and-wear clothes, overdedication to playing with the children, being meticulous about some small aspect of the house or your personal life to the exclusion of the truly important jobs which need to get done are just other ways of procrastinating. We're often trying to avoid the big jobs.

Sentimentality and Regard for the Old-Fashioned Ways: Baking your own cakes or bread, buying 100 percent cotton that needs ironing, doing windows the hard way, avoiding Mop & Glo or other shortcut products, mixing your own cleaning products, or collecting trinkets for display which need dusting are time-consuming jobs which are so unrewarding that we avoid doing them. Do you have some dusty pieces of clothing stored somewhere right now in a basket waiting for you to find time to iron them?

These are ways to escape from the *important* jobs we don't want to do. We do the easier jobs or more familiar jobs or the ones that we have to react to immediately because we have allowed an emergency to arise rather than setting goals and working toward those.

Stop and evaluate your use of time. Make a record for three days showing how your time is used. How much time do you actually allow for *planned* household tasks? You might be surprised that the statement "I don't have time for housework" is absolutely true because you make it that way.

How to Make Decisions

Another reason people procrastinate is that they hate to make decisions. Mary Beth was like that. Even going out to a restaurant that had a big menu caused her a lot of confusion. Deciding where to store things in the house or when to do a job overwhelmed her.

Mary Beth's problem is a common one. She had grown to feel that her decisions were not always the best ones. Mother would criticize or suggest changes to improve Mary Beth's work. She always urged her to do better. Consequently, Mary Beth learned not to trust her own judgment. It was less painful not to decide than to run the risk of making the wrong decision. As a result, she became a procrastinator. It was so hard to decide how to organize her closet that she just left it alone. Leaving it alone, of course, *was* a decision—a decision *not* to tackle the job.

This hesitancy to make a decision and to start a job is due to anxiety and a poor self-image. On the other hand, making a decision can be an opportunity to feel in control, to assert one's desires, and to enhance one's self-image. It is a way for us to control, rather than to be controlled by, life.

What is the solution, then, to the inability to make decisions? How do you resolve the problem of procrastination? Several suggestions may help:

1. **Narrow your choices.**Give yourself permission not to try to do everything at once. Let's go back to Mary Beth's problem of deciding on what to order at a restaurant. "I used to have that problem," her friend Esther said, "so I decided ahead of time on a pattern. When I eat out, I choose pork, beef, fish, and chicken, in that order. If I had fish last time I ate out, I know this time I'll choose chicken. It narrows my choices and makes my decisions easier."

2. **Predetermine many things.**The strength of the Flipper is this principle of deciding ahead on household chores.

3. **Set goals.** All decisions we make will move us in some direction. We need to determine ahead of time where we want to go. Then our decisions will be based on what we want to accomplish.

4. **Start!** The hardest part is starting because there are so many unknown decisions to be made, especially in a new activity. The reason that beginning is so important is because it is as we begin that we see what information we will need. We can also see how the job is going to be organized. Remember, "A job begun is half done."

5. **Ask yourself, "What is the worst that could happen?"** Suppose you are afraid that the decision you make will not be the best. Ask, *What is the worst that can come of this?* Frequently the answer will surprise you. The big bad decision isn't as big as you thought when looked at in this light.

6. **Be willing to make a mistake.**You are not perfect, and you will make mistakes. It is a part of life.

7. **Get information.** Lack of information makes decisions harder than they need to be.

8. **Clear the base.**When the house, checkbook, laundry, and life in general are confused, it is no wonder that we have trouble deciding about anything. When our house and our schedule come under control, we have a better view of what we need and how to get it.

9. **Take control.**The turning point in decision making will come when we adopt the attitude that a decision to be made is an opportunity—not a threat.

Once we start to make decisions, we will have greater control over our tendency to procrastinate. Procrastination is not some vague weakness in our personality; there are definite causes for it. Find the demon in your life that causes you to procrastinate, and you will find that procrastination becomes a problem of the past.

PROCRASTINATOR'S CREED

Knowing that procrastination is, at least in part, a matter of habit, I will do the following as a matter of breaking the procrastination habit:

I will make the bed as soon as it is empty.

I will fill the ice tray immediately and put it away.

I will put the toilet paper on the roll before it is half used.

I will clear the table, do the dishes, and clean the kitchen immediately after eating. I will consider cleanup a part of the meal.

I will put away what I get out and will not say I will be using it again soon.

I will put away my painting, ceramics, sewing, and other crafts when I am finished for the day, even if I will be using them tomorrow.

I will handle the mail as soon as I pick it up and will not leave it in a pile to consider later.

I will hang up my clothes and put away my shoes as soon as they are off my body.

I will be visually sensitive to anything out of place.

I will remember those three tender little words:

DO IT NOW!

which my conscience whispers when I am tempted to procrastinate.

15

On Making And Saving Time

What can be done at any time, is never done at all.

ENGLISH PROVERB

Frequently we say we do not have enough time to keep house. This may be true in some cases. There are people who have so overscheduled their lives that they really don't have "enough" time at home to keep the house the way they would like to.

Aileen is one person who comes close to that state. She has a husband and handicapped son in the house. She works six days a week and on one of her free days a month she goes to the garden club.

That leaves only three days a month free. Such a schedule makes housekeeping very difficult. Yet despite that, Aileen is making real progress because she is following the principles of good time management. There are women who seem to be able to handle a schedule that is larger than life. For most of us Messies, however, it is wiser to schedule enough time to do what needs doing without Herculean effort. We are, after all, not superwomen.

When we say we don't have enough time, usually we have an organizational problem. We do have a few minutes here and there, but because we are not prepared with plans or don't remember what those plans are, the time slips by without our noticing. There are a lot of "little minutes" to be found between large blocks of time if we are just prepared to use them.

It is strange to think that the simple management of minutes can make such a difference in our lives. Actually it is at this point that Cleanies differ markedly from Messies. Cleanies value little minutes. They use little bits and pieces of time whenever they have them and consequently get a lot done without ever seeming to have to do long hours of housework. They do such things as clean the tub as soon as they get out, wipe the sink after they brush their teeth, hang up clothes as soon as they take them off.

The use of these little minutes will make the difference between success and failure. Success is very important to peace of mind and productivity.

A peculiarity of mine, and perhaps of yours, is the habit of thinking only of big jobs. If there is a little piece of paper on the floor, I say to myself, *Sigh! I guess I'll have to vacuum the floor*, and walk on by. My Cleanie friends would stoop down, pick up the paper, and the job would be done.

I think this idea of THE BIG JOB is a peculiar attempt at organizing on our parts. We react to the idea of doing a job rather than just doing the part that is a problem.

The reason for this no doubt is because we are "thought people," not "visual people." We would rather plan an activity in an orderly fashion and then do it (or maybe never do it; but at least it is neatly planned), than do a little bit at a time. Perhaps this is an attempt to stop the flitting around and distractibility that afflicts the Messie. But, like other good ideas that don't work, it needs to be abandoned.

Nevertheless, some jobs require a certain amount of thought and planning. Meal preparation is one example.

Cooking and shopping for food take a great deal of time. To speed up that process, plan menus and shopping lists for a week or so in advance. Sample menus and a shopping guide for one week are given on the following page.

Messies Anonymous Food Planner
Sample Weekly Menu

Sunday— Baked soy chicken, rice, brussels sprouts, rolls.

Monday— Hot dogs, sauerkraut, macaroni and cheese, sliced tomatoes.

Tuesday— Spaghetti with meat sauce, mixed green salad, Italian bread.

Wednesday— Fish sticks, baked potato halves, peas, slaw.

Thursday— Cheese omelet, sausage, broccoli, biscuits.

Friday— Tuna-noodle casserole, green beans, applesauce.

Saturday— Broiled fish fillets, parsley rice, glazed carrots, rolls.

Weekly Shopping Guide
(Sample shopping guide for one week)

Chicken
Hot dogs
Hamburger (half lb.)
Fish sticks
Cheese
Frozen fish fillets

Brussels sprouts
Sauerkraut
Tomatoes
Broccoli
Green beans
Carrots
Parsley
Rice
Potatoes
Peas
Applesauce

Macaroni
Italian bread
Biscuits
Rolls
Noodles
Mushroom soup

Also:
Toilet paper
Cat food
Bread
Mayonnaise
Margarine
Laundry soap
Toothpaste
Bath soap
Dishwasher soap
Lunch meats
Lunch snacks

Also, look for easy-but-good recipes. I love the ideas in Peg Bracken's book, *The I-Hate-to-Cook Book; McCall's* puts out a quick cooking magazine; and there are many other publications at the magazine counter of the grocery store with the same emphasis. A recently published book you may want to look at is *Keep It Simple – 30 Minute Meals From Scratch*, by Marian Burns. Occasionally, bringing in take-out food will take the pressure off during a busy day. This idea loses its fun if it is overdone, but it certainly can be a help from time to time.

Double cooking is always a good idea. Make twice as much spaghetti sauce or bake two chickens so that another meal is basically started.

One of the ideas I like best is for the husband to take his turn at cooking. In my family, my husband is the head barbecuer. In Florida, where we have so much warm weather, this can mean a lot of barbecuing.

Don't let the family fall into the habit of eating at different times. This will wreck time schedules and is not ideal for family life.

Then, of course, there is always eating out. It, like takeout food, is nice for a change, but it gets tiring if overdone.

Question: What does the busy wife make for supper?

Answer: Reservations!

But our shopping needs are not limited to food. Consider how much time you spend shopping for nonfood and even for nonclothing items.

Catalogs save shopping time and energy. Sears, Penney's, and Montgomery Ward issue large, familiar department store-type catalogs. I like catalog shopping because of its convenience and because there are things offered in catalogs that aren't carried in the stores. You go from one department to another with the flip of a page. Ordering sizes has problems, but these usually can be worked out. Hard-to-get sizes are carried in the catalog, too.

Gift house catalogs carry many items I have found useful for organizing my house. Frequently the items, like storage shelves of certain types, are not easy to find in the store, but are staples of this kind of catalog.

Whatever you are shopping for, don't waste time while you do it. If possible, shop when the crowds are down. A full-time homemaker said to me, "It is a sin for me to grocery shop on a Saturday or a Friday night." If you can, avoid shopping on those days.

Everybody has twenty-four hours a day, but some people seem to manage those hours better than other people do. Consider how the following time stretchers could add minutes or even hours to your day:

1. Double up entertaining. Once the house is company ready, invite guests on two back-to-back days;

and/or

Have twice as many people over as you usually would. This makes *one* evening, *one* cooking, and *one* cleanup;

and/or

Have an open house for a very large number. Then you entertain many in one fell swoop, saving gobs of time.

2. Know where things are. How much time is wasted looking? Have a hook for keys just inside the door; have an eyeglasses holder; have a file for bills.

3. Plan for easy maintenance. Don't buy white rugs, clothes that need ironing, long-haired dogs, or knickknacks that need dusting. When you buy something, ask yourself, *Will it cause me work to maintain it?* Usually, because we are in love with the idea of how nice it will be to have an item and because we don't regard maintenance as very important, we buy what we like no matter how poor a choice it is from the maintenance standpoint.

4. Don't *do* so much. If you sat down and listed all your activities, you would probably be shocked at all that has crawled into your life while you weren't looking. Look at your schedule with clear eyes. Then begin weeding out.

Vegetables that are planted too close together jam each other so tightly that none develop properly. In order to have full, healthy vegetables, some good plants have got to go to leave room for the others. Some of us have so much jammed together that none of our activities are really producing well. The quality of life improves as the quantity of activities is reduced, if we have overscheduled ourselves.

5. Store things where they will be used. Store cleaning materials in each bathroom. Store towels in the bathroom, if possible. Keep the dishes by the dishwasher and the pots and pans by the stove. And know where they are stored. Nothing wastes time in a more frustrating way than looking for a lost or misplaced item.

6. Manage telephone and visiting time. If a lot of time is wasted talking, either in person or on the telephone, set your own time limits. If you clean house until 10 A.M., don't accept calls before then. If 6 P.M. to 8 P.M. is your time for the children, explain to the callers that you are busy and will call them back.

7. Move fast. In my interviews with Cleanies, I was surprised at the recurring comment, "I move fast," or, "I don't waste time getting it done." Cleanies want to get their housekeeping goals accomplished and move on to other things. As a Messie, I must admit that I took a more casual approach. One reason Cleanies move fast is that they have a definite time goal for the completion of their schedules.

8. Ask for help. In Proverbs 31:15, the chapter about the ideal woman, you will notice tucked away a mention of her maidens. This woman had help with all her enterprises! We need outside help, too.

We need a certain number of electronic maidens to help us with our work. Electric dishwashers, washing machines, dryers, microwave ovens—all can save time and energy in our busy days.

There is a point, however, at which too many gadgets become counterproductive, and we have to spend more time cleaning appliances and more space storing them than they are worth. In short, don't overdo in this area.

9. Buy time. Everybody has twenty-four hours a day, but there are different demands on each individual's twenty-four hours. If you have more jobs than time to do them in, buy somebody else's time. In short, get a maid or a cleaning service to help you. Don't feel guilty about it, either. You are not neglecting your responsibilities; you are just buying more time when you need it.

Unfortunately, a maid is not the answer to the basic problem. One woman said she had a full-time maid but still had a problem. The maid just kept her piles dusted. Another said her maid charged her ten dollars more to clean than she charged a neighbor, because the work at her own house was so much harder. Basically, *you* are the only one who can organize for yourself.

Then there is the problem of cleaning up for the maid. We would be embarrassed to have anyone come in and see the place like this. Some houses aren't ready for the maid yet.

Sometimes you can hire a maid to come and help with your organizational project if she is someone you feel you can work with in this way.

After you have developed your organizational system and have listed the chores for each day, you can give the maid the jobs of your heavy day and be free to do what you like. She is best used for maintenance. This is when she can be of real help to you.

It is tempting to try to use her to do what a maid cannot do, keep the house all week with just a one-day visit. You must follow your own daily plan of maintenance and break old habits if your house is going to look nice for more than one day a week.

If you decide to use a maid, the most satisfactory way to find one is through the recommendation of a friend. If you don't know anyone who can help you with a recommendation, ask around to find out how people in your area have found help.

116

But with or without a maid, you are going to need the cooperation of your family. In the next chapter, you are going to discover how to get the kind of cooperation you need without nagging (or at least without a whole lot)!

RULES OF THE HOUSE

If you open it ———— close it
If you get it out — put it away
If you sleep in it — make it up
If you drink out of it — wash it
If you take it off — hang it up
If you turn it on —— turn it off
If you drop it ———— pick it up
If you clip it ———— file it
If it hurts ———— comfort it
If it cries ———— love it

16

Getting The Family To Cooperate

If there is one place where your program will run into trouble, it will be with getting your family to cooperate. Read the following letter:

Dear Messies Anonymous,

The house is a mess now, and I don't feel very good about myself for it. I look out the window quite often to make sure no company is coming. One time I was in the mood for cleaning and my children said, "Who is coming?" Now that's bad! I have three children, ages fifteen, eight, and eighteen months. Since the baby was born, it really got worse. I wish I was very neat, but I am not.

Is it normal at all to have a messy house? I see some mess in my house and it depresses me. I am ashamed. I know I need help. My fifteen-year-old daughter helps when asked but even that doesn't help in the big mess. My eight-year-old son does not help, even when asked, nor does my husband. I should not have to ask. I should be able to do it all. But I don't. I know I will never win the "Tammy Tidy" award, but there must be a better way.

Please help,
M.F.

It is easier to rule a kingdom than to regulate a family.
JAPANESE PROVERB

This lady's problem is typical. Let's be realistic. Just because you have a desire to live a different life doesn't mean the rest of the family is going to have the same desire at exactly the same time as you do. And you must realize that you may be largely responsible for the bad habits that have developed, especially in the children. Habits are not broken in a day, or in a week. It takes patience and determination within ourselves to overcome these obstacles. A big dose of humor and love toward our family is important.

But we should also develop a plan of approach. First, you will need to communicate your dream. Have a family meeting about three weeks after you begin your new program. You will have established your credibility by this time. Write out a goal-setting daydream to read to them.

You may also want to share the following letter with your family:

To the family of a Reforming Messie:

Someone close to you has become involved with Messies Anonymous. She wants very much to change her way of life so that the house is not a problem.

The decision to change is a significant one and she will need your help in that decision. Keeping house is a very complex job. The Reforming Messie is one who has become bogged down in that complexity but is not willing to live that way anymore. She feels a change is necessary—no, *imperative!*

The house is our home base. It is the extension of ourselves into our surroundings.

When visitors come unexpectedly and we are embarrassed, when we cannot invite friends over because it is too much work to prepare, when we can't find the important papers (birth certificate, insurance bill, income tax information, and so on), our way of life suffers and so does our self-concept.

And then there is the confusion. Why does so-and-so have such a neat and lovely home while I struggle and fail? Is there something wrong with me? If so, what is it?

On the other hand, when the house becomes neat, orderly, and beautiful not only on the surface but on the inside as well, a sense of control, confidence, and worth comes to replace frustration and guilt.

As the Messie begins to put this program into practice, you may notice some peculiar differences. There may be several responses from you to this change.

If you are a Cleanie—If you tend to be what we call a Cleanie (one for whom keeping the house neat comes easily), you may applaud what you see. All the confusion and clutter has been driving you crazy. At last you see a ray of hope. Let me encourage you to do what you can to help, but be patient and understanding. Now is **not** the time to take over and give all those hints and suggestions you always wanted to give. Don't rush things. The change must come from within, even if it comes more slowly than you would like. There may be slips backward that will discourage both you and your Messie. But remember, a detour is not a dead end. With encouragement things will get on course again.

If you are a Messie—If you yourself have the tendency to be a Messie, you may have difficulty adjusting to this new way of life. You may be a Messie who has frustrated yourself with this problem of messiness. You, like the Messie you live with, have been upset by this lack of control and the problems it brings to your life. Maybe you feel ready to tackle changing and join in the changing. For you the adjustment will be easy. You will be relieved. Or you may want things neater and more organized but may not be willing as yet to make any changes yourself to bring order. Or you may be one who says, "It doesn't matter to me what the house is like. I wish she would just leave things alone." What you need to realize is that having a nice house is very important to someone close to you and you have an important part in it.

When a person decides to change housekeeping habits, it involves the family in a way other changes do not. If a person decides to stop overeating, drinking, smoking, or the like, it is pretty much an individual endeavor requiring only encouragement and patience from the family. In the area of housekeeping, the family is much more involved in the change because the family functions in that house each day. The once easygoing Messie now becomes concerned if you get out the telephone book and don't put it away when you are through. Your shoes in the living room, once ignored, now become a problem. You may wonder if things weren't better before all this "wonderful" change started. Many times you will be **positive** things were better before all this neatness craze began.

Your understanding at this point is crucial. What the reforming Messie is undergoing is a new experience. For the first time, the house is a priority and for the first time she feels that there is hope. For the first time she is struggling with control in an area she has been defeated in before. When new things are attempted, it takes practice — for her to know how to approach you about the change and practice for you to know how to respond. So be understanding, be patient, and above all, be cooperative.

Change is always hard, but it *is* worth it—not just to the Reforming Messie but also to you. You will probably find after a time that you are changed and wouldn't want another way of life for the world either.

Love,
Mom

But communicating your dream will not be enough. "Many hands make light work." Translated into home life, this means that every member of the family must help with the solution since every member is part of the problem. In the book *Bonnie's Household Organizer*, there are four chapters that deal with getting children involved in the housework. Bonnie's new book *401 Ways to Get Your Kids to Work at Home* is great. Part of the reason that my friend Marcella's house is always nice is that her six-year-old has been well-trained and always puts her things away.

One way to do this is to put in writing every task that you want your family to help with. Then it is not you saying the job must be done; it is the written instruction which requires that the job be done. Writing, especially typing, is much more official than Mom. Mom's voice fades quickly and can be forgotten. Writing stays there until it is dealt with.

The Flipper will set up your household tasks in writing with a place for a check to show that the job is done. You can say to your son, "Jack, I want to mark off the job of taking out the garbage on today's card, but I can't mark it off until you do it. I really want to get this off my mind before I start dinner, so could you do it now?"

Don't forget to let him mark it off or see you mark it off, and don't forget to say "Thanks" as you do so. I have found people are amazingly cooperative when you are working with a checklist and not just telling them out of your own mind what to do.

In addition to communicating what you want, you must let kids know you are serious about what you have them do by checking it after it is done. People do what you *IN*spect, not what you *EX*pect. Don't assume or hope that what you tell them to do will get done; inspect it and give praise or rewards for a job well and quickly done.

This is where many of us fail with our children. It is so much easier to assume they have done what they should without actually checking. And being distractible, as many of us are, it is hard to remember to check each time. But kids need to know that the job *will* be checked each time.

Finally, don't let the kids make a big mess. Kids can make a bigger mess than they can clean up. One reason we have a hard time getting them to clean up their toys—the tent made of sheets, the tea set out with all the dolls sitting around it, the pillows propped around for furniture, and the cookies, and the thermos with juice in it—is simply because it is too much for them to handle. It doesn't make sense to allow them to bring it all out and not make them put it back, does it? "You kids brought all this junk out and now you are going to put it right back where you got it. I want all that stuff put away before your father gets home. Now let's get busy!"

It is much easier for children to get things out of their proper places, to unfold the sheet and so on, than it is to fold the sheet and collect and wash the pieces of the tea set. Besides, now they are tired and their attention span is spent.

What is the answer? I frankly love to make a big mess. There is a certain wonderful freedom in living without restraint if only for an afternoon. I don't do it anymore, however, because really I don't want the problem of cleaning up a colossal mess or living with it if I don't clean it up. The "freedom" is not worth it to me. But because I know the joy of making a big mess, I tend to let the kids do the same thing, thinking I am doing them a favor. Then they are left with the problem I have learned to avoid in my own life. That's really not fair to them.

So the answer is to help the kids plan. You put some limitations on how much they can get out, where they can put it, how long they can play. They will want more things and time than you will allow, but soon they will get used to living less excessively and you will get used to directing them in a more moderate way. At first you will have more work to do because you won't be able to leave them on their own. I have noticed that children of Cleanies play more neatly than mine because the limitations on their activities were started earlier in childhood.

Be sure to tell your children ahead of time how long they can play, tell them ten minutes before the time elapses that they will have to quit and clean up in ten minutes. Then stick by that time schedule.

Behavior modification is another method to change sloppy habits of children. This requires serious thought to set up a plan for your needs. First decide what one specific habit you want to work on changing. Is it leaving toys in the living room, dropping books by the door, not making the bed, not hanging up the clothes? Work on that one thing and offer a reward for improvement. If there is more than one child, have them work together as a team. If the team succeeds in breaking the habit for that day, they are rewarded immediately. If one falls down, the team has to wait until the next day for the opportunity to achieve a reward. Be careful to encourage an upbeat atmosphere. Don't criticize the one who fails. Cheer success.

Remember you don't want to cause a mess in your family life while trying to straighten out the house. The house is for the family, so care is required to maintain love and good humor while making the change.

As in all things, love and patience go a long way in making the transition. It also helps to have some nice activity planned for them when they have finished with the clean-up.

Husband training is another matter, and I could not presume to tell you how to work most effectively with your husband. Each marriage is different and each relationship different. If you make housekeeping an issue between the two of you, you may lose more than you gain.

In my family I find the most effective method is to get the house in very good order; then things out of place stand out glaringly. Nobody likes to mess up an orderly area.

However, this is not always the whole answer. After twenty-three years of living with me, my husband had developed some poor habits, too. It is hard to say what he would have been like had he married a Cleanie. One day when I had concluded he was not showing the proper concern for my goals in the house, I decided to do what I suggest my students do: "If you have a need, talk about it."

So I talked, not in a grudging way, but in a way that expressed my feelings. To my amazement, my husband told me his view of how things were going and it made sense. I had not noticed some of the ways he had been contributing, and his heart *was* with me. Knowing this took a lot of pressure off my mind.

Sure, things go awry now and again. Sure, I have my weaknesses and he has his. But he lets me know about mine, and I let him know about his, we make adjustments and move on—usually in the right direction.

Perhaps you have tried talking but it made little difference. You might try *writing* how you feel to him:

Dear Hubby,

First let me say I love you. You have brought so many strengths to my life and to our marriage, and I really appreciate that.

I am bringing to you a problem that I have. For a long time I have been struggling with myself and with the house trying to get control over the clutter. And believe me, it is a struggle.

The only reason I keep trying is because it bothers me so much to live never knowing where things are or having to wade through so much stuff to look for something. It worries me that important papers may be lost in the piles. (I know they are probably there—but where?) I am afraid people may drop in unannounced. I want to be able to have guests over without having to go through Herculean efforts.

Most of all I guess I want to live in a beautiful house that I feel is under control. Perhaps you and I are different in how we feel, but I'll bet that if things were beautiful and under control, you would feel the same sense of joy I would and be proud of how the house looks. So I would like you to do two things:

First, I hope you will share with me my goal for a new way of life. Only if we stand together in this will we even begin to make any progress.

Second, I want to ask you to help by putting away the things you get out like ice cream bowls, magazines, shoes. Also I want you to help me clean up and get rid of the unnecessary things around the house.

It will be a big job and require a lot of effort from both of us, but let's do it together.

I can't wait until we have made the change.

Loving you,

Now you may expect any number of responses, from enthusiasm (not likely), to bafflement, to reluctance or maybe worse. Work with whatever attitude you get. If your husband's response is not satisfactory, have patience. Patience, I have found, is a big ingredient in marriage. Usually it pays off if it is born of love and commitment to each other.

Newton's law of inertia says that any body of matter at rest tends to stay that way unless some force moves it to get it started. Translated into housework, it means it won't be easy to break old patterns. Do as much changing as your husband will permit at a time, and you will probably find the going gets easier as you move along. It is not easy, but it is worthwhile.

How to get help around the house:

• Hide the kitten, then ask your daughter if it could be trapped under the junk in her closet.

• Tell your teenage son it's time his new girl friend was given an escorted tour of the house — including his room.

• Let your husband's socks lie where they fall until he panics at 6 A.M. one cold morning.

• Leave the dog's half-chewed bone where it is — between the bedroom and the back door — then wait until your husband has to let the dog out at 4 A.M.

More Tips On Organizing

Doing housework the hard way is for those who have nothing better to do.

It is my goal for all of you, and for me, too, that we should get and keep our homes organized in the least possible amount of time. I don't think it is unrealistic to say that our work can be accomplished in two or three hours each day. If you work and don't spend all day at home you will have less time and less energy for housekeeping. Nevertheless your goal *can* be achieved!

To accomplish this, a lot of cluttered surfaces need to be cleared. Special temptations for clutter are the top of the toilet tank and the bathroom window ledge. Kitchen windows, and kitchen counters, too, fairly beg to have things put on them: bottles, jars, tissue boxes, and appliances. The clutter turns any dream of cleaning these surfaces into a nightmare. There is no such thing as a quick swipe at the bathroom or kitchen in your morning cleaning when all these things have to be moved.

The best way to achieve order in the bathroom is to get a shower caddy and put the shampoo and conditioner bottles, the soap, and the washcloths on it.

127

In the kitchen, I suggest an almost bare counter. For a long time I fought this idea. I noticed that two of my Cleanie friends had almost completely bare counters. Still, I resisted clearing my kitchen counter because I thought it was an unnecessary and rather extreme step.

Then, in reading Anne Ortlund's *The Disciplines of the Beautiful Woman*, I again came upon the bare counter idea. That made it official! If it's in a book it carries more weight, so I tried it. What a difference it made!

Clearing my kitchen counter and color coding my clothes in the closet were the two moves that had the most satisfactory results for me. I didn't think either one was particularly important, but both turned out to be significant helps. I took the canisters off the counter and distributed them in several separate places in the kitchen cabinets. I put the blender under the counter in a place that had been cleared by throwing away some unused item. I felt I had to leave my toaster and my coffee maker on the counter, although my Cleanie friends keep theirs underneath. But since then I have gotten rid of my toaster, so that spot on the counter is empty. When my family wants toast, I broil it in the oven.

Now you are going to tell me that you don't have room under your counter. I know the problem. I am sure that men design kitchens and have no idea how much room is necessary for storage.

However, let me tell you of one woman's experience. She had her kitchen remodeled. During the remodeling, she put her kitchen equipment on a table on the back porch. After the remodeling was finished she decided to leave it on the porch and to get items to be stored in the kitchen only as she needed them. At the end of three months, half the things were still on the back porch. If you used this method, how much would be superfluous and left on the back porch?

I know the potato ricer belonged to Grandmother and the pots were Uncle Henry's, but you have the here and now to think of. Can you think of a way to clear out the space under the counter so you can clean off the top?

Another way to cut down cleaning time by changing organizational patterns is to plan not to let things get dirty. An ounce of prevention is worth a pound of cleaning up. Thus, you can put rugs both inside and outside the entrance doors so that dirt and trash will get caught there before being dragged into the house. You can put foil on the bottom of the oven so that if anything spills, all you need to do is change the foil rather than clean the oven. You can use cook-in bags for things that might splatter. If you don't have a cook-in bag, at least use a pot with very high sides.

One of the hardest problems for me to deal with was soap scum in the bathroom from the hand soap. It melts into the soap dish and foams over the side, hardening into semi-cement. I hate it.

Luckily, just at the time I was ready to do something about it, soft soap became popular. That was my solution. The only problem is that it is quickly used up by my teen-agers. So when it is time for a refill I fill the container with dishwashing liquid. Sometimes I put slivers of bar soap in it together with a few drops of perfume. It works fine, making a perfumed creamy soap. This way, too, I can get rid of those pieces of soap that are too little to use but which I am too frugal to throw away.

Another method to speed up cleaning is to spot chronic problem areas and look for a solution. I had a trash can for throwing away food in my kitchen. It had no top because I thought it would be too much of a problem to remove the top each time, and it would be too difficult to do with scraps in my hand. The can was not very satisfactory because it was unsightly and the food kept splattering onto the white wall behind it, requiring frequent wiping with bleach and soap.

When I finally awoke to the fact that this was a chronic problem which needed a solution, I was tuned in to solving it though I didn't have any idea how I would do it. Soon afterward I was wandering through a discount store and saw a garbage can with a lid and a foot pedal that opened the lid. This kept the food scraps covered and when the top lifted back it protected the white wall from streaks and spots of garbage entering the can. I had seen these cans frequently but, until I had identified my specific cleaning problem, I had not really noticed them. If you identify a problem with a view to solving it, often the solution soon comes knocking at your door.

The final way to organize for order is to put things away. This is a very hard habit to get into, but it is a top priority.

I learned a little about this on the day after Thanksgiving. The shopping center was really crowded. The shoe store salesmen were bustling around. Shoe boxes and shoes were everywhere, some piled by the customer and some where the customer had been before.

There came a slight lull and the manager began clucking around the store, "Are these your shoes, Bill? Are these yours, Cal? Check these boxes—whose are they?"

When I asked him how he kept all these boxes and shoes straight, he gave me these tips:

1. Don't let too much time go by between straightening up. Keep things up.

2. Each salesman has his own area of the store for his responsibility so the manager has an idea who is falling down on the cleaning job when he sees what area is messy.

3. Every time a salesman goes in the back to get another shoe, he takes something with him whether it is his or not.

4. The fourth thing he did not tell me—I saw it. It was that he had his standard and he personally saw that the system worked.

The application to the home is obvious:

1. Keep short accounts — don't let things get too far behind.

2. Devise an easy-to-manage plan, so you can check on how each person is doing his job.

3. Everybody does his part and works as a team to get the job done.

4. We don't rely on the plan working by itself. We check on it and nudge it along. Remember people don't do what you expect, they do what you **in**spect.

These tips apply to all aspects of home management — even grocery shopping.

When you bring the groceries in, put them away, fold the bags, and either store them immediately or throw them out. No fair using the groceries out of the bag or, worse still, out of the car. You've got to put them away.

This principle applies to laundry, which should be folded and put away immediately, and to mail, which should be thrown away or filed immediately, too. When I write a letter, I put it in the mailbox immediately. So far it hasn't been stolen or rained on. Business executives, early in their careers, learn the value of handling papers only once. As executives of our own homes, we can apply this principle to our own work. Handle small chores as they come up; don't wait for them to add up to a mighty mountain of work.

But where and how do you get charged up for your work? Read on!

TEN COMMANDMENTS
OF HOUSEKEEPING

I Thou shalt not try to do everything thyself. Get help from children, husband, and maids as you can.

II Thou shalt have a goal, for without a goal, nothing will be accomplished.

III Thou shalt have a plan and stick to it.

IV Remember the family to treat them in love while you (and they) are changing.

V Thou shalt not over-schedule and thou shalt not say yes to everyone who asks. Set your own priorities and say yes or no in line with them. Take control of your activities.

VI Thou shalt dream and keep dreaming until your life-style fits the dream.

VII Thou shalt reward thyself for jobs well done and milestones met.

VIII Thou shalt make housework easy to do by organizing for efficiency, because only as work is easily done, will we do much of it.

IX Thou shalt find joy in beauty and order. We are not accomplishing these goals only for utilitarian purposes. Only as we joy in our accomplishments will we be willing to continue.

X Thou shalt not procrastinate. Keep things up and do jobs as soon as thou shalt notice they need doing. Do not leave it out to be put up later.

Energy: The Spark Plug Of Housekeeping

In the book of Proverbs (31:17), Solomon continues about the ideal woman, "She girdeth her loins with strength, and strengtheneth her arms." Apparently this woman knew some way to strengthen herself deliberately. There are ways we too can find energy to do our work.

As we work we can conserve what energy we have by wearing comfortable shoes, such as nurses or waitresses wear. If you work outside the home, make sure you do all you can to arrive home at the end of the day as strong as possible. If you must stand in one place all day, buy a spongy rug to prevent tiredness of the feet and legs. If possible, use air conditioning or bring your own fan if circumstances allow.

While I am teaching math classes in our junior high school, I use only a fan when it is not *too* warm because the air conditioner makes it necessary for me to talk louder which exhausts me. Instead of standing to write on the chalkboard, I sit on a stool and use an overhead projector on which I can write without moving from my stool. This has the added advantage of permitting me to face the class while I write, so I am able to keep an eye on my students while the overhead projector reflects the work on the board behind me. This is how I solve some of my energy-draining problems. Can you think of adjustments you can make to save some of that hard-gotten energy?

Another source of energy is nutrition. My daughter's miniature horse, Wild Thing, lives in a fenced-off section of our yard. When we first got the horse she had been eating sweet feed, a high-energy food. The veterinarian recommended that she should be switched to rolled oats because sweet feed gave her too much energy, and that would not be good for her in the somewhat confined area in which she lives. If rolled oats had proved to be too energy-producing we could have switched to horse pellets, which provide even less energy.

I am not suggesting that you should buy sweet feed. I am suggesting that the same principle applies to people. Find that combination of food that works to make you feel your best. Don't think it will come naturally; it probably won't. You'll have to search for the proper foods.

I have friends who claim that if they miss their vitamins one day, they feel a letdown the next. If vitamins help you, don't neglect them.

Medicine prescribed by a doctor for a special condition should not be overlooked. I take thyroid medicine because most of my thyroid has been removed and what is left should remain dormant. If I were to forget to take the medicine for any length of time or get the idea that I could exist without it, I would be a basket case before very long. Take health seriously, for the sake of your house and yourself.

Perhaps the quickest way to get a surge of energy is to improve your looks! A good haircut at frequent intervals is a must for me. I have heavy hair which tends to be oily. If I let it get long, it becomes heavy and droopy. Then I begin feeling heavy and droopy, too.

Another quick improvement can be made in the area of makeup. I go to Merle Norman shops because they are the only shops I know where people will carefully advise me.

Better department stores have cosmeticians who will help, but I feel a bit uncomfortable sitting on a stool in the middle of a department store, putting on makeup.

A warning is in order, though. Cosmetics are expensive and it is a good idea to go with some spending limit in mind. Buy a little now and go back for more later if necessary. Let me also recommend the book *Color Me Beautiful*, by Carole Jackson, as a guide to help you decide which colors will set you aglow.

Since my house has been organized, my mind has cleared up, too. Now I can give attention to details such as jewelry. I don't dress up every day using accessories, but I am happy to have the right ones when I need them. Previously, things were in such a jumble I had trouble knowing what I had or how to find it.

For those who spend the day at home, there is a temptation to bum around in the same old junky outfits. Buying a new outfit or two will put pep in your step. Getting up early, showering, dressing, putting on some makeup and a new smock, a shorts outfit, or whatever you find best to wear for comfort at work, will get the day off to a good start. Dragging around in a gown and robe telegraphs to your body that you really are not ready to work yet. The book *Dress With Style*, by Joanne Wallace, can show you how to add zip to your looks at home and out. So dress with purpose!

Above all, DON'T GO BACK TO BED! Sleeping is a temptation because it helps one to forget about the things to be done.

A long-range change in your weight will also produce energy. Too much or too little weight will wear a person out. It also discourages improvement of any kind in some people. Weight Watchers, Overeaters Anonymous, 3D, or several other organizations are groups to turn to for help. The first two can be found in the phone book if there is a group in your city; 3D is a Christian group that works through churches of all denominations and can be reached at Diet, Discipline, and Discipleship, Inc., 2710 Chili Ave., Rochester, NY 14624. Undoubtedly there are other groups around the country which could help you with your weight if that is necessary.

There is one organ of the body which has a great reservoir of energy waiting to be tapped. That organ is the brain. Have you ever noticed that when there is work to be done the body becomes very tired, but if there is fun to be had energy seems to come from nowhere? Having a messy house is tiring. William James said, "Nothing is so fatiguing as the eternal hanging on of an uncompleted task." He was right! Having all those odds and ends to do makes the day look like an unpleasant mountain to climb. Energy will come from order, and from success in gaining control of the work in the house. You will be buoyed by the order and beauty around you.

Success brings more success, and that brings energy. Three weeks after one of my students started on the program, her husband sent her flowers with a note saying, "The house looks great, Honey!" What do you suppose that did for her energy level?

Remember, too, that we all need breaks to keep our energy high. Some of us spend so much time trying to bring order out of the chaos of our houses that we don't take any time off for relaxation. We don't feel it is right to play until our work is done. And our work is never done.

Take one day a week for fun. Plan not to work on that day. Then when you get back to work, you'll get a lot more done.

Spiritual faith is another source of strength. In the book of Isaiah we read, "He gives strength to the weary and increases the power of the weak.... those who hope in the Lord will renew their strength. They will soar on wings like eagles; they will run and not grow weary, they will walk and not be faint" (Isaiah 40: 29, 31 NIV). I really feel that much tiredness in housekeeping is tiredness of life as it is. Only if the soul is joyful can the problem be overcome.

An important habit to break is the soap opera habit. The people in these shows are losers — interesting losers, but losers none the less. They are immoral, too, and this is bad input for anybody.

I mentioned earlier that I was once hooked on a soap opera. I say *hooked* because I had to structure my day around the soap opera. I could not go out to do errands if I could not get back in time for the program. In short, I found I needed my daily "fix" or I was uncomfortable and hard to get along with.

Then the program was moved to a time when it was not possible for me to watch TV. What an answer to my need! I vowed never to get into that kind of bondage again.

One part of the program I did miss was the beautiful house the characters lived in. The folks were wealthy and had maids. One of the few spots of order and beauty in my life was that soap opera. Now it is much better to have order and beauty in my own house.

Good books of the right kind can be motivating and uplifting. But they, like television, require that you take time from your work. So use them sparingly at first if you are inclined to be a book addict.

Reading the Bible or another spiritual work first thing in the morning can lead us into that right relationship with the Lord from which we draw strength. If you don't know where to start I suggest the Psalms and the Book of John. From there you can branch out on your own.

We have decided. We have organized. Now we have time to paint a few dreams.

When I was younger, the house
was cleaner,
As I got older, the dirt got meaner.

The babies came—they're all
such joys,
And each one owns a thousand
toys.

They begged us just to get one cat,
A gerbil and dog soon followed
that.

Each teen brings home at least
one friend,
The dirty dishes just won't end.

Yet soon our chicks will fly the
nest,
Our house will shine, like all the
rest.

I'll love it when you make a mess,
Because the messy years are the
best.

The
Payoff

PART FIVE

19

Painting on Your Clean Canvas

*Everybody needs his memories.
They keep the wolf of insignificance
from the door.*

SAUL BELLOW

The nice thing about being organized is that it enables you to do what you want to do, to paint what you want on your nice, clean, prepared canvas. This is particularly important for your personal life whether you live alone, with someone else, or in a family. Now you have time to establish your family or individual traditions.

If you are single you may think this section is not for you. Tradition is for families, right? Poppycock! I think tradition is even more important for singles to attend to than for families, because in families you have tradition more or less thrust on you by the kids or by your spouse.

If you are single, you are pretty much responsible for your own traditions or lack of them. Some people can carry on traditions for their own sakes. I can't. If I don't have someone to share it with I hardly think it is worthwhile. So I would have to build people into my tradition if I were single. They might be other singles like myself, senior citizens, families, or students.

I knew a single college librarian

who regularly invited students to her room for waffles. She had coconut waffles, pecan waffles, all kinds of waffles and syrups. A touch of home cooking meant a lot to us. Students would bring back special waffle toppings from their vacations. I am sure her life was enriched by her tradition. And so was ours.

If you are single, don't let what could be very rewarding traditions slip by because of lack of thought.

If you live near your family, many of your traditions will involve them. But don't settle for that. Be imaginative! Start your own!

With families, traditions are lying around for the taking. Bedtime stories, special foods, birthday parties, and holidays can hardly be avoided.

The problem with traditions is that they require a lot of effort. You have to be organized to keep a good tradition running.

If you put the system in this book to use, you will have a handle on things. You will know where the Christmas things are; you will know where the Halloween things are. In short, things will be under control.

You will be surprised how knowing where things are can enrich your life. Somehow it gives starch to the mind. Flabby, half-formed ideas will march out in full dress uniform for your family to enjoy. Things that were just too much bother will be done because now you will have the time and energy to do them.

What are some of these traditions? There are the usual things like displaying the flag on holidays now that you know where the flag is, and there are bedtime stories now that you have all the children's books gathered together.

Special foods from your own ethnic background or traditional family favorites are important. In my family we eat black-eyed peas on New Year's Day and believe the more peas a person eats the more money he will get.

A friend of mine adds a unique twist to this tradition. In her family they add a clean silver dime to the dish containing the peas. Whoever gets the dime gets double luck in the new year. They use the same dime year after year.

Then there are birthday celebrations. In the birthday cake you can bake a peanut. Whoever gets the piece with the peanut gets a special prize. Let the birthday celebrant be the one to select the menu for that night.

Recently we have added another aspect to birthday celebrations. At the table we each tell what we most appreciate about the person whose special day it is and then we give him or her a Bible verse.

Thanksgiving and New Year are at the beginning and end of the big holiday season of the year. I think Thanksgiving is my favorite holiday because it is, for me, a purely personal relationship between me and God couched in the context of national Thanksgiving.

It is a good thing that this refreshing holiday comes first, giving strength for the days to come up until New Year. But of course Christmas is the highlight of the season for us as a family.

You really have to be organized to have a satisfying and joyful Christmas. First you have to know where the Christmas things are stored. Hopefully they are all together in boxes labeled "Christmas" and stacked alphabetically in the garage, basement, or attic. But if they are not, you should have the places where they are stored listed in your Box under the special heading "Storage" so that you can find them when preparation for the big day comes.

Buying presents, putting up decorations, and cooking are the big three of Christmas celebration. Gift buying is best handled by spreading it out through the year so that by the time December 25 comes you are ready.

It is also a good idea to wrap each gift as you buy it so that you are not hiding in the back room on Christmas Eve wrapping gifts by yourself when it would be nicer to enjoy time with the family in the living room. Put the names of the people for whom you are going to buy gifts during the year in the monthly section of your Box at the beginning of the month in which you plan to buy them.

Decorations come out from year to year and carry more importance because of the memories tied in with them. The star you lifted three-year-old Johnny up to put on the tree is now put up by Johnny because he's the only one tall enough to reach the treetop.

Christmas tree balls are the most important of decorations. One of the saddest experiences of my early married life was the first Christmas my husband and I spent together alone. When the time came to put up the tree, a little blue table-top one, we had to go out to a store to buy decorations. There they dangled, strange Christmas balls, hung by string instead of metal hooks, since I fancied we were too poor to buy metal hooks. As a result of that experience, I decided my kids would have their own Christmas balls, with heavy tradition attached, to take into their own homes.

So each Christmas I buy four matching balls. One ball is for my husband and me to keep. The other three are for each of our three children. If possible we mark the year in an unseen place on the ornament and include the name of the child if it is hard to tell one ornament from the other. Some of them were made by the children at nursery school. Some we painted on summer vacations at the cabin. I guess it is too much to hope that the young people our children marry will bring a similarly collected selection of Christmas ornaments to be merged on the tree for their first Christmas together.

By the way, we still come across a Christmas ball now and again with a string attached instead of a metal hook. So even that first sad experience became a Christmas memory of the bittersweet kind.

Christmas foods tend to run in families. A special kind of turkey dressing, a favorite eggplant casserole, all are happily anticipated before they are actually enjoyed.

For a great book on Christmas get *Take Joy*, by Tasha Tudor. When you open the book you can practically hear the jingle of sleigh bells and smell the Christmas cookies baking.

It has songs, recipes, and best of all, loads of tradition. And when you have your house clean and neat, your storage under control, and your time planned, you can enjoy these traditions too. I bet Tasha Tudor is a Cleanie. One of the nice ideas she suggests is the Kris Kringle tradition. In her family around December 12, they each draw a name of a family member secretly. During the days between then and Christmas it is the Kris Kringle's job to do nice little things in secret for his or her special person. On Christmas Eve each person tries to guess who his Kris Kringle was and the secret is revealed.

Some of the hardest things to manage are children's treasures. These are papers, awards, school pictures, and other memorabilia your child brings home. Where can they be kept? The answer is a Treasure Box. This is a box about orange crate size which you can cover with sticky, plastic paper like Con-Tact. Inside put manila file folders—one for each year. If you like, you can decorate the outside with the child's picture and name. In each folder put some of the school papers from each year along with certificates and other mementos. There is also room for some of the bulkier treasures of childhood like the box with the frog skeleton.

Don't overdo. A sample of each thing will be enough to prod the memory.

In the regular flow of family life some nice everyday traditions can develop now that the house is not holding you back. For example, we like to have family night from time to time. For us it is usually a Friday night. A friend of mine could not come to a meeting one Saturday because she and her husband and teenage son had planned a family day for that Saturday. I like that.

I was talking to my daughter about our family traditions which had plugged along enthusiastically if not efficiently during my Messie years. She enjoyed the ones I mentioned, but she was really enthused about our traditional church activities.

I realize that not all churches provide the same support for the individual and family in spiritual and social ways as ours does. Our church is a kind of extended family, and the people are warm and genuinely interested in each other. They contribute a lot to our family.

It is important for us to get up and go to church. On Sunday morning, I like to keep the same schedule of popping out of bed, doing the dailies, eating breakfast, and getting off, leaving the house tidy in case somebody should come home with us.

If it is too much effort to make a big breakfast, have sweet rolls and sausage served on paper plates and let the children drink out of plastic cups. Throw the plates and cups away after use and you are ready to go.

From my personal standpoint, the Sunday morning church service is the highlight of my week. And it is much easier to go and really enjoy it if the house is in order and ready to send me off and welcome me back. It leaves me in a good frame of mind so I can relax and enjoy the day. Because I feel good about the order that is around me, I feel good about myself, and I am able to look forward to the fresh, clean canvas of a new week.

FAMILY TRADITIONS

Old Christmas decorations are the prettiest. New ones picked out or made by a child come next. Plastic ones fall short, unless they carry the baby's toothmarks.

For boys, enormous gift packages are the best. Middle-sized ones that rattle come next. Anything that looks like it came from a clothing store doesn't count.

For girls, tiny boxes from the jewelry store are best. Middle-sized ones that rattle come next. Some years, even boxes from the clothing store count.

The Fourth of July needs a parade and a cookout. It doesn't need rain. It definitely doesn't need the thought of Summer School.

20

The Real Beginning For You

You now know just about everything I know about how to leave the morass of messiness for an ordinary life.

I struggled for twenty-three years to play the housekeeping game, and for twenty-three years I lost. The methods I have shared with you have changed my life. They can change yours, too, if you choose to put what you have learned into action.

First, recognize that you are a Messie but that it is not necessary to live like one. It is possible to move up the scale. Commit yourself to becoming a 5, a 6, or a 7, and then analyze yourself to see just exactly which habits are creating the most difficulty for you.

Next, set some short- and some long-range goals for yourself, and then use the Mount Vernon method to organize your home. Be sure to discard everything that isn't useful or beautiful. Take your time and save your energy, because the changes you are about to undergo will revolutionize your life.

Once your house is organized

and free of the accumulation of the years, purchase the necessary tools to keep it that way—a Flipper, a Box, a Notebook, and a File. Always remember that procrastination can defeat you, and use your tools as effective weapons against it.

Involve your family in your endeavors and remember that it may take them some time to adjust to your efforts.

The plan works. It works marvelously, but only if *you* make it work. You must sprinkle the magic dust. I'd love to hear from you to know of your successes.

Good luck, and may God bless you as you begin to set and accomplish your goals. As for me, I have to go and dust my fuse box. A dusty fuse box is an unhappy fuse box.

The Messie Motivator

*New Strategies to Restoring Order
in Your Life and Home*

TO Ivan

who loved me in spite of it all.

Appreciation

to Tina—who typed my creative (translate
"disorganized") manuscript and kept
a backup copy of it so I wouldn't
have to worry about losing mine.

to Marie—whom I seek whenever I want my
self-worth bolstered. Unknowingly
she inspired this book.

Contents

INTRODUCTION

The story is told of a South Sea islander with the unlikely name of Johnny Lingo who went to bargain for a bride. The father and mother of the girl he had chosen to marry were outside the hut waiting for the big occasion. Villagers, who knew of all the happenings in the village, gathered around to follow the negotiations. Some of the men murmured that Johnny was an accomplished bargainer and would undoubtedly get a good deal. The going price a groom had to pay for a bride was between two and five cows. The women often compared the prices they had brought. Those who had fetched five cows wanted it known. The bride-to-be was a very shy girl and just a shade short of homely. Embarrassed and fearing humiliation, she had, to her family's dismay, climbed a tree some distance away to watch the proceedings.

Johnny arrived and squatted before the girl's father in the South Seas fashion. When the greetings were finished, he promptly offered eight cows for his intended. *Eight* cows! The deal was quickly concluded. The bride was bought. She and Johnny were married and sailed away for their honeymoon on a neighboring island.

When they returned, the owner of the general store went to their hut to deliver a package that had arrived in their absence. Johnny had ordered a beautiful ornate hand mirror as a wedding gift for his bride. When Johnny and his bride came out of their hut to greet him, the storekeeper was amazed at the transformation in the woman. Gone was the shy, homely girl the villagers knew. In her place was a radiant beauty, basking in the confidence of her husband's love and esteem. Johnny gave his bride her gift.

After she had gone into the hut, the storekeeper remarked about the startling change he had seen in Johnny's wife.

"I have loved her since she was young," he said. "I have always wanted to marry her, but I knew she felt unworthy to be my bride. I bought her for eight cows so that she would know and all the village would know how valuable she is to me. That knowledge brought the change you see."

This book is the Johnny Lingo story. The change in your house will be permanent only when you know what a valuable person you are. People of our quality do not live in clutter, do not hurt or embarrass ourselves by living disorderly lives. We are not two-cow people or five-cow people. We are eight-cow people. When we fully know and accept this about ourselves, the change in our houses will come about naturally and permanently because it will come from the inside of us and be outwardly reflected in our surroundings. The war against disorder will be won at last.

I am an eight-cow woman—a wonderful, valuable, eight-cow woman. I want to shout it to the world, to let the whole village know I am worthy, I am valuable. And so are you!

The Messie
Motivator

Facing
the
Enemy

PART ONE

1

The Winds of War

We has met the enemy and it is us. POGO

There's a wonderful wind blowing in your life. It is the wind of change and it brings the hope of a new spring of order and beauty, leaving behind the winter of clutter and disorder.

The wonderful thing about spring is that it happens so easily and so naturally. Winter loosens its grip and slips effortlessly away.

That is not the way it is going to be with your housekeeping problems. They will not go away automatically.

I've got bad news and good news for you.

The bad news is that *you* must do it. The good news is that you can.

Let's get some idea of just how bad this winter is. There are approximately 33 million Messies in the United States. Some are men; some are women. Some are adults; some are kids. But it is on the Messies who are adult women that the problem falls the hardest. The reason is that adult women are the recognized organizers of the world. This is true at home or in business. It is true of wives or of secretaries. If you are the "senior" adult woman of a group, you are expected to be the organizer.

Notice I did not say that senior adult women are the organizers because they are good at it. You may be good or you may be awful at organizing. The job of organizing is simply given to this group because they are "supposed" to do it. This position has some good points. The person in charge of organizing can make things go the way he, or in this case she, wants them to go. For an organized person, being the organizer is a position of power. Power gives a person strength and a feeling of well-being. We see this in the lives of our organized friends. The friend who proudly shows you around her immaculate house (even opening her closet doors to show the tidy rows of clothes, shoes, purses, and so on) is not doing it for your benefit primarily. You may indeed be fascinated, even flabbergasted, to see this incredible order. But the real reason she is showing you her organized house is to flex her organizational muscles—to reassure herself of her power. She is experiencing a surge of well-being, a lift, from "showing off" the order she has created. There is a certain magic of energy that comes from being in control. By showing you around, she is raising her energy level.

There is motivation there, too. When she feels that surge of strength and energy, she wants to continue keeping the house in order so that she will keep on feeling that strength, that power.

This is true at the office as well. When certain information is needed and you can reach out and produce it with efficiency, you get a surge of confidence. This kind of motivation works especially well if someone else, the boss maybe, is standing there waiting. You want to continue keeping things in order so that you can experience this success again.

But it is not necessary to have someone else "see" in order to get this power. Every time a housewife opens the door to her organized closet and every time the business man or woman reaches for and gets information efficiently, they assure themselves that they are powerful. They are in control.

Do you as a Messie wonder how some people keep up their motivation over the long haul? Many are motivated by this power principle. When they feel control slipping away, they automatically shift into high gear. They cannot stand to feel frustrated or embarrassed. They cannot stand to feel power-less. It's frightening to them and they won't have it!

The 33 million Messies in the country are missing out on this feeling of power. They feel powerless and frustrated because they cannot get control of the house. They feel embarrassed and humiliated because others see their impotence. They feel harassed and degraded because those who must live with them complain constantly about the clutter and disorganization they are forced to live in.

Women from all walks of life have written to me, eloquently expressing how it feels to be a Messie out of control. Those of you who are not Messies will not understand the emotions of those of us who are fighting the battle with disorder and losing. Perhaps you thought we Messies didn't care. How wrong you are. We care desperately.

> "I was drowning in a sea of clutter and was becoming paralyzed, apathetic, and numb in an attempt to preserve my sanity!"
>
> Doris, Oklahoma

> "The last few years I have felt hopeless because of my disorganization."
>
> Shelly, Colorado

> "I'm tired of running around like a chicken with its head cut off."
>
> Heather, Massachusetts

> "I lived for years in near-desperation because of my housekeeping problems."
>
> Dot, Washington

> "I knew there was something wrong with me, that I was a failure as a person."
>
> Lynn, Idaho

Living in the winter of messiness is a very severe problem.

> "I have just been thinking about the humiliation and loss of self-respect we suffer as the result of a messy and disorganized life. It is so destructive."
>
> Betty, California

"I have been in complete despair."

Lois, Illinois

If you are a Messie, you know how it feels. We long for success and power. Too often we get frustration and failure.

But the winds of hope are blowing; surely spring is on its way. Perhaps before it is over we may call the winds of war the winds of hope.

IT'S TIME TO DECLARE WAR WHEN . . .

You find a four-month-old dry cleaning receipt in a coat pocket; you don't remember what clothes you took in and what's worse, you haven't missed them.

Your mother-in-law has submitted pictures of your home to Ripley's Believe It or Not.

You sort and wash a bag of clothes you found in the basement—then realize they were the clothes you had set aside for the Goodwill.

Your collection of ceramic mice that you've been collecting since eighth grade has filled three knickknack shelves, two coffee tables, the top of the refrigerator, your baby's old crib, and half of the bottom drawer of the guest bedroom dresser.

Your husband has painted over the basement door the words from Dante's *Inferno*: *Lasciate ogni speranza, voi ch'entrato*— All hope abandon, ye who enter here.

THE AGONY OF DEFEAT—
SYMPTOMS OF A DEFEATED MESSIE

Embarrassment "You'll have to excuse the mess. I, uh, well, the U.S. Olympic Pillow-fighting team just had practice here, and I, uh, haven't quite ... just push that aside ... well as you can see, uh. ..."

Humiliation You open the refrigerator and the cat jumps out.

Frustration "Always winter but never Christmas." The treadmill of knowing what should be done and beginning with good intentions—but never finishing. There is probably nothing more frustrating than not finishing.

Anxiety That nagging existence in which something is always lost, late, or spoiled. (Akin to the concept that anything you like is either illegal, immoral, or fattening.)

Powerlessness Sort of like having a Rolls-Royce with a dead battery—what's the point?

Harassment Daily bombardment by the needs of family, home, and self. A domestic version of the London Blitz: mostly annoying, but with the possibility of real disaster.

Out of Control Suddenly your life takes on *Alice in Wonderland* qualities—and you find yourself shouting, "Off with her head," at the neighbor's pet cocker spaniel.

Apathy That point where you say, "If you care so much, *you* clean it."

Lack of Confidence *"I'll* never get this house clean."

Lack of Hope "I'll *never* get this house clean."

Lack of Luster "I'll never get this house *clean.*"

2

The Thrill of Victory

Discipline is the soul of an army. It makes small numbers formidable, procures success to the weak, and esteem to all.

GEORGE WASHINGTON

The Messies Anonymous group was born so that Messies could gain support and comfort from one another. Living as a Messie is a lonely life. No Messie really talks about housekeeping, not with any depth anyway. The people who talk about their messy houses are the Cleanies. Cleanies are those whose houses are always immaculate, except, perhaps, the rug has not been recently shampooed. With few exceptions, Messies suffer alone. Many, many Messies think, as I did, that they are the only ones who are having these strange, unexplainable problems with housekeeping.

Let me share with you their feelings. Since Messies Anonymous really is "anonymous," I will use only the first name and state. Some Messies would not care if they were known worldwide. Others might. Therefore, the anonymity.

"I don't feel quite so alone knowing that I'm not the only person who has this problem."

Regina, Delaware

"My first reaction was relief that there are others like me around (I always thought I was unique!)."

Betsy, Pennsylvania

I guess I should have known that others were having the same problem with organization that I was having, but somehow I must have tuned out the problems I saw in the houses of other people. I guess I thought their problems were temporary and surface. I knew mine were permanent and went down deep into the recesses of the bottom drawer of the most remote dresser.

Other Messies were not fooled as I was. They had other reasons for feeling that no one could understand their problem.

"I have been embarrassed, frustrated, disappointed, and ashamed. I knew I wasn't the only bad housekeeper in the world, but I thought most of the others I knew were just lazy. Not me—I worked from daylight till dark and never got the house clean. It was a relief to find that there were others like me."

Martha, Texas

Now, right here, before I continue telling you about members of Messies Anonymous, let's back up to explain how I discovered all of these fellow Messies.

Messies, as you must know by now, are those people who daily struggle with and fail at the important job of building the base from which they and their families work—their homes, or more specifically, their houses. They are not lazy. By now you know that they are not content with things "that way." On the whole, they show remarkable strength and good humor considering the ordeal under which they chronically live. Within each Messie lies a dormant pile of enthusiasm just waiting to be ignited by a spark of hope.

If you have not already guessed, I also want you to know

that I am a Messie. For twenty-three years I lived with the same frustration my fellow Messies have been living with. Finally I found a method that worked—really, wonderfully worked—for me. So great was my delight that I put a little ad in a local paper, advertising a class to share the program that helped me. Because I was a school teacher, this way of sharing came naturally to me. Because I was not really convinced that there were other Messies like me who would come to the class, I had some friends come sit with me at the appointed time and place. To my delight and surprise, twelve Messies arrived upon the scene. They were kindred spirits in search of the secret of successful housekeeping.

This was the first Messies Anonymous group. The name says it all. The word *Messies* has sort of a funny ring to it showing that we have a sense of humor and an upbeat approach to the problem. *Anonymous* shows that although we are working in a positive way to overcome our problem, it is still a personal thing. We don't necessarily want to include in our confidence those who may not understand. The two names together indicate that there are a bunch of us who want to be identified together for support and comfort. We have a definite program and plan to change—the Messies Anonymous program.

I tried other more positive names; I really did try. Apparently, people who are Messies are not interested in skirting the truth. Names like Happy Homemakers, Homemakers Unlimited, Domestic Doers did not make a ripple. Messies Anonymous did; it made a big splash. People who are Messies, and don't want to be, are interested in plain talk. They want it told like it is. So Messies Anonymous was the name.

As news of M.A. spread across the country, thousands of letters poured in. It is from a few of these letters that I quote.

In response to this outcry for help, I wrote *The Messies Manual, The Procrastinator's Guide to Good Housekeeping. The Messies Manual* is must reading for any reforming Messie. It explains all the basics of the M.A. program. One of these basic parts is the Mount Vernon method. Briefly explained here, it is, like all good ideas, simple and effective.

The Mount Vernon method is the first step to organizing your home. One of the Cleanies I talked to some years ago in my desperate search for help, told me that on a visit to Mount Vernon she was so impressed with the maintenance that she made it a point to talk to the woman in charge of housekeeping. She asked the housekeeper about the method they used. The housekeeper responded that she directs her cleaners to start at the front door and work around the inside periphery of each room. They dust and wax from the time they come to work early in the day until it is time for the public to arrive. A few minutes before opening time the workers collect their boxes of cleaning supplies and leave. The next day they begin where they left off and keep going from room to room until it is time to leave again.

But it's easy to keep Mount Vernon clean. George isn't there to mess it up. We are not going to use this method for dusting and polishing. Basically, we will use it as a method for organizing—not cleaning. You may want to clean a little as you organize, but don't emphasize the cleaning part.

Let's begin at the front door. You start with the first piece of furniture you come to which has a nook, cranny, or drawer. This is where you begin. Then you go around the inside periphery of the house, cleaning out these kinds of places.

You begin by throwing away all the junk you have accumulated in that drawer. Put it in a throw-away box. And be serious about it. Don't keep the pen that only works half the time and the year-old calendar even if it does have nice pictures on it. Your freedom from clutter is more important than these things.

Be willing to take a risk that you may later want what you have discarded. Also, realize that it may cause temporary pain to throw something out. Remember, however, it also causes definite pain to keep it. Throwing it out is mild pain compared with the pain that comes from having to live helplessly with all the clutter that finds its way into our houses. An exhilarating feeling of freedom comes once you make the decision to take control of the house and actually start by beginning to throw out things.

You do not worry about cleaning walls, drapes, upholstery, and so on as you go. Basically, you organize each spot. Along with your "throw-away" box keep with you a "give-away" box and a "store-elsewhere" box.

When you have done enough for one day, stop, and start again tomorrow.

Don't overdo. This is a marathon, not a sprint. Don't wear yourself out. Pace yourself. Take a day off each week so you will have a break to look forward to. Reward yourself when you get over a big hurdle.

Make a list of several items you plan to do each day. There will probably be from three to seven jobs on your list. Each day do these before you begin the Mount Vernon method.

You'll find real control developing before you know it. Boy! What a relief!

This is the method I taught at that first class. It has remained the basic get-control method for Messies Anonymous.

As the organization grew, I held seminars around the country, taking the M.A. message to lots and lots of enthusiastic Messies. But the number I reached was only a drop in the bucket compared to the many, many more Messies who wanted and needed help. So the job of Messies Anonymous was to find out how to reach and help them in a way that really would make a difference—a permanent difference.

The amazing thing was that it worked. It worked for women who came to the seminars. It worked for women who bought *The Messies Manual* and read it alone in their homes, finding for the first time that others understood there were real reasons for their problems, and that there was real help available.

Just as I had been thrilled, they were too and wanted to share their delight. I received letter after letter:

I am beginning my Mount Vernon. While Mount Vernoning the living and dining room, I'm also repainting them in a lighter, brighter color. This may not be a recommended approach, but the painting and seeing the growing picture doubles my energy and enthusiasm.

I'm not yet where I want to be, but it's getting closer, and I'm getting excited. When I feel overwhelmed, I close my eyes and see where I'm headed. It's lovely.

I think I'm ready to face the world; well, at least close friends. Soon, the world.

Lynn, Idaho

I have my self-respect back again and so much confidence. My daughter-in-law came by unexpectedly about 7:15 this morning and everything was clean and in order. What a wonderful feeling! One month after I started, all I have left to do is one shelf in my hall closet and one in my pantry.

My family is delighted. In fact, I'm a star in my own home and everyone is so eager to do their part to keep everything clean.

I had gotten to the point where I never entertained anyone and when someone knocked at my door, I would block the door with my body so they couldn't see in.

This past holiday season I wouldn't have any of the dinners at my house because it would have involved too much cleaning, but next year will be different and wonderful. Now there is a whole new me.

Pat, Louisiana

I have truly enjoyed discovering your *Messies Manual.* I have been using it in my home for the past six months. Using your directions I have made dramatic improvements in the appearance and organization of my home.

Alice, Florida

3

New Recruits: Volunteers Not Draftees

It is not enough to fight. It is the spirit which we bring to the fight that decides the issue. It is morale that wins the victory.

GEORGE CATLETT MARSHALL

It takes a lot of courage to be willing to take full responsibility for the condition of things. It is much easier to insist that we are victims of some outside force. The fact that we are not naturally good at housekeeping, that our houses are too large or too small, that we have low energy levels, that we work long hours, that we live with messy people, does not prevent us from having the houses we dream of. Our houses look the way they do because we have given them permission to look that way.

You and I are people of infinite value. We are people of dignity. We are not slobs. We are not undeserving. We are super, wonderful people. Somewhere in our hearts we know this. If we did not know it, we would not strive so hard to excel. And we do excel! All of us are successful in many ways. Where we are successful depends to a large extent on how we think about success.

Let me tell you the story of two women, each of whom was striving for success in her own way.

Beth is a composite of the Messie who feels that her value lies in what she is able to contribute to the world around her. She collects mementos because she feels that it is her responsibility to preserve the past. She is intelligent. The stacks of books, newspapers, and magazines in her living room show her interest in ideas. Her hobby materials scattered about attest to her creativity. The bits and pieces of leftover craft materials indicate her frugality. She has no time to stay home and do housework because she is so much in demand to do things she has volunteered for outside the home. When she is home she plays with the children or helps them with their projects. The house reflects this, if you know what I mean.

Here we have a successful woman. Beth is intellectual, frugal, generous with her time and energy, aware of the importance of her heritage, and an attentive mother. She certainly is creative. She uses her creativity to prove that she is a worthwhile person. Her value is there for all to see the second they enter her house.

"Come on in! Excuse my mess! I've been doing ceramics all morning," Beth says, often calling attention to the confusion around her, almost proud of it. Sometimes it is canning all morning, sometimes it is painting, but always it is clutter.

Woe unto Beth if she decides to become an elementary school teacher, a Sunday school teacher, or a Scout leader. She goes at every project with gusto. Charts, song sheets, posters, flannel-graph materials, and flotsam and jetsam for some possible future project would take over the junk room, overflow onto the bedroom floor and maybe even onto the bed to be removed to the floor each night.

I will not mention the problems she would have if she ever decided to take up refunding and coupon collecting seriously. (As a Messie, I know I can never be an elementary school teacher or coupon collector. I have tried both and found they require a much higher level of organization than I am able to maintain. For me to attempt either one of these jobs would be like an alcoholic trying to be a bartender. Some Messies can handle these activities with a lot of effort. I found it was easier to seek alternatives.)

Beth feels that because she is able to do all of these things she is successful. But the people who live with Beth are very frustrated; they hate the clutter. They let her know it in no uncertain terms. The children hesitate to bring friends home. Beth is frustrated and hates the clutter, too. Even she doesn't understand why she doesn't change. No matter how often she tells herself that the house is not that important, she continues to be bothered by its condition. But she won't change because this clutter shows, however poorly, that she is an important and valuable person. Beth continues to work at all these tasks to prove how valuable she is. Perhaps if she felt her own sense of worth more strongly, she would not have to keep proving it to others and to herself. The bottom line is that somehow, in proving her worth, she lost her dignity.

I first noticed how like Beth I am in oil painting class. I found that when I got paint splotches all over me, I wore them with pride. I was a painter! When I teach school, I end up with yellow chalk on my skirt and blue ink from the overhead projector on my hand. I don't really mind. I am, after all, a teacher. These messes set me apart as special.

Karen is also a successful woman. She has a strong sense of dignity and feels that her self-worth is threatened if her dignity is threatened. She feels that her home is an important reflection of her inner worth. She plans for its beauty and order to speak graciously of her. For her, the house is not just a location in which she *does* things. She feels that the house is a very personal extension of herself. Where does she get this feeling?

We are all made in God's image. God is a God of order and beauty. Karen feels this push to beauty and order very strongly whether she puts it in those words or not—whether she believes in God or not. We were designed by Him to feel at peace when things are in order and to feel frustrated when they are out of control. Karen may do fewer activities than Beth because she realizes she can't do as much as Beth tries to do and still maintain the way of life that she insists on. Besides, Karen doesn't think that abundant activity is necessary or desirable. She doesn't feel she has to prove her worth by producing. The activities she does decide to tackle, she does in the same way she keeps her house—an orderly and deliberate way.

Both Beth and Karen are successful in ways that are im-

portant to them. Beth values creativity; Karen values beauty and order. But Beth's success is not satisfying. She and her family are frustrated. Unless Karen goes to an extreme and becomes obsessed with order, she and her family will have a strong base from which to do the work they feel is important to them.

Beth set out to live a certain way and she succeeded. That way of life brought her misery. She had not bargained for this. The thousands and thousands of letters I have received pour out the trouble this way of life has caused. But the Beths of this world keep on trying to live happily following the Messie lifestyle. Many will not change. It is painful to change. They are willing to lose every shred of dignity in order to hold on to the unsuccessful path to self-worth they have chosen. But without dignity, there is no true self-worth.

When it becomes more painful to live in a cluttered house than to change, success is on the way. But not until then.

Let me share with you the story of one Messie as it is told by her son, whom we will call Roy. As always, personal details have been changed.

For years my mom has been collecting things either for sentimental value, or because she might need them some day. Through the years, the whole family has tried in every way we knew to get her to let go of much of the "stuff" that she kept. When we were younger, we were always embarrassed to bring our friends home, and we rarely had company. Mom realizes that her house is a "mess" and is very embarrassed and insecure about it.

Through the years, she has gotten more depressed, has lost almost all self-worth, and has had many, many very painful experiences because of her pattern of thought and because of the methods that we used to try to change her. I don't believe that any of us ever meant to injure her; we always believed that we were trying to help her. But Mom's self-image is so damaged, and she is so set in her habits, that I had really given up all hope, and frankly felt that she would probably either go to her grave early or lose her sanity early because of the friction and incredibly low self-esteem.

You so perfectly described my mom. She *is* a very devout perfectionist. She goes to great lengths to keep her home "germ free" while piling papers and many potentially "useful" things around till she can't even use most of her cupboards and closets.

Roy's mom did not get into this mess primarily because of low self-esteem. When she first started, things seemed to be going well. She found comfort, pleasure, and a sense of personal value in her hurried, collecting, creative way of life. Soon both she and her family began to be frustrated. Things slowly got out of control. In order to regain the comfort and self-esteem we all need, she turned to past gratifiers—collecting and activities. Unnoticed, dignity slowly slipped away down the stream of her unordered way of life. When she and her family noticed it was gone, nobody knew where to find it.

Perhaps you recognize something of yourself in the story of Roy's mom. All of us do. In searching for personal value in things outside ourselves, we lose the sense of dignity within ourselves. But there are certain steps we can take to find that lost or misplaced sense of dignity.

4

Basic Training: Action Steps to Dignity

dig·ni·ty/dig-nət-ē *The quality or state of being worthy, honored, or esteemed.*

Losing our dignity is rarely the result of a cataclysmic event. Oh, there are major traumas that can result in a temporary loss of dignity. But a real sense of dignity and feeling of self-worth are lost only after months and years of chipping away. Land stripped of the trees and grasses necessary to secure and protect the earth will erode. Maybe not noticeably at first, but after one or two years without protection, the topsoil is completely washed away and the soil becomes ugly and unable to nurture growth. Dignity is like the earth—unless we secure and protect it, it will erode; washed away in the rain, hidden behind the clutter, lost in the mess.

There are steps we can take to uncover and secure our dignity. The key is how we treat ourselves. We can begin to plant trees that will shade and nourish for years to come. We can cultivate the flowers and grasses that provide beauty and comfort. We can learn to restore the earth, to replace the lost nutrients and to give it rest when necessary. And as we begin to nurture and cherish our own dignity, others will come to respect it as well. Not only respect it, but enjoy it with us.

Dress With Dignity

☆ *A person of dignity dresses with dignity.* ☆

If we often dress sloppily we think poorly of ourselves. Some will say it works the other way—that people who think poorly of themselves dress sloppily. It works both ways. But we can easily control how we dress. I never cease to be amazed at the kind of clothes I allow myself to wear. I am constantly having to whip myself into doing better. It is only because I am trying to develop in myself a life-style of dignity that I have thrown away the underwear with stretched elastic that does stay up under panty hose, but not well. I forced myself to get rid of the drab housedresses that "do" around the house. *Panty hose that have tears and runs will be all right for wearing under slacks,* I used to tell myself. Poppycock! Am I not important enough to wear undies with good elastic and panty hose without runs? I certainly am! And I will! So I have thrown away the old "make do" stuff. Under the beautiful exterior I present, is respectable underwear. And it's not because I might get in an accident as my grandmother used to warn. I wear nice undies because *I* see and *I* care. A person of dignity wears nice **underwear.** It is a personal thing. *We do it for ourselves.*

Needless to say, the exterior follows the same trend. People who wish to upgrade their own self-esteem must make the effort to upgrade their outer appearance. Hair should not be neglected or droopy. Frequently, it is hard for Messies to realize the importance of this. We feel ideas and ideals are important. What we put on our bodies seems less important. Because we tend to neglect it, we must pay special attention to how we dress. It is the first step in our search for dignity. It will be the first clue to others that a change has begun in our lives.

> A person of worth wears clothes that are clean, neat, and in good repair. This means no stretched-out elastic, no panty hose with runs, no torn slips. She always maintains high personal standards, even on the things that don't show.

Speak With Dignity

☆ *A person of dignity speaks with dignity.* ☆

Recently I was at a small committee meeting. The chairman was a man of considerable dignity. He commanded the group basically by the way he spoke. Let me first of all say that he was British and had to his advantage an elegant British accent. That would not have been enough to command respect, however, if he had not used other techniques well. He spoke deliberately and somewhat more slowly than most. But perhaps most important, when he made points, he leaned forward slowly and looked directly into the eyes of those in the group. It was done ever so naturally, but it was commanding.

I would say that most of the people in the group spoke in a similar way. (The members of the group were mostly men who were in positions of leadership in their occupations.) When they spoke, they expected to be listened to, so they did not have to speak loudly or rapidly. In short, they spoke with confidence. What a contrast to many chatty, excited women's groups. Studies have shown that women are interrupted much more often than men. We feel we have to talk louder and faster to "get it in."

This matter of speaking with dignity has two sides. If we feel confident and in control, we will speak in a way that reflects it. It works the other way, too. If we speak confidently, deliberately, not in a high, fast voice, we will command respect from others. This will reinforce a sense of confident dignity in ourselves.

Agatha Christie, in one of her mysteries, describes just such a characteristic way of speaking. "Dr. Nicholson was a big man with a manner that suggested great reserves of power. His speech was slow, on the whole he said very little, but contrived somehow to make every word sound significant. He wore strong glasses and behind them his very blue eyes flittered reflectively." (*Why Didn't They Ask Evans?*)

People who respect themselves express their own feelings more often. They also speak more politely to other people be-

185

cause the people to whom they are speaking are considered valuable and important and should be treated with dignity. Instead of asking a favor ("Will you hand me the phone?"), confident people are much more likely to make a statement of their feelings ("I would like the phone, please," or, "I would appreciate it if you would hand me the phone"). It is the language of authority. It gets quicker action. Making statements about what you want carries much more weight than asking for what you want.

I saw an example of this at the committee meeting I mentioned earlier. At one point, when the work of the committee was slowed by unnecessary backtracking, the chairman leaned forward. In a quiet and open way he said, "I feel I must tell you that if we continue going over material we have already covered sufficiently, I shall become impatient." I was amazed to see the change. The backtracking stopped immediately.

Most of us would have said, "If we keep going back, the meeting will run late," or, "If we keep going back, we will confuse the issue." But he was a man of confidence. His feelings were in the best interest of the group. He spoke them freely.

Messies tend to be too friendly, too giving, and too open. Just as wearing sloppy clothes to save money is an unwise idea when carried too far, being too accommodating encourages people to treat us without respect. The way you talk can help correct this. Express your feelings clearly and unemotionally. You are a person of worth. Your thoughts and feelings count.

People of dignity speak of themselves in positive ways. Although they may be very open about their weaknesses, and we all have them, people of dignity do not speak of themselves in derogatory ways.

I am not encouraging a bragging attitude. Bragging is offensive. It is beneath a person of dignity. Perhaps it will be easy to see what I mean if you watch someone whom you really admire. See if they don't speak rather openly, *when appropriate,* about their strengths and successes. You should, too.

If you are an excellent seamstress and someone asks if you can sew, tell them. Say with a smile, "Yes, I am a very good seamstress," not, "I sew a little sometimes."

Finally, people will respect you if you have something valuable to say. Messies, being idea people, frequently are avid readers. We may read the morning newspaper, the *National Enquirer,* or *The Wall Street Journal*—but we generally do read. As a result, we are usually in tune with what is happening in the world. This will enable us to hold our own in most conversations. Keeping up with current interests will make us interesting people. That is certainly a plus. If you feel that you have let a little sluggishness of mind creep in and you need a jolt of enthusiasm or interest, why not consider going to college for a refresher course or taking a correspondence course? Studies have shown that people who have large vocabularies are more successful than those who have poor or mediocre vocabularies. You might enjoy getting a book on vocabulary improvement to rev up your word power. Have the cares of life pushed you away from the intellectual stimulation you really need to help your self-esteem and strengthen your concept of the importance of your own personal dignity? In your search for the dignity that may have slipped away, you must be sure not to neglect your own personal development.

A word of caution is needed, however. Don't sign up for anything that will take too much time and force you into that hurried and harried way of life that is robbing you of so much dignity already. Get things more under control before you begin any extensive commitment.

One more thing is necessary; being interesting is really not enough. Speaking in the proper tone or making the proper eye contact is not enough either. You must have something really worthwhile to say. People will *want* to hear what you have to say if it meets their needs—either their need to have certain information, their need to have the answer to a problem, or their need for understanding. Parroting clichés or talking in a surface way about unsolved problems will cause people to think less of you. They will know that you are not interacting with reality in a meaningful way. We need depth to our speech.

I am not suggesting that we attempt to change our personalities and become very stiff, looking over horn-rimmed glasses and issuing deep dictums. Many of us are bouncy, bubbly, and full of fun. Great! If that is you, be bouncy, bubbly, and full of fun. Perhaps you have a subtle but persistent sense of humor that pervades every aspect of your life. You can't keep it down. Wonderful! Hold on to that quality. I just want to remind you and myself that if we are interested in fun, humor, and friendliness only, we will lose that important aspect of our lives that makes us take ourselves seriously enough to care about the dignity we all enjoy. That will be reflected in our houses. People of dignity do not live in clutter. They live in order and beauty.

If you are depressed and your depression is affecting the house (or the house being so messy is affecting the depression), now is a good time to begin picking up one or two shreds of dignity at a time. Perhaps you can start to speak more confidently in your home or on the phone. Perhaps you will start stating your needs openly in a nonemotional way. Perhaps it will just be a new haircut or new underwear. Whatever it is it will be for you—because you are a person of worth.

A person of worth speaks confidently and politely, clearly expressing her ideas and feelings without apology.

Act With Dignity

☆ **A person of dignity acts with dignity.** ☆

All of us have our doubts about our own personal value as people, if not at all times, at some times. It is at times like these that we need to remember some helpful things we can do to reinforce our own self-esteem.

It is always a good idea to seek out people who value you. Even if you are not going through a time of self-doubt, you need a friend, an acquaintance, or co-worker who thinks you are just great and knows how to tell you in a regular and responsible way. Family members play an important part here, but we may feel that they think we are great because they are prejudiced. I find that the more objective opinion of someone outside the family has a clearer ring of reality when the going is tough. Nothing, however, can take the place of constant reassurance and appreciation from family members on a day-to-day basis. Some people find that dogs or other pets who always love and admire them and think they are wonderful, give them a strong reinforcement of self-esteem.

Of course, the basis for it all is God's assessment of us. We *need* to know He thinks well of us. David was amazed at God's view of man and expressed it so beautifully in Psalms 8:3–5 (NAS) as he talked to God. "When I consider Thy heavens, the work of Thy fingers, the moon and the stars, which Thou hast ordained; What is man, that Thou dost take thought of him? And the son of man, that Thou dost care for him? Yet Thou hast made him a little lower than God, and dost crown him with glory and majesty!" The point is that people of dignity find ways to maintain the sense of worth they know is really theirs. (More will be said about this in chapter 9, "Rethink Your Position.")

A person of dignity acts like a person of dignity by refusing to let himself be put down by others. Just as he knows that putting down others is wrong because they are made in God's image and deserving of respect, so he does not allow it to be done to him. There are several ways to avoid being treated rudely or in a disrespectful way.

The first way is to just avoid people who do not have the good judgment to treat you properly. If there is someone who is "on your case," simply make it a point to see or speak to that person as little as possible. Don't avoid him or her because you are angry. Avoid them with the same sensible attitude that makes you avoid repeatedly putting your hand on a hot burner. It just does not make sense to continue an unsatisfactory action.

Many of us Messies, being open and friendly, find it hard to do this. As a moth is drawn to the flame, we come back again and again to the rude person because we think that surely we can get it straightened out. We think that if we are nice enough, friendly enough, clever enough with the retorts, or caustic enough with our answers, we can somehow change the person so that we will be treated properly by him. I have seldom found this to be the case. The person who has the poor judgment to treat me rudely in the first place, seldom has the good judgment to stop it.

Sometimes, because we work with certain people or because they are members of our families, we cannot avoid them completely. In that case, some other approach must be used to correct the situation. But correct it we must. We do not deserve to go on indefinitely being degraded by another person.

The first thing to do is to recognize that it is happening. Frequently, the put-down is subtle or disguised as humor. Face the fact that you are being put down and determine that it will not continue. After that it will not continue. Somehow, whether through humor, talking to the person in an unemotional but direct way, transferring elsewhere, speaking to the boss about the problem, or, in some cases, through a breakthrough in friendship (how about asking that person out to lunch?), we will make a change.

Let's back up a second and note specifically what we are not talking about. We are not talking about criticism. All of us do things that someone needs to tell us about. That's not disrespectful if it's done properly. We are not talking about a slipup of rudeness toward us. Everybody can make a mistake on a bad day. It's best to forgive and forget these things as quickly as possible.

We are not talking about everyday give and take which some of us who have sensitive spirits and low self-esteem may construe as rudeness. In that case, we should try to improve our own sense of self-worth and be a little more laid back in how we view our treatment. What we *are* talking about is a chronic, derogatory treatment, which is shown by the kind of criticism, the tone of criticism, the frequency of criticism, or derogatory humor.

I guess we all have had the misfortune to be involved in some of these situations. I recall once when the mother of one of my junior high students called me about a problem. As I talked to her, her attitude became belligerent; so I quietly said, "I'm afraid we are going to have to discontinue this conversation. I make it a policy not to talk to people who treat me in a disrespectful way. It would be better if you talked to the principal about this." She was flabbergasted. "You mean you won't talk to me!" I repeated my statement about my policy and I ended the conversation on a polite note. The problem was handled through the principal.

I follow this plan with my junior high students as well. On rare occasions students will be rude, sometimes without realizing it. If I talk in an explanatory way to them, letting them know that they are behaving in a way that, whether they mean it or not, is not respectful, they will usually change easily. (By the way, I always talk to them about their behavior in private because junior high students are very sensitive in front of their friends. I want to protect their dignity as well as my own.) If they continue to be rude, I immediately have someone else talk to them because, as you now know, I do not continue to talk to people who talk to me in a disrespectful way. Nor do I talk to others disrespectfully, at least I sure try not to. So far things have worked out well in these areas. In areas where I have less control over what goes on around me, things are not always so simple.

It may help to explain that I never ask for an apology from anyone who has been rude, whether child or adult. That is a personal decision on their part. I don't feel the need for one myself because I don't take rudeness as a personal affront so much as a failure of judgment on the other person's part.

Having said all this, let me hasten to mention that there are times when we bring trouble on ourselves. Not long ago, I was in the market for my first pair of glasses. It had been one of my New Year's goals, "Get an incredibly attractive pair of glasses." My sixteen-year-old son, a young lady friend from Trinidad, and I stopped in an eyeglass store in a mall. I tried one style and then another. Some looked funny. I put some on upside down. We got pretty silly. When I asked the man if he would open the case and show me a pair of glasses I had seen, he refused, saying that we were not seriously in the market for glasses. I felt he had been rude. He should have opened the case for us, I suppose; but looking back I can see that I brought it on myself. The man had no sense of humor. Perhaps he was tired. In actuality, I was an accomplice in his behavior.

Sometimes this happens to people on a much broader scale. Some people find that they get very little respect as a regular thing. Rodney Dangerfield has made a comedy career of it but when it happens in real life, it's not funny at all. If you find that from place to place with many different groups of people you are getting no respect, it is probably that you, like me in the eyeglass store, are cooperating. Most likely you do not know what brings on this treatment. Perhaps you think you know. "It's because I'm fat (or ugly or clumsy)," you may say. It is not any of these. One of the most respected men I know is a high school teacher with cerebral palsy. He speaks with a slur, cannot fully control the muscles of his face, and to top it all off sometimes comes to school wearing tennis shoes, army fatigue pants, a dress coat, and a tie. High school kids can be cannibals if they sense weakness of self-esteem. This man has not had any trouble. Someone has instilled in him a self-respect that has taken him many places more able-bodied people have not been able to go. It is not because of anything physical that we are treated badly. Physical problems sometimes become the focus of disrespect, but they are far from being the cause.

If you find that lack of respect follows you around like a cloud, try to find out why. Go to a counselor if you can find one who will work with you on social morés. Ask the counselor, "What can I do differently which will bring me the kind of acceptance that I deserve?" Pinpoint problems and work on them.

If you can't find outside help, try reading books on success. Begin to implement some of the techniques in this book. It is important for you to do this because you are a special person. There is nobody more deserving of the proper treatment than you.

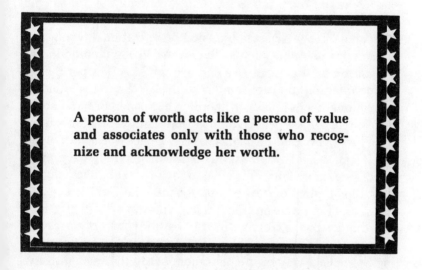

A person of worth acts like a person of value and associates only with those who recognize and acknowledge her worth.

React With Dignity

Messies tend to live in a particularly troubling world. On the one hand, we are aware of our own good capabilities, our strengths. On the other hand we find ourselves doing some very peculiar things which make us feel as though any confidence in our own worth is misplaced. The characteristics that make housekeeping difficult for us, also make us relate to other areas of life uncertainly.

We may forget important things, we may not notice obvious items, or we may mistake simple facts. We may try to overcome our weaknesses by using organizational techniques. We can use planning such as the Mount Vernon method to get the house under control. We can use the M.A. Flipper System (see chapter 12) to keep it under control. We can use other organizational techniques for handling our schedules and activities. But there are certain things that cannot be planned for. Once I wore my pull-on slacks to school backwards. I thought I was losing weight when I noticed how baggy they were in the front. Two hours later I discovered my mistake. There is no organizational plan for how to put on pants. You don't make a list that says, "Put pants on frontways." There is no organizational plan that keeps me from letting my bathtub overflow because I forgot it. Everybody makes a mistake once in a while. When this becomes a way of life, as is commonly the case with harried Messies, it can get very discouraging. It eats away at self-esteem.

If we do klutzy things in front of others, we feel even more like dunces than ever. How we react *after* we've done these things is very important. Let's look at some mental approaches we can prepare ahead of time.

We have already talked about avoiding those who put us down regularly. When we do something particularly dumb in front of others, we must be prepared to handle it. Even people who are usually nice may be tempted to make a hurtful or funny crack. Don't let it throw you. Accept yourself and it will be easier. If you wear your pants backwards and someone mentions that this is the situation, tell them that you are a trend setter. If the tub overflows, tell them that you are doing a really great cleaning job on the bathroom floor—and the hall floor, and the bedroom floor.... It *is* upsetting to do these things. We would much rather be like those in-control people who have never done anything awkward as far as anyone can tell. Messies work with a high degree of error. The point is that we must work harder to overcome our upset as quickly as possible. As our self-esteem grows, the time between our misstep and our forgiveness of ourselves will shorten. We will be able to accept ourselves for what we are, warts and all, and enjoy those aspects of our lives that are more successful.

When awkward things happen, avoid the tendency to make excuses. As I was outlining this chapter one Wednesday morning, happily anticipating my final day of vacation before returning to school, I suddenly realized that WEDNESDAY *was* the day I was supposed to return to school. The faculty meeting was scheduled for 8:30 A.M. and it was already 8:45. My first impulse was to berate myself for my oversight while frantically scurrying around, then race to the meeting. Once there, I could mutter my flustered excuses. But I remembered my own advice. I am a person of dignity and worth. No dumb thing I can do can alter that fact. I had been looking forward to making a nice appearance at school on my first day. I had recently had my hair done in anticipation of school beginning. I wanted to fix it right. So I forgave myself, got dressed carefully, did my hair and makeup, and drove carefully to school, enjoying the beauty of the morning. I arrived unusually happy and joined the meeting which, as it happens, had begun late. I was just in time to introduce myself as though I had been there all along. No one asked me why I was late, if they noticed at all. Several people did tell me how nice I looked.

I am a person crowned with glory and majesty by God even when I am late to the school meeting, forget my bathtub, wear my pants backwards, or do any of the thousands of other things I am likely to do which are not so easily solved.

But what happens when we get really down and very dis-

195

couraged with ourselves and things begin to unravel? What happens when our faults catch up with us and we are overwhelmed by self-doubt?

The best thing to do is to remember the successes. There are certain things about myself I am proud of. You have some, too. Tell yourself, *I know I goofed up here but I* _____ (fill in the good stuff here). Everybody should have something to remember in more rational moments.

But sometimes no amount of talking to ourselves can convince us that we have *any* good qualities. We are depressed. We do not deserve to feel like that. Outside help from a psychologist may be needed.

You are valuable, not because you think so or because others think so but because God thinks so. Even if you are so depressed you don't ever get out of bed and you never pick up even one piece of clutter, you are infinitely important. You don't even have to believe it one little bit for it to be true. Just count on it—you are marvelously, wonderfully valuable. Period!

A person of worth reacts with grace and humor to the people and events of life—even embarrassing ones—without apology or excuse.

Treat Yourself With Dignity

☆ *A person of dignity treats herself with dignity.* ☆

The basis of being a person of dignity is our own self-respect. When we respect ourselves, others will respect us. We must think of ourselves as people of great value. It will make a big difference in every aspect of our lives, including our houses. Our houses reflect our own personal attitudes about ourselves.

You will notice I have shared a number of things about myself which some people might wish to hide. I freely share that I work with a high degree of error because my own worth does not rise and fall in relation to how many dumb things I can cover up. I am made in God's image. I am important to Him. I am one of that special group of people known as *Humanus Wonderfulus* subspecies Messie.

This is precisely the reason that we don't make excuses. We do not need to hedge in our nobility by pretended perfection. It exists perfectly well without our paltry efforts to protect it.

Excuse me while I adjust my crown.

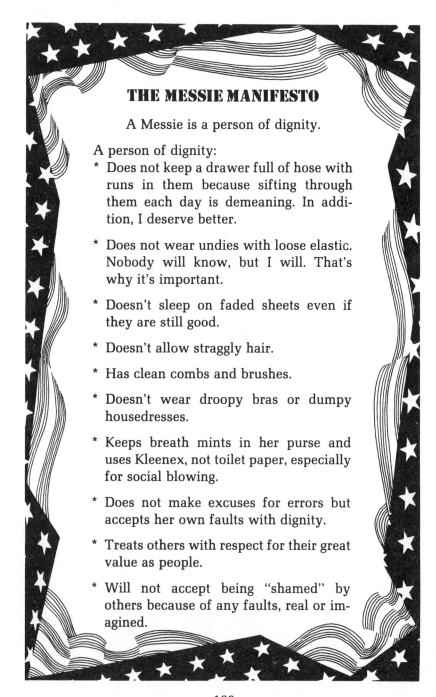

THE MESSIE MANIFESTO

A Messie is a person of dignity.

A person of dignity:
* Does not keep a drawer full of hose with runs in them because sifting through them each day is demeaning. In addition, I deserve better.

* Does not wear undies with loose elastic. Nobody will know, but I will. That's why it's important.

* Doesn't sleep on faded sheets even if they are still good.

* Doesn't allow straggly hair.

* Has clean combs and brushes.

* Doesn't wear droopy bras or dumpy housedresses.

* Keeps breath mints in her purse and uses Kleenex, not toilet paper, especially for social blowing.

* Does not make excuses for errors but accepts her own faults with dignity.

* Treats others with respect for their great value as people.

* Will not accept being "shamed" by others because of any faults, real or imagined.

Profile of a Messie (Part I): The Reasons

Messiness is, for the most part, something we are born with. I have been a Messie all my life, but I didn't know it until I tried to organize my house for myself. Until that time, I had lived in the organization that my mother, the Cleanie, produced. When I had trouble with organization, she always kept me steered in the right direction and floated me along when I floundered organizationally. All of this help I took as a matter of course and didn't realize how messy I was when I was on my own.

Lurking in my brain was a closet full of destructive thinking and a trunk full of characteristics that would later sink my organizational ship. Right from the beginning of my marriage, when I started housekeeping on my own, I started in the wrong direction.

Many Messies share characteristics that make it hard for us to succeed in housekeeping. Let's look at some of these characteristics Messies have in common.

199

Distractibility

Like a flea in a frying pan, Messies hop from one task to another, leaving a trail of half-done tasks behind them. Without actually deciding to leave one job, they find themselves another. The cluttered nature of the house invites this. We hop from one job to another because in order to put away things from one pile, we must clear a shelf to receive the overflow from another shelf, and so on.

Finally, husband comes home and it is left for tomorrow— or whenever we can get back to it.

The Flipper system, which is described in chapter 12, is designed to give direction and purpose to our labor so we won't squander our energy on playing musical messes.

Visual Tune Out

Messies don't really "notice" how bad things are because they don't actually focus on things visually. You might say they *think* nearsighted. They may have good visual acuity, but they don't "look" at the condition of the house. Messies have a sort of tunnel vision. They can see only a little part of the house at a time, working like crazy on that. This accounts for one part of the house being in super shape while the rest is a shambles.

Tendency to Overdo

Because they really do want to succeed in the house and know they are distractible, Messies frequently get so tense that they overdo. They are so intense that they keep on too long. If Messies could relax and stand back from the whole issue of housekeeping, they could make a lot more progress.

This overdoing can show itself in several ways. Peg, for instance, wants desperately to have a nice orderly home so she begins with the drawers of the dresser. All day she sorts socks, folds clothes, lines drawers, and so on. Meals are left uncooked and laundry is left undone. So anxious is she to succeed and so strong is her concentration that she becomes rigid. She cannot shift into other jobs when they need doing. The house is too disordered to clean. But the drawers are neat.

Mattie has a different problem but the result is the same. Mattie is able to see the bigger picture. Her goal is to do the whole house—to get control once and for all. It must be done. She is determined. Hour after hour she labors, doing a Herculean task spurred on by desperation. She cannot slow down because her concentration on success is so strong. If the children interrupt, as they always do, she cannot handle the shift she must make for the interruption. She may become angry at them and quit the job altogether. She cannot shift from the house to the kids and back to the house.

Peg becomes discouraged because the really troublesome parts of the house are not done and Mattie becomes exhausted. They both quit for a long rest. Again, they overdo. This time they overdo resting. The house gathers dust while they read (or whatever) to escape the burden of overdoing.

Now they have a really good excuse to tell themselves: *I tried but it was just too much for me.*

The Mount Vernon method is designed to keep a person from getting on the wrong unproductive track like Peg or on the overdoing track like Mattie, while getting the house under control. "Inch by inch it's a cinch" is our motto. But the inches must be directed in the right direction or we quit.

Slow Movements

Some Messies move slower than other people. Our Dan Marino, super Miami Dolphins quarterback, has what physical therapists call a "fast twitch." His synapses and nerves just work quickly. He'll be standing in the pocket under pressure and all of a sudden the ball is gone. He moves like lightning. He was born with a fast twitch.

Many Messies have slow twitches. We seem to be working at the same rate as others but less gets done. Those who do have fast twitches sometimes use it as an excuse to procrastinate because they will get it done quickly once they begin. But they put off beginning.

These and other similar characteristics actually interfere with housekeeping successes. Cleanies aren't troubled with these hindrances.

Messies Anonymous assumes that anybody who is a Messie wouldn't be that way if it were a matter of choice. But we were born with these characteristics, just as we were born with our hair and eye color. There are other hindrances we bring on ourselves. These are ways of thinking we pick up along the way to help us adjust to our messy way of life. In the end, these "adjustments" add to the problem.

Many Messies are just "laid back" types. That's why we need a specific, easy-to-follow plan, designed to fit personal characteristics. Perhaps some of us had the spirit of the 1960s. We persuaded ourselves that it was not necessary to be too intense about life. We were already disorganized by nature, and the undisciplined life-style was in vogue. This combination moves a Messie a long way down the road to disastrous housekeeping.

To add to our problems, Messies are able to absorb vast quantities of personal stress. We are used to having things out of control. We can take it. We know we won't die if the phone is disconnected (they can reconnect it), if a check bounces (they'll put it through again), if there's no food for breakfast (we'll have SpaghettiOs), if a report is not ready (nobody's perfect), if we can't find the tax receipts (it's only money). This kind of living is devastating to a person's self-esteem. Because we can handle it, we let it continue, not realizing how devastating it really is to us. Messies cannot allow their dignity to be trampled on. We should not allow ourselves to "take it."

A banker I know told me that he had customers who knew they were overdrawn and who had the money to deposit but just did not bother to come to the bank to make the deposit. "Lazy," he called them. But I wonder. Why would a person be willing to take the consequence rather than put forth a little effort to avoid it?

Perhaps one reason is that same rebellious nature that causes some people to procrastinate. *You aren't going to tell me what I have to do,* they think consciously or unconsciously, and so they break the rules and take the consequences.

Finally, Messies kid themselves by hanging on to unproductive ideas. The energy-saving idea of leaving things out so the items don't need to be taken out again just makes a mess. But the idea *sounds* good. The idea of piling, not filing, doesn't work either, but it seems like such a time-saver. The fruitless idea of having six boxes of Band-Aids around somewhere so when I need them surely I'll be able to find one, doesn't work either. These ideas make for a messy way of life. They must be abandoned if a new way of life is to emerge.

While the Messie is struggling to overcome her natural characteristics and her unproductive ways of thinking, other people are entering into the picture. Husbands, children, and parents who are disturbed by having to live in this commotion eventually begin to state their feelings about the way things are.

"You need to put things away so I can find them."
"Why don't you keep the house looking like Carrie's mommy does?"
"I don't have any clean underwear to wear today."

We can react in several ways to their chiding. We can—

Rebel. I have already referred to those Messies who react in a rebellious way, become angry, and don't change—just for spite.

Retreat. Some Messies react by withdrawing. They get too upset to do anything. Sometimes they become depressed and spend long hours in bed or reading or just doing a few things they are successful at and ignoring the rest.

Use smoke screens. This is a Messie who may seem always to be working or about to work or talking about work or planning to work, but she never gets much done. She may really be trying, but not to accomplish what her family wants—a beautiful house. She uses talk to cover her lack of actual accomplishment. When she does work it is not to accomplish the job, it is simply to say she's done it. This Messie is not goal oriented, she is task oriented. She does not pick up the house because she wants it to look beautiful and work efficiently. She cleans because that's what is expected of her; that's what she's *supposed* to do. She may vacuum at the end of the day because it's on her list. A Cleanie would vacuum in the morning because she wants a lovely home all day.

Messies play all kinds of games with themselves but they always come up losers. When Messies realize they have some characteristics that make organization difficult, they can compensate for them. Accepting ourselves with our weaknesses will help relax us and free us to work more efficiently. When we realize there are ways of thinking we need to abandon, success is just a thought away.

Profile of a Messie (Part II): The Personalities

"Imitations abound but there's only one YOU."
FLORENCE LITTAUER (Personality Plus)

Twenty-five years ago I was introduced to the four basic temperaments originally propounded by Hippocrates, the Greek physician who is generally credited with being the father of modern medicine. All through the years, people have tried to divide humans into some type of meaningful classification. Although no system really divides people with perfect accuracy, this ancient Greek classification certainly can give us some significant insights into ourselves and those we live with—and try to understand. The names for these temperaments may sound Greek to you, but we will stick with them so as not to buck twenty-five hundred years of history.

Here are the four types with their basic personality traits:

> *Sanguine*—Lively, sunny outlook
> *Melancholy*—Dark, moody outlook
> *Choleric*—Active
> *Phlegmatic*—Slow temperament

No person is purely one temperament. We are all combinations. Most people, however, have one dominant personality type. Understand your basic type and the types of the people you live with and you will understand some of the problems you have been having with yourself and with them. Since it is true that opposites attract, this is important!

Characteristics of the Personality Types— Which Type Are You?

Sanguine. Sanguine types are outgoing, lively, and exuberant. Generally optimistic and not easily bored, they have many interests to which they can turn and are frequently involved in crafts, art, and volunteer work.

Sanguines tend to have spotty memories. Things like names, dates, and places tend to fade rapidly.

Because Sanguines live in the present, the past fades rapidly from memory and they are unable to visualize the future with any clarity. I believe this is the reason so many Sanguine Messies collect things. They know, intuitively, that the past will fade and they will not be able to remember it. In order to compensate, they make a Herculean effort to insure that it doesn't slip. They take and keep gigantic amounts of snapshots. They keep old programs, canceled ticket stubs, shells from the beach, and baby shoes. They have good reason to: Without them, they probably won't remember the past with the richness they feel it deserves. Being responsible people, Sanguines want to be prepared for the future. Since they cannot visualize the future well (and who can know exactly the future?), they go overboard on being prepared. They keep old medicine, magazines, and makeup "just in case." The problem with this is that unless they are highly organized, they can't enjoy or even *find* all these items they have collected. Even the organized Sanguine finds that all of this organized "collection" becomes too much burden to bear.

This living in the present with little regard to the future is also a problem when it comes to keeping a time schedule. Even though Sanguines may know they have to be someplace at a certain time, they find it difficult to pace themselves to get dressed and drive there in the proper amount of time. When it comes to remembering things to do in the future, Sanguines are very unreliable, often forgetting events or getting the time or day mixed up. Because I am a Sanguine, as are many Messies, I missed the opening day of school, as I mentioned earlier. This is also one of the reasons bills are allowed to become overdue. The time passes quickly before the Sanguine realizes that the date for sending the payment has passed. It seems as if the bill just came a few days before.

Because Sanguines live in the present, they have difficulty with long-range goals. Although they may take on several projects and volunteer for many worthy activities, they have a problem following through. The goal begins to fade quickly. Other, "fresher" activities catch their attention. The goal that was so important yesterday, drifts into the murky past.

Many Messies have the basic Sanguine nature. If they live with another Sanguine, there is double trouble for the house. They will be cheerful but always frustrated with the state of things in the world around them.

Melancholy. Melancholies have a very rich temperament. They are very sensitive, which means they usually enjoy the fine arts. Indeed, they may be musicians, artists, inventors, philosophers, or theologians.

Melancholies are sensitive to the needs of others. They do not forget them like the Sanguine does. They remember and analyze the needs of the person, because they love to meet needs whether personal or of some other nature. They are idealistic, purposeful, and organized.

Most Melancholies are perfectionists. They love to analyze things to see how close to perfection they come. They also love details and are very visually sensitive. Melancholies love to make charts, graphs, and lists. They live best in a house that is orderly and serene. Because of these characteristics, they make good housekeepers—evaluating what needs to be done and doing it efficiently. They are economical, as well. If you are part Melancholy, you can use this artistic and sensitive characteristic to encourage yourself to keep going. Go to model homes and displays of beauty. Dream of the beauty and order that will be yours if you keep going with your plans. You can make your home your art.

If you live with a full Melancholy, he or she is probably grieved at your messy tendencies. The disorder and lack of perfection drives them crazy. Nothing a Messie does is ever good enough for a Melancholy. He will redo it or be forced to say something about it, blurting out hurtful things. He may even exaggerate some problems, making you feel further confused and frustrated.

If you are a Sanguine personality, all of this perfection and depression from the Melancholy you live with can drive you crazy and eventually discourage you from trying. If you are a Messie with some Melancholy tendencies, these traits can cause you to procrastinate or put yourself down because you take so seriously your own faults.

Choleric. Cholerics have optimistic, take-charge, goal-oriented, dynamic personalities. They are always trying to change things for the better and are frequently put in positions of leadership for that purpose. What's more, they know how to organize and delegate work.

Does this sound like a person who would be controlled by a messy house? Not on your life! If you are a Messie who has even a touch of Choleric, use it. Nurture it and use it. It will help you immensely to get on the right track.

If your husband or mother or mother-in-law is a Choleric, you may find yourself being highly pressured and criticized. Because they are goal-oriented, they sometimes (perhaps frequently) ignore the feelings of the people they relate to. They look down on people less capable than themselves.

If you live with a Choleric who has not learned to tone down his pushy nature when dealing with you, you may find your relationship strained by this bossy approach. This may discourage or anger you to the point that you do an even poorer job of keeping house than you would have otherwise.

Cholerics are hard to change. If a Choleric is interfering with your life by his abrasive approach, you need to let him know that. He is sure he is right and that if you would only change, he would not have to push you. However, clear communication, oiled by love and caring, should begin to make a change. A person of dignity, Messie or not, doesn't allow herself to be chronically put down, no matter how capable the one who puts us down is.

On the other hand, Messies can use the organizational abilities of Cholerics once the tension between them is dispelled. The Choleric can help guide a Messie to success, if the Messie is the one who initially asks for advice. Thank God for Cholerics. They are the movers and shakers of the world. Let's get them to help us, not boss us.

Phlegmatic. Phlegmatics are easygoing people. Many Messies have a large touch of Phlegmatic. They are steady, low-keyed, patient, and accommodating. Phlegmatics are good workers in any organization. They may not set the world on fire with enthusiasm or creativity, but they can be counted on to get the job done.

Most Phlegmatics are happily reconciled to life and are not pushy. Although they do not take control of situations automatically as do Cholerics, if put in a position of responsibility they feel they can handle, they will usually do a very good job.

Phlegmatics are good listeners. They are not restless to get on to other things as Sanguines are. They make good, easy-to-get-along-with friends and are always there when you need them.

Phlegmatics may have fewer weaknesses than other types, but the weaknesses they do have are significant to Messies with Phlegmatic tendencies.

Phlegmatics are not easily motivated and do not have much get-up-and-go. They prefer not to make plans to do things such as go out to a play, remodel the house, or upgrade housekeeping. It's easier not to. The saying, "Let's not and say we did," fits the Phlegmatic. In its most extreme form, this low motivation is called laziness.

Phlegmatics prefer to *think* about things to do rather than *do* them. The fact that they have thought out a job carefully often substitutes for actually doing it. Mentally, they are very efficient, always thinking of how to save energy by doing things in an easier way. They feel content knowing they are all prepared mentally to do the job if they ever get around to it—but they usually don't get around to it.

When it comes to housecleaning, the big job which would be necessary to get things in order just overwhelms them. They have a low-energy level. They may go to a seminar or read a book and be content with knowing *how* to change even if they never do.

This is low motivation further compounded by the Phlegmatic's tendency to be stubborn. If a Phlegmatic decides not to change, even a Choleric cannot persuade her to do so. The low motivation is "set" by stubbornness. An easygoing good humor often disguises this trait—but it is there.

Finally, Phlegmatics tend to be indecisive. Melancholies are indecisive because they want to make only the "best" decision in their perfectionistic way. Phlegmatics, however, hesitate to make decisions for more practical reasons. First of all, they are so easygoing, they don't really care about some choices. "Coffee or tea," "milk or Coke"—what difference does it make? None, to Phlegmatics. They let others order first and get what the majority wants.

The other reason Phlegmatics hesitate to make decisions is because they are protective of their energies and commitments. They do not want to make a decision that will later require them to do more work than they really want to do.

If a Messie woman lives with a Messie Phlegmatic man, she may have a tough time getting him to cooperate in her desire to change the house. After she gets the house in order and is wonderfully proud, he will not compliment her because he really doesn't care whether it is neat or not. Don't let this discourage you. It is his nature. Besides, you care even if he doesn't.

The Messie Temperament. Perhaps there is a fifth temperament which combines the temperaments of the other four groups in such a way as to make it a separate temperament—the Messie temperament.

Messies are frequently confused and frustrated by their own temperament. It contains a combination of conflicting characteristics of the other groups in varying combinations.

Messies have the friendliness, poor memory, cheery disposition, distractibility, and reluctance to say no of the Sanguine. Most Messies are basically Sanguine.

You can take advantage of this part of yourself. Use your friendliness and cheerfulness to encourage yourself to clean up the house. Invite people over, schedule get-togethers. This is a perfect reason for the Sanguine Messie to get the house in order.

Messies also have the Melancholy's sensitivity and desire for true values of life such as art, beauty, and learning, which causes great stress to their soul. So they compensate by using their natural ability to not notice the mess. To complicate things further, Messies are frequently perfectionists like Melancholies. This perfectionism along with the habit of collecting are the major impediments to progress. Perfectionism is a most frustrating characteristic because it works against itself. It has the seeds of destruction built in. As you know, the perfectionist Messies want to do it right or not at all and, too often, "not at all" wins. However, the Melancholy part can be one of the Messie's strongest motivations. Because this part makes them desire a quality way of life, they are often able to overcome hindrances and keep going over the problems until success is achieved.

The Phlegmatic part of the Messie that can be the most troublesome is low motivation—the feeling that everything is "just too much." The Messie with this trait needs to set up a reasonable program for herself. She should do a little Mount Vernoning every day. And when she sets up her Flipper, she has to make sure she doesn't overschedule and thereby discourage herself because it is too much.

Use Your Knowledge

Knowing about these temperaments can help you see yourself with all your strengths and weaknesses. You can then encourage your strengths and work either over or around your weaknesses. Weaknesses are never excuses for failure. They are only hindrances to avoid as you aim for success. Remember, whatever your temperament, you will succeed if you have a goal, have a keen desire to achieve it, and have a plan to do so.

If some of the characteristics you see here are those of the people you live with, learn to use and draw upon the positive characteristics and to overcome the negative ones.

Winning
the War
and Keeping
It Won

PART TWO

Victor or Victim: It's Really Up to You

Habit is habit, and not to be flung out the window by any man but coaxed downstairs a step at a time.

MARK TWAIN

Somewhere, hidden away, is our desire to improve our way of life. We must find it and nurture it. We must come to the realization that we and we alone are responsible for the condition in which we live. This understanding may come slowly or with the shock of a glass of cold water in the face. But it must come. The impact of this realization will result in a delightful life change you have been afraid to dream of.

We must realize that the house, with all its clutter and disorder, is the direct and deliberate creation of our own desires. The decisions we have made created it. We may not like what we have created—but create it we did! And only we can "uncreate" it.

Mother is not going to make the change for us. No fairy godmother is going to do it. No psychologist is going to come with his truck and haul stuff away. Neighbors or the health department are not ultimately responsible. We are.

True dignity begins when we plant our feet squarely in the middle of our lives and say, "I am responsible."

219

What a burden it lifts from our backs. No longer do we have to search for some cure, hoping and wondering from whence it may come charging up on a white horse, with some magic formula for success. We are the cure.

There is no secret of success written on a green stick hidden in the forest as Dostoevski thought as a child.

Once upon a time there was a man whose chief goal in life was to make his fortune by finding diamonds. He left his village to search the world over for these diamonds. He spent his life in this fruitless search and died a poor man. When his friends in the village dug his grave, they dug up incredibly valuable and beautiful *diamonds!* He had been searching in the wrong place. What he wanted had been close at hand all the time. Yet he died unfulfilled.

The answer you seek is close at hand. It is within you. If you keep searching in other places, you will waste time and miss out on the incredibly beautiful and wonderful life that is available for you. Grab it! Insist on it! But first admit, "The answer is within *me.*"

It is not easy to admit this. We have been telling ourselves for so long that we must save unnecessary items, that we must keep busy, that we deserve to rest, that we must follow the self-destructive path we have been following. It is hard to admit to ourselves that we have been wrong. We've been feeding ourselves destructive thoughts. It takes courage to say, "I have been wrong." Find that courage! You must—if you are ever going to find the answer to your dilemma.

Life often works on paradoxes. We have sayings to show that. We say that we "get by giving," we say, "more is less," and so on. In the area which we are talking about there is a similar principle—we improve by not trying so hard. Messies are rather intense people. Our intensity drives us to a frenzied life of saving, studying, doing, and going. To us everything is *so* important. We *must* keep this. We *must* do that. This way of thinking leads to cluttered lives and cluttered minds.

Just *relax!* Every detail of your life is not all that important. So you threw away a pan yesterday that you hadn't used in years but could use today. Who cares? You have another one that will do. Things don't have to be as elaborate and perfect as you've been telling yourself they need to be.

You are not the only person who can direct the school carnival which saps your life every year. Relax, let somebody else do it. Even if it is not done as well as you would have done it, who cares? It really is not all that important that every detail be done exactly as you would have done it. Even if (horror of horrors!) the school carnival isn't held unless you head it up, so what? Is there that little interest on the part of all of the other parents? The history of the world will not be changed if the school carnival is not held.

"Oh, but I love to do it," you say. "The children have so much fun!" But how about *your* children when they come home? Is it fun to have clutter all around or no clean socks when the morning rush comes?

We cannot have everything, and, what's more, it is not important that we do. Wake up to that fact and you will find the freedom to begin having the great life you want. You don't need to do everything. You don't need to *keep* everything. You don't need to read the newspaper through each day *and* do the crossword puzzle. "Thou shalt read every newspaper religiously," is not the eleventh commandment. After a while all the clutter and activity we gather to ourselves confuses us so much we don't even know what we need or want. We are just on a treadmill of bad habits.

Stop! Deliberately step off that treadmill. Decide now that you will *not* continue the way you have been going.

Somewhere in the past you decided, decision by decision, to get on the treadmill. Today, you can make a decision again—the decision to get off. Choose what you want now.

Perhaps you are afraid to get off—to let go of the way of life that you have told yourself makes you valuable and fulfilled. Perhaps you are afraid you will lose part of yourself. On the contrary, only as you take control will you be able to find your true self.

If you will not get off you have become a victim of your thoughts. Nobody knows the fear that comes to the heart of a Messie who must make that decision. We have become so attached to our destructive ways. I know there are Messies reading this right now who are afraid to think about letting go of these destructive patterns. The change may come with regrets—it may come with tears, first tears of loss and then tears of relief. You may valiantly start to let go and later turn back. That's okay as long as you know that when you have gotten the courage again, you will return to the new way of life you have chosen.

Challenge your fears. Tell yourself out loud and in writing that your life will be better when you quit striving so hard. Tell yourself that it will be okay for you to relax and not work so intensely on every detail. Tell yourself you will not lose part of yourself. You will gain the dignity and self-esteem you lost in the scramble of that other way of life.

There are two different approaches that readers who want to change will take.

Some who read this chapter will be infused with a fighting spirit. "How dare this house do this to my life!" they'll say as they get angry and roll up their sleeves to begin the fray. This attitude is very important. When we get angry, we will fight to make a change.

In California, a serial rapist had accosted and raped many women and no one seemed to be able to stop him. One young lady was jogging in the daylight hours when this same rapist jumped her from behind, knocking her to the ground and falling on top of her. He was much heavier and stronger than she but she was infused with anger and indignation. She would *not* be a victim. In her determination, she did her best to fight. All she could do was hit him in the throat with one free hand, but she did it so convincingly that he gave up and presumably went in search of an easier victim. The women who told this story were running a program on self-defense. They told how some of the women they talked to were reluctant to fight. Women attending the class said that they would fight to protect their children but would hesitate to fight to protect themselves. Our children are important, but we are important, too. Their statement was that self-respect is the basis of self-defense. Self-respect is the basis of our self-defense against messiness, too. When we respect ourselves, we will fight and win.

There is another helpful attitude which is good to adopt. In the long run, this attitude is probably one that will sustain the Messie over a longer period of time than anger because anger is hard to sustain. Sometimes in a flash of insight, the Messie will see the ridiculous nature of her situation. On a cloud of self-respect, like having an out-of-body experience, she rises above the house and looks down. She feels powerful. She laughs at how foolish she has been to have been dominated and defeated by the house. She will not fight the house. *We only fight with equals,* she reasons. She will not give the problem the courtesy of being considered an equal. The problem is large but she sees suddenly that her ability is so much larger. Almost regally, she begins banishing the problem. She doesn't fight it away. She simply dismisses it a little at a time. Slowly but surely it disappears because of the force of her mind. She has changed her thinking about herself and her house. In a sense, she loves the house into order. This attitude is a powerful force. The mess, no matter how big, cannot resist its power. This book may be the thing that opens your eyes to your own power.

A wonderful way of life awaits you. You can have the life you want. The secret really is within you.

Six Strategic Steps

The desire to change carries within it the seeds of its own fulfillment.

NAPOLEON HILL

Those Cleanies on the opposite end of the continuum from Messies are remarkable people. As I circulate across the country representing Messies Anonymous, I meet many different kinds of people, including that remarkable group known as Cleanies.

Cleanies hearing about Messies Anonymous feel this is an opportunity to tell me about the condition of their houses. They feel compelled to talk about it.

"My house is always perfect," the older professional man was telling me with his Spanish accent from behind his big desk. I had come to see him for business reasons but he had digressed to a subject he cared greatly about.

"I do not expect anybody to come visit me but if you were to come home with me right now, my house would look like a picture in a magazine. And I throw things out—always throw things out. I cannot stand things out of order. I don't know why. It is a sickness with me."

So went the conversation. It was like many other conversations I've had with Cleanies who love to talk about their beautiful houses. With Cleanies, the order of the house at this moment—right now—is a big thing.

What makes Cleanies different from Messies? When you really understand this basic difference you will know the secret of success. The thing that makes Cleanies so successful in controlling their houses is *desire*—a strong, burning, consistent, heartfelt desire to have a beautiful home at all times.

You already have some of that desire since you are reading this book. If you can make it intense enough, it will be the force behind your changing. We are not talking about a general wish or a vague hope. When you can see the house in your mind, when you can feel the joy you'll have when it's that way, when you cannot imagine things continuing the way they are now—then you have the desire you need for success.

In 1937, Napoleon Hill wrote a gentle, insightful book with the startling title *Think and Grow Rich*. This book, reprinted many times and still going strong, was probably the first book to expound the power of thought to accomplish what you want, provided you know what you want—and we know that, don't we! We want lovely, orderly houses! That's it, Mr. Hill! Mr. Hill should have written a book entitled *Think and Grow Neat*. The power of thought works for any goal, provided you know what you want and have the desire to accomplish it.

There are six steps to accomplishing what you want. These have been adapted many times to various goals. We will apply them to having a beautiful house because that's what we want.

1. *Decide exactly what you want.* Don't say, "I want a generally nice house." Decide *exactly* what you want. Make it definite. Do you want it nice in the public areas at all times so guests can always be welcomed, even unexpectedly? Or do you want it beautiful so you can enjoy being at home and seeing it? Or do you want it to be uncluttered so that the house can reflect your own personality? Or do you just want to quit losing things? Perhaps it is all of the above. Whatever *you* want. De-

225

cide now. Stop a minute to pinpoint your desire. Say it out loud to yourself before reading on.

2. *Decide what you will do to get it.* "There's no such thing as a free lunch." Keeping the house orderly is going to cost you; but living with it the way it is now is costing you already. The price you pay in lost time, lost self-esteem, lost money because of waste, misplaced papers, and so on is enormous. Decide what you are willing to give (or give up) in order to get what you want. That is your payment for a lovely home.

3. *Set a time limit.* Put a date on *when* your goal will be accomplished. Stop a moment and fix a definite time. Be realistic. It took me three and a half months to do the Mount Vernon method to my house and it is not large. After the Mount Vernon method, the Flipper System takes over (more about that later). Announce your target date out loud.

4. *Make a plan.* Decide on exactly *how* you will accomplish your goal. The Mount Vernon method, including a few daily jobs, is the way to start. Begin right away, whether you think you are ready or not. Include any other steps necessary to your plan.

5. *Make the above steps definite by writing them down.* Get a piece of paper and pen. Write exactly how you want your house to be and tell what you'll do to get it that way. Put down a time limit. Put that piece of paper in this book right now so you won't have it just floating around the house. If you want to put it on the refrigerator or bulletin board, that's okay, but have a definite place and keep it there.

6. *Read aloud the statement you have just written twice a day.* Read it when you get up in the morning and when you go to bed. Form a mental picture of your lovely house as you read. Feel the elation as though your house is already exactly as you want it.

Now you are mentally ready to begin. Success comes to those who are ready for it.

Strange as it may seem, your past failures may be just the trigger you need to flip you into success. If things had not gotten as bad as they are, you wouldn't be as willing to change as you are.

In my case, though, I had lived for twenty-three years in a chronically frustrating state of messiness that was growing very tiresome, indeed. It was a leak in the sink that finally made me change. I had kept stacks of newspapers under my sink because I might need them "just in case." The sink sprang a slow leak, but, because the newspapers soaked up the water, I didn't know about the leak until the floor of the cabinet had rotted. This was the final indignity. I suddenly saw the state to which my faulty thinking had reduced me. I was angry at what I had done to myself. It was the beginning of the end of my chronically Messie way of life. I didn't know how, but I knew I would change.

How much I have changed was pinpointed this morning as I made plans for the day with my husband.

"I'm going to the university library to write for a few hours," I said.

"You can't," he answered in a surprised voice. "My mother is coming for an overnight visit. Don't you need to clean house?"

"What needs cleaning?" I asked. "The bed is made. The dishes are in the dishwasher washing. The rug was just vacuumed and the furniture polished. There's nothing to do."

"You could do the toilet, the tub, the bathroom sink."

"We don't have a bathroom sink," I reminded him. (We had had it replaced but the replacement was faulty, so we were "between sinks." It certainly cuts down on cleaning the bathroom.)

"Well, okay," he said. "I have some straightening up to do with my books and papers."

So here I am at the library, overlooking a green, manicured lawn which leads down to a pond mirroring the trees beyond. My mother-in-law is coming. The house is in order. How did my cluttered, topsy-turvy life come to this point? It began when my kitchen sink cabinets rotted.

In other words, I reflected the attitude of the newsman in the movie *Network* who shouted, "I'm mad as hell and I'm not going to take it anymore." When the embarrassment, frustration, and anger go, they are replaced by a steel-cold determination to change. And we do.

What's peculiar about this whole story is that my long-suffering husband at times still carries the fear born of years of living with things out of control. It shows how hard it is on everybody to live that way.

"It is always darkest before the dawn." The reason this is true is because we can stand only so much darkness. Then we *make* the dawn come; we insist that it come. Are you ready to make the dawn come? To insist on it coming? Not to rest until it comes—and soon? That's desire. We must have it.

Thoughts are powerful things. We make our own situations by our own thinking. Like a genie, materializing from a cloud in a bottle, our thoughts turn into the life we see before us. Thoughts are indiscriminate. They work positively as well as negatively. If you direct them toward neatness, the house will materialize in an orderly way. If you don't direct your thoughts toward neatness, the empty space will be filled with disordered thoughts and the house will materialize in that way. Your desire to live in beauty and order is significant. If you can conceive it, you can achieve it.

Go back to the six practical steps at the beginning of this chapter. It is very important that you follow them exactly so that your mind will conceive clearly the goals you wish to achieve.

You will not always find clear sailing. There will be discouragements and failures. Don't let that stop you. Every failure carries an equivalent seed of success.

There is another you, different from the one you have been living with. She is a successful, powerful person in her house. She is your other self, not a new self. She's been there all along. Your other self has the ability and power to obtain beauty and order.

Be open-minded about yourself. Open your mind to the possibility of success. It will come.

Now It's Your Turn

The six strategic steps to accomplishing what you want are:

1. Decide exactly what you want.

2. Decide what you will do to get it.

3. Set a time limit.

4. Make a plan.

5. Make the steps definite by writing them down.

6. Read aloud the statements you have just written twice a day.

Use the following space to outline your own goals.

Step 1. My goals include:

_____

_____

_____

_____

_____

Step 2. In order to achieve my goals, I am willing to: (What changes in my life am I willing to make?)

_____

_____

_____

_____

_____

Step 3. I will reach my goals by: (Use specific dates; be realistic.)

_____

_____

_____

_____

_____

Step 4. In order to reach my goal, I plan to:

_____

_____

_____

_____

_____

Step 5. You just did it!

Step 6. Read the above out loud twice a day—when you get up in the morning and when you go to bed at night. You're on your way!

9

Rethink Your Position

Thoughts rule the world.
RALPH WALDO EMERSON

Whatever we tell ourselves consistently and repeatedly becomes a part of us whether it is true or not. Once it becomes a part of us it begins to become true. Because thoughts are so powerful, they can make things happen. Once they take root, they grow and attract thoughts of the same kind. Soon the mass of thought grows to an overpowering force. If we convince ourselves something can be done, it will be done. It must be done. It is already done. We just need to follow through on effecting it.

Let me use an example. I have a strange problem with my weight. Apparently my mind approves of my body weighing ten pounds more than the rational part of me wants it to. I know this is true because the last time I weighed myself I saw that I had lost about four pounds. *That only leaves six more to lose,* I told myself. However, I noticed that another self somewhere in another part of my mind was saying, *That means you can eat more. You have four pounds you can gain and still be okay.*

I suppose we all have ambivalent feelings about certain things. On the one hand, I want to weigh six pounds less and on the other I feel I can weigh four pounds more.

Concerning the house, on the one hand I want to have a beautiful, orderly house and on the other I want to live a casual, disorderly life. The question is "Which one will win?" The answer is, the one whose thought process is stronger.

As for my weight, I have found a wonderful way to tip the scale of desire the way I want it to go. I use an autosuggestion tape to reinforce my goals. I reaffirm to myself twice a day that I want to lose six pounds. My weight slowly, but surely, begins to drop.

The self-hypnosis tape is nothing more than a way to concentrate on reaffirming my desire and my plan for weight loss. Listening to that tape is one of the nice things I do for myself. It helps me be the person I really want to be.

Denis Waitley, in his book *Seeds of Greatness* (Revell, 1983), suggests that people use this repetition to reinforce thinking that will help them achieve their goals. He has found that "self-talk" statements recorded on an audio-cassette tape in the person's own voice against a background of slow baroque music are very significant helps.

To make a tape, write your self-talk down, go to a quiet place, play slow baroque music, and read your statement aloud to yourself in a normal voice. Make your statement personal by using the words *I, me,* and *my.* Make them affirming statements in the present tense such as:

I am relaxing.

I feel my muscles growing relaxed and warm.

My breathing is regular.

My heartbeat is slow.

I am entering a state of relaxation.

I am a person of great dignity.

I am a person of significant worth.

It is good to be alive.

I make many good contributions to the world.

I feel happy and positive about my life.

My house is beautiful and orderly.

I am relaxed and happy.

I enjoy being here.

The sunshine and breezes enliven my life and home.

I am excited about the opportunities in life and what I am accomplishing.

My home is beautiful and orderly.

Being in my home gives me strength and energy.

I thank God for my life and this day.

Repeat each statement three times. The music should be slightly louder than your voice. The self-talk should be clearly audible, but not dominant. As you listen, feel the joy of success.

As you relax, your mind will accept the statements you are making. You are not lying to yourself. You are simply listening to your "other self," the one who wants you to have a lovely house and to reach all your goals.

You and I are always talking to ourselves, whether we do it with a tape recorder or not. Frequently, we think negative, destructive thoughts that make us weak and ineffective. Messies in particular, being high-quality performance people, must keep telling themselves positive things lest they mislead themselves. Using this method, you will make sure that your thoughts are the right thoughts.

However you do it, whether by reading your goals aloud to yourself twice a day as mentioned in chapter 8, or making a self-talk tape, or purchasing an autosuggestion tape, definite repeated retraining of your thoughts is essential to success.

I was listening to a very successful man being interviewed on the radio. When asked the secret of success, he said that during his childhood, his father encouraged him to memorize a little poem. Through the years, this poem ran through his brain affirming and reaffirming that success was possible even when it seemed impossible. Although others discouraged him, he was successful in attaining his goals. He attributed it in large part to this poem.

It Couldn't Be Done

Somebody said that it couldn't be done,
　　But he with a chuckle replied,
That "maybe it couldn't," but he would be one
　　Who wouldn't say so till he'd tried.
So he buckled right in with the trace of a grin
　　On his face. If he worried he hid it.
He started to sing as he tackled the thing
　　That couldn't be done, and he did it.

EDGAR A. GUEST

Each time he was challenged, that little ditty ran through his brain. His father had given him a great gift—the gift of powerful thoughts. These lead to definite purpose and plans. Applied with persistence, they culminate in success.

In order to cement your desire further, you need outside reinforcement. A great deal of strength is found in working with others. Coals that are separate lose their heat much faster than coals all piled together. You *can* make the change alone; however, it is so much better if you find another person to succeed with. This is one case where one plus one equals more than two. Somehow the bond between those striving together for a goal becomes a third power. If you have more than two in a self-help group working positively together for a goal, you have a very strong power for change. Messies Anonymous self-help groups are designed to put this force for good to work for you. It only takes two or three to make a self-help group.

For those who do not have a self-help group in their area and don't wish to start one, letter writing may be a catalyst for success. Many important plans have been formulated and born through letters. The idea for the unification of the thirteen colonies was begun through correspondence among those who were later to lead the revolution. If writing appeals to you, write to a Messie you know who wants to reform. If you need to find a pen pal, send for the Messies Anonymous "Connections" list of those who wish to correspond. If you'd like information about starting a self-help group or if you would like a copy of this M.A. "Connections" list, send a stamped, self-addressed, legal-sized envelope to Messies Anonymous, Department B, 5025 S.W. 114th Avenue, Miami, Florida 33165. Include a word or two about yourself so we can add you to the list.

Retraining our thinking so that a messy house becomes unacceptable and only a beautiful orderly house is acceptable to our way of thinking is imperative. Only a real change in thinking will produce the persistence we need to keep on when the going gets tough—and it *will* get tough.

There will be times when you think you can't keep on, that it is not worth it. There will be times when family and friends will criticize you for how or what you are doing. There will be times when their lack of cooperation will be discouraging.

You will give yourself many excuses for quitting:

> I don't have enough energy.
>
> I don't have enough time.
>
> I don't have enough desire.
>
> My house is too small.
>
> My house is too large.
>
> My family is too messy.

A strong desire to change will keep a reforming Messie going when these discouragements come. Without persistence, there will be no success.

Remember the chapter title "Victor or Victim: It's Really Up to You"? You are the only one who can make it happen. Your desire to change is newborn at this time. Feed it, strengthen it, protect it, so it will grow into a strong, persistent, satisfying way of life.

Close your mind to the possibility of failure. When I first started changing, I was tempted many times to quit and go back. But I didn't because that old way of life was so painful to me. I was *determined* never to live that way again. Only that kind of determined attitude along with solid retraining of thinking will insure success.

10

Active Duty or Why Messies Are So Busy

Most Messies are very busy people. We dash from activity to project to activity and back, anxious to fill our hours with worthwhile pursuits. A few super-organized people might be able to keep a schedule like this without having their lives come all unraveled. Messies cannot. Born into the world with characteristics that make organizing difficult, Messies' lives stagger under this kind of schedule.

Why do we work so hard? Why do we keep ourselves so very busy?

There are several reasons, some of which are all right; others which are not.

Pride

The busier we are, the more highly regarded we are in our society. When we enter a doctor's office that is crowded to the rafters, our admiration for the doctor is reinforced. We may have to wait too long and the doctor may be stretched beyond his capacity to perform well because of overscheduling, but we still think, *He must be such a good doctor; look how busy he is.*

Busyness means we are needed; we are wanted. Pride of the wrong kind, the desire to impress others above all, pushes us to behave foolishly. Our schedules, our personal lives, our genuinely good activities suffer. People may notice and admire us. Busyness *is* encouraged by society. But what a price we have paid to have our egos boosted!

Laziness

It takes effort to organize my time. It takes energy. It takes discipline for a Messie who loves to please to say no to someone who asks for time and energy for their needy activity. This may include our children and our husbands as well. Certainly, we may help others and should. But only within the boundaries predetermined by us. We must set our own schedule in accordance with our priorities. We must accept only the activities that fit into our schedule.

Gordon McDonald, in his very excellent book, *Ordering Your Private World* (Moody Press, 1984), tells of how he took command of his time schedule. It all revolves around his calendar. Eight weeks in advance, he blocks in his personal schedule. He schedules time for reading, time for meditation, time to be with his family and friends, and time for study.

When he has requests for his time, he consults his calendar. If the time requested has already been blocked out for himself, he asks for an alternative time, one that fits his plans better. He sets his priorities for the use of his time early. Other plans flow around those priorities.

It would be so much easier from the planning standpoint to just do whatever comes up day by day—to respond to the immediate, to the demands of other people. That is the lazy way. It is also the nonproductive way. We won't have time to do the work important to us, and that includes the house.

Enthusiasm for Life

Messies are generally very creative, outgoing, enthusiastic people. We tend to overdo, to be too expansive in our living. Like children in a toy store, we view life as chocked full of wonderful activities and opportunities for us to enjoy. We want to be involved in hobbies, crafts, and fine arts. We can't pass up the opportunity for reading and seminars. Of course, our children's activities are so important and fun, we *must* get involved. Like that child in the toy store, we gather into our schedules all of the activities that attract our ebullient attention. We forget that there will come a time when we'll have to pay. Nothing is free. We pay for these activities with time and energy. If we pay too much for them, we don't have time and energy left for the essentials of life. As a result, the family may have to eat one more lick-and-promise meal, the unwashed dishes will wait a little longer, and we begin to cut back on the basics that determine our quality of life. Without a quality life in which the home and family are cared for properly, these other good activities lose their luster.

A peculiar thing begins to happen as the home front deteriorates. We begin to search for more activities outside the home. Who wants to spend time there? We begin to daydream and read. As a result, a downward spiral develops, and the home suffers more and more.

We know we are overbusy when we forget appointments, lose things, fail to return important calls, put things in piles until we get to them, let deadlines for things like driver's licenses or tag renewals slide, forget to record checks, and spend time doing small nonessential things just to make ourselves believe we are trying to get things in order. For instance, an overbusy person will spend her time cleaning the oven when the kitchen is a shambles and then wonder at the end of the day why the house looks so bad after she worked so hard. We jump from one activity to another trying to make a dent.

Soon the stress of the way of life we have created begins to take its toll. We become nervous because things are out of control. We have an uncomfortable feeling that we may be in trouble and not know it. Has the driver's license lapsed? Or the insurance? Could we find the Band-Aids if a child got cut? Have we put that refund check in some pile or thrown it away by mistake? Did we forget and leave clothes in the washer soaking? Do the children have clean clothes for school tomorrow? We begin waking up early just to worry.

The family becomes nervous, too. When the children have to hunt and hope for their clothes and, as a consequence, miss the school bus, they are upset. When the check bounces because we let the banking get confused, our husband is upset. When these incidents multiply, it becomes a nightmare.

Personal relationships begin to unravel because we are overbusy. Our conversations become mere reacting instead of satisfying communication. Messies cannot handle a heavy or nonplanned schedule. We must cut back on our activities until we find the level of unbusyness in which we can maintain a quality life. Perhaps you will need to cut way back at first and slowly add a few activities at a time. Always add with care.

There is one type of Messie who is not overbusy. She is suffering busy-burnout. This Messie may have tried so hard and so long without success that she has quit trying. Perhaps she is so traumatized she is immobilized by depression. No more busy schedule for her. She has quit and simply withdrawn from it all.

For the still overbusy Messie and the one who has quit, there is one commonality: Both feel a gut-level, heartrending dissatisfaction with themselves. Life is no fun anymore. The busy Messie doesn't take time to admit it. The withdrawn Messie suppresses it. But the dissatisfaction is there and must be highlighted before any help comes. Until we see how much this overbusy way of life is hurting us, we won't stop it.

When we decide to cut out many of the busywork activities, just as we get rid of unnecessary stuff by the Mount Vernon method, it is hard to decide what activities to discard. Some Messies will insist that they are doing only the bare minimum now, only the essentials. When they look for something to do away with, nothing can go. All of the activities seem so essential. We must do them all.

Let me tell you my experience. When my daughter, Lucy, was a newborn infant, just home from the hospital, she developed a distressing habit. She had trouble going to sleep and staying asleep. I took time from my busy schedule to rock her to sleep and put her into her crib, only to be recalled by a startled, screaming baby a few minutes later.

You must understand that I had determined earlier that the baby would not slow me down. I would be Mrs. Superwoman. I could do it all. This sleep problem was certainly challenging that. My important plans were suffering.

In desperation I called Dr. Wilson. We lived in rural

northern Indiana at the time. The phone lines were old. A call to Dr. Wilson a few miles down the road in Columbia City was long-distance. The connection was bad. Loudly, I explained the problem.

"IT SEEMS LIKE SHE IS HAVING NIGHTMARES," I shouted.

"SHE MAY BE," he crackled across the line, and then he went on to prescribe help for the problem.

"DR. WILSON!" I said, trying to be heard, "I MUST NOT HAVE HEARD YOU CLEARLY. IT SOUNDED LIKE YOU SAID THAT I OUGHT TO HOLD THE BABY FOR *EIGHT HOURS A DAY.*"

"THAT'S WHAT I DID SAY. I BELIEVE THAT WILL SOLVE THE PROBLEM," he replied only too clearly.

All my busyness came to a screeching halt. Baby and I certainly got a lot of rest. She slept and I watched TV. We were both happier and calmer. My busy schedule went to pot. We were both better for it.

Perhaps you have had times when your busy schedule was interrupted by a broken arm or by having to leave town for an emergency. Surprisingly, things do not destruct without you. In most cases, things continue very well in your absence. (When others know you won't be there to do your jobs, they step in and do them.) Cutting back on your schedule is a little like a vacation. People get along without you then, don't they? You really don't *have* to do it all. The trick when you're not on vacation is to make sure others know that you expect them to begin taking over if they want jobs to be done.

We must do a Mount Vernoning of our schedules. Get rid of all the activities that are cluttering up our lives. We give away unwanted clothes, don't we? Now let's give those unwanted activities to someone else or just throw them out entirely. What a relief it will be!

When our lives begin to right themselves from the topsy-turvy mess they are in now, we will be calmer and happier. We will have confidence that our lives are under control. The best thing is that we will then have quality time for ourselves—to read, to think, to plan, to dream. On my key chain I have these words from eighteenth-century poet William Cowper:

> A life all turbulence and noise may seem
>> To him that leads it wise and to be praised.
> But wisdom is a pearl with most success
>> Sought in still waters.

lit·tle min·utes/lit-əl min-əts   short periods of time generally left over from or in the middle of larger projects. "Little minutes" occur when your ride is late, when dinner is ready but the kids aren't home, when you're stuck in line or in a traffic jam or in a waiting room. The most popular example of "little minutes" is a television commercial during which most Americans have learned to fix a three-minute snack. Other examples include making the bed while waiting for the coffee to brew, writing letters while waiting for an appointment, rinsing the sink and wiping the mirror while waiting for the curling iron to heat, washing dishes while waiting for the family to gather for dinner. Used effectively, "little minutes" reap many hours of pleasure and relaxation.

11

Hurry Up and Wait— Why Time Management Techniques Don't Work

Procrastination is the art of keeping up with yesterday.
DONALD ROBERT PERRY MARQUIS

The book market is full of books on time management but they won't help the Messie whose problem is procrastination. She will just procrastinate putting the time-management techniques into use. The reason is that procrastinators really want to procrastinate for reasons they themselves do not usually understand.

Procrastinators have a distorted sense of time. Actually, they live apart from the restraints of time to some extent. I do not wear a watch and almost never know the date. I only check the time or date when it seems important for me to know them. My judgment of when it is important is not always accurate. That is why I almost missed the opening day of school.

Time passes erratically for the Messie procrastinator. Usually time goes more slowly for the Messie than for other people so she is surprised to find she has procrastinated so long. Occasionally, time speeds up, unexpectedly. When she thought she had enough time to do a job, she finds the time has passed by too quickly to get the job done. So a deadline is missed.

Procrastinators suffer from a complexity of thinking that works against their doing what really is in their best interest to do. They also generally suffer from a feeling of low self-esteem. Procrastinating is one way of protecting their self-worth from being lowered.

Messie procrastinators also feel, conversely, that they are very capable people and that they are capable of accomplishing many excellent goals if they could just "get it together." If pushed, they might confess they have thoughts of greatness or genius in certain areas. They are perfectionists in their own way.

Because they are perfectionists, Messies take a long time to decide *what* to do. Then after they decide what to do, they wait a little longer to see whether or not anything comes up to cancel the wisdom of that decision. All of this mulling things over takes time. This kind of procrastination seems rational to the careful Messie who is already low in self-esteem. She doesn't want to make a mistake.

The low self-esteem and perfectionism combine to make a recipe for failure. Let's look at several examples of how this works.

Joan wants to upgrade her house by redecorating, so she spends hours looking through sale catalogs, browsing in stores, and visiting model homes. She's been at this project for some time, but the house is still waiting for the wonderful transformation. Why? Joan is not sure of her decorating ability or her ability to maintain a beautiful house. As a substitute for doing the decorating, she talks about her big plans, she shows catalogs and magazine cutouts as proof of her sincerity. Because she is afraid of failure, she never actually *does* the job. She can't be criticized for doing a poor job if she never really does it. She tells herself she has to get the house straightened up before she begins beautifying it. Here we see a combination of her poor self-esteem and perfectionism. Her procrastination has shielded her self-esteem from being hurt.

Mary, another procrastinator, wants to get her house in order. She feels she must, however, do some other things first. *People see the outside of the house more often than the inside,* she tells herself as she does what she knows how to do well—

yardwork. No one would guess how the inside of the house looks. She never fails at the job she does on the inside because she never starts it. She's too busy in the yard. She tells herself that if she ever did get to the house, it would be beautifully maintained. After all, isn't the beautiful yard proof of that? On those occasions when guests are invited, Mary starts late and does a quick surface job to make the public area look okay. She tells herself that if she had had the time to do it, the house would have been thoroughly cleaned. She did not fail to keep the house nice—lack of time was the problem. Procrastination has protected her self-esteem. She has a fear of failure. Mary's true ability in the house has never been tested. She avoids trying so she can avoid failure. She has an *illusion* of ability.

People also procrastinate because of fear of success.

For various reasons, Messie procrastinators sometimes sabotage their own success. We may tell ourselves several things.

"Perhaps the kids and my husband would feel it wasn't 'home' anymore."

"What would I do with my time—why would I even be needed at the house—if everything got caught up?"

"If I get the house under control and keep it nice, people will begin to expect it and I might begin to slip back into my old ways. It's too much pressure to keep it up."

"I am a Messie, a wonderful, creative, procrastinating Messie. If I succeed in the house and things are neat, my creativity will be stifled."

"Mother, bless her heart, is such a Messie. Like mother, like daughter. It is a bond between us. I don't want to make Mom feel bad."

"Mom is such a perfectionist in the house. Even though I'm grown, my messiness keeps me dependent on

**I'LL THINK ABOUT IT TOMORROW—
AFTER ALL, TOMORROW IS ANOTHER DAY**

her like a child. If I get control of the house, I'll have to take my place in the adult world."

So sometimes we procrastinate in the house because we fear the changes success might bring.

Jodie has a messy house. Her mom is always after her to fix it up. Her husband and kids complain, but the house stays messy. Jodie is a capable adult woman. She feels that she should control her own actions and not be controlled by others; so she says no to their pleas. To her it is a sign of power. Any imposed schedule is a challenge to be defeated. As a matter of fact, it may be that this rebellious attitude toward being dominated accounts for Messies ignoring time. *I will do what I want, when I want. I will defeat the restraints of time,* she thinks deep in her heart. It gives her a feeling of power and control but is disastrous as far as success is concerned.

This rebellious attitude may also make the Messie procrastinator impervious to the restraints of the usual housekeeping rules. *Other people may need to put things away but not me! I'll keep everything out. I can remember which pile it is in. It will be so much easier to get to. I can handle it.*

I remember a woman in an organization workshop I attended saying she had a mirror that sat on the floor waiting to be hung for years. But she wasn't going to hang it because it bugged her mother so much that she didn't.

Sometimes people procrastinate paying bills out of resentment. They feel the taxes or utilities are too high or they don't like the doctor's treatment so they make them wait for their money.

When the Messie procrastinator begins to see that all of this procrastination is painful and hurts self-esteem more than protects it, she begins to consider changing. But how?

It is important to set specific goals and to commit ourselves to them aloud to some sympathetic person. The Messie procrastinator likes to make vague, general grand plans for change. This makes accomplishing the goal *vague* and *general*. However, it is important to set very specific, easily observable goals which have a time target.

When you tell your goals and time target to the sympathetic person you choose to help you, also tell her the steps you are going to take to accomplish your goal. Messies must learn to look specifically at the job to be done.

When the Messie first begins to change it is hard, because Messies appreciate only final accomplishments, not intermediate steps to the final goals. It is important to value each step toward the final goal.

In the same grand way of thinking, Messies want to work only when they have large blocks of time to work in. A few minutes here and there are disregarded as unimportant when they actually could be just the time needed to get many jobs started and well on the way. Frequently, a big job can be conquered by doing it in short time segments such as five or fifteen minutes. When the set time limit is up, the work stops. Messies find it hard to start doing things this way.

It may be that Messies like large blocks of time because they feel they cannot be jumping from one activity to another—that is not a productive way to work.

Messies learn to fear this fitful, distractible way of working. They are aware that in the past they have found themselves unaccountably jumping from one job to another, not following through on any. This is frustrating and unproductive, so Messies tend to avoid short-term jobs. Messies have to concentrate so hard on a job to get it done that it is hard for them to shift gears to another job.

The difference between being distracted and this plan I am proposing of using "little minutes" to get a job started or to continue on a job is that in the latter case using little minutes is deliberately done. Using little minutes productively and deliberately is a skill learned by many people who are very accomplished producers.

Another reason Messies don't like to do small jobs is because it takes a Messie more time and effort than most people to take out and put away any items needed for a job. It does not seem worthwhile. For instance, the Messie procrastinator may have lost the bills, or the pen, or the checkbook to pay the bills. The Messie procrastinator may not be able to find the dustcloth and spray wax to do a quick polish job on the living room furniture, or the envelopes or stamps to send a quick letter. To Messies, all jobs are big jobs, so we procrastinate. It is imperative that the Messie procrastinator set up the house so she can quickly get her hands on whatever she needs to do jobs easily.

Because Messies are perfectionists and have a low self-esteem, they are easily discouraged. Any problems they run into make them feel stupid or dumb so they retreat to their old standby against failure—procrastination.

To experience success in overcoming these problems, the Messie procrastinator can be helped by special support either from an understanding friend or a support group. Messies Anonymous support groups or "Connections" writing partners may be just the help needed.

Knowing the roots of our procrastination may help to weaken the hold these roots have on our lives. It is not noble to be a perfectionist. It is just an excuse not to work. Fear of success, fear of failure, and a rebellious attitude of self-assertion all work to hurt us. We must change our attitude about our former behaviors.

The real key is to build a realistic picture of ourselves as people who are valuable even when we try and do not achieve. Remember, we are people of dignity. We don't need to protect ourselves from failure by procrastinating.

William Knaus, an expert on the problems of procrastination says,

The object [of changing attitudes] is to help people create an image of themselves as doers; not stewers. They have to overcome their self-doubts and build tolerance for frustration. Too many people just don't want to put themselves out. They think somebody will take over for them or bail them out (*U.S. News and World Report,* October 24, 1984, p. 11).

Spotting and Untying
Organizational Knots

A. Put a check to the left side of any areas in your life that are not organized—where you think further control is needed.

___ 1. Finding things (Glasses, keys, purse, etc.). ___

___ 2. Meal planning and preparation. ___

___ 3. Cleaning the house. ___

___ 4. Paper (Finding, filing, and sorting). ___

___ 5. Keeping finances in order. ___

___ 6. Laundry (Washing, drying, folding, and putting it away). ___

___ 7. Keeping things picked up. ___

___ 8. Dishes (Washing, drying, and putting away immediately). ___

___ 9. Grocery shopping. ___

___ 10. Delegating jobs. ___

___ 11. Being on time. ___

___ 12. OTHERS

___ _____

___ _____

B. Put the letters of the category below that *best* explains the reason for lack of organization in the area that you checked. Put the letters to the right of the category in the space provided.

LF   Lack of Follow Through—Getting the main part of the job done but failing to finish it up.

LP   Lack of Planning—Not planning for the future. Maybe you prefer spontaneous living.

AD   Lack of Attention to Detail—Thinking only in terms of the "big picture."

IP   Impatience with Paper Work—Easily frustrated.

PT   Perfectionistic Thinking—Finding it hard to decide the best way to do the job.

PG   Orientation toward *Present* Gratification—Wishing to have it easy now, even though it will make the future harder.

TC   Too Compliant—Letting others dictate what you do and letting others ignore your plans.

EC   Excessive Confusion—The situation is so complicated and confused that it is difficult to begin.

C. Describe in your own words what keeps you from getting organized.

12

Special Tactics

All's fair in love and war—and we are waging war on disorder. A good general always has a few secret weapons to pull out when the going gets tough. In this chapter I'm going to let you in on three of my favorite special tactics.

The Maid and I

In Messie days of yore, I would occasionally have a maid come help around the house. I found it helpful to have someone who could swoop in, bring order and some degree of clean, and swoop out again. For about half a day things would be so nice and then gloom would descend slowly as clutter crept out into my orderly house. Dirty dishes would creep into the sink, dirty laundry would sneak into the hall, and shoes would appear under the living room sofa.

And then there was always the problem of preparing for the maid. A certain amount of cleaning and straightening must be done. The piles needed to be somewhat corralled before she could come. Getting ready for the maid was no small job in itself.

One of my seminar attendees said that a maid she shared with some other ladies in the neighborhood charged her five dollars more to do her house because of the clutter. This incident was the catalyst that made her finally decide to find some way of making a change. In almost each seminar I give I have a maid attend. In my last seminar I had a lady who founded and ran a maid service. Just because you can clean another person's house does not mean you can organize yourself.

I was more prepared one Saturday recently when I called a local maid service and asked them to send a maid. I asked for a fast thorough one. They sent Debbie. I wanted to be there when she came to show her the products to use, where they were, and how I wanted things done. For six hours she was there. I wondered when we started how she could fill six hours. But she did! And I worked with her much of the time. Beds were moved and floors mopped and waxed. Everything was vacuumed. Furniture and cabinets were dusted and waxed.

I found out two things. In some areas I did the work better than she did. In some areas she was better than I was. We worked well as a team, and a lot of behind-the-scenes cleaning got done. I was pleased. The price was high, but it was, for that time, worth it. It was a lot better than the time I hired a maid to come clean while I was gone and my husband was home. I told him what to tell her to do because my mother was coming for a visit and *something had to be done*. When I arrived home from work, I found she had cleaned the stove very well—but little else. That was a disaster.

Perhaps my experience can offer some guidelines if you are searching for a maid.

1. Decide whether you want a slow but thorough maid or a fast surface cleaner or a combination of the two and make your preference known before you hire her.

2. Be prepared to work with her the first time. There are so many ways to do things and each house has its peculiarities, so you need to guide her in your way for your house.

3. I had never used a maid service before but found this experience very satisfactory. You might inquire if there

is one in your area. You will find them in the yellow pages under *Maids.* If you want heavier cleaning done such as windows, rugs, etc., call a company under *Cleaning Services,* which advertises they do residential work.

4. Don't be too picky. I thought she left too much water on the floor after she mopped. But don't let your perfection make you tune out any help from a maid.

Now the clincher. My husband doesn't generally want to be bothered with a change in his routine by having a maid come. He was not sure it would be worth the money. (I had to sort of ease Debbie in over his grumbling.) Last night, *he* suggested it would be nice to have her come back in a month or so.

Miracles do happen.

BADARACCO

The Flipper

In chapter 2 I explained the Mount Vernon method for organizing your house. But any Messie knows that the real problem is not getting the house in order—it's *keeping* it that way. The Flipper is the heart of the Messies Anonymous organizational program.

Let's think of the Flipper as a recipe for a cake.

When you get through with your recipe, you will have twenty-four cards set in a book.

At one sitting you decide your cleaning schedule. On each of these cards you put a few of the jobs you would like to get done during the week. Spread them all out so everything doesn't pile up for Saturday. Each day, look at the Flipper and do the jobs indicated. Like all good ideas, it is simple. For Messies to use it efficiently, it has to be simple.

This is the basic idea of the Flipper.

Now let's get back to the recipe.

Ingredients:

One small photo album. The kind that has twenty-four plastic sleeves with blank cards in the sleeves. These clear plastic sleeves are supposed to hold snapshots but we are going to put in cards listing our housecleaning chores.

One Vis-a-Vis pen. You can buy these at any office supply store. Get the fine line if you have a choice. Use this pen to mark off the jobs as you do them each day. The pen marks will wipe off easily so you can use the Flipper again and again after you finish going through it the first time.

One paper clip. Preferably plastic, because metal rusts. Put that on the card you are working on because Messies have poor memories. If we forget which card we're on, being perfectionists, we won't want to continue until we remember just exactly which one it was.

This brings up the problem of what to do when you get behind. You have two choices:

1. You can try to get caught up to where you should be.

2. You can forget about what you have neglected and start from the day you would be on if you had kept up.

The correct answer is number 2. Forget about what you neglected. Start from whatever day it is. The Alcoholics Anonymous creed of living "one day at a time" applies here. Forget the past. Start today and make today a success.

Some paper and a pen. Perhaps a pencil will be better because you'll change your mind as you think.

Write down the jobs you would like to accomplish twice a week. Put those on the appropriate cards. For example, if you wish to mop the kitchen floor twice a week, put that down on first-week Tuesday and Friday cards, second-week Tuesday and Friday cards, and third-week Tuesday and Friday cards.

Then select the jobs you wish to do once a week. Write those on the three cards for the day you choose, say Wednesday of each of the three weeks.

Next decide which jobs you wish to do only once every three weeks. Choose any convenient days from the cards to do that job. Write each job down. Now you are finished with the day-of-the-week cards.

This is the basic cake. Now for the filling.

There are some jobs you would like to do daily. There should be no more than six or seven. These do not go on the day-of-the-week cards; they go on three daily cards. Don't include jobs that are already a habit.

All these cards represent three weeks of housework. One card will be Monday, first week; then Tuesday, first week, and so on, until the first week is finished. The second and third weeks follow consecutively. Notice there is no Sunday because everybody needs one day a week off, at least. You may choose Sunday and/or any other day you want.

1st Week Menu	
1st Week Daily	
1st Week Monday	
1st Week Tuesday	
1st Week Wednesday	
1st Week Thursday	
1st Week Friday	
1st Week Saturday	
2nd Week Menu	
2nd Week Daily	
2nd Week Monday	
2nd Week Tuesday	

2nd Week Wednesday	
2nd Week Thursday	
2nd Week Friday	
2nd Week Saturday	
3rd Week Menu	
3rd Week Daily	
3rd Week Monday	
3rd Week Tuesday	
3rd Week Wednesday	
3rd Week Thursday	
3rd Week Friday	
3rd Week Saturday	

Cards which are located at the beginning of each set of weekday cards look like this:

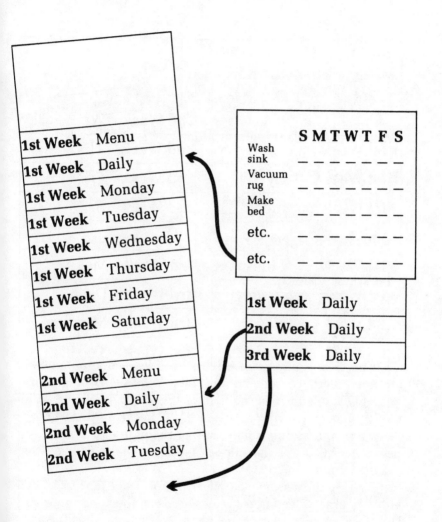

We've got the cake and filling. Now we need the icing. You will notice that the card above the daily card is empty. Use that for your menu planning. Decide what schedule of eating you want, write it down, and slip it into the sleeve above the daily.

Sunday: Chicken, rice, peas

Monday: Tuna casserole, salad

Tuesday: Chili, cheese toast, Jell-O

Wednesday: Meat loaf, potato, limas

Thursday: Quiche, fruit

Friday: Fish, macaroni & cheese, peas

Saturday: Spaghetti, French bread, slaw

1st Week Menu

1st Week Menu

1st Week Daily

The cake is almost ready. Just a little decoration and we are done. Perhaps you did not include the menu or perhaps your photo album has more than twenty-four sleeves. Add motivational sayings from this or any other book you want.

Now your recipe is finished and ready to use. Don't, I repeat, DO NOT use the Flipper until you have finished the Mount Vernon method.

The Mount Vernon method is done only one time to get the house in order. The Flipper is used to keep the house in order. Use the Flipper regularly, erasing the marks when it is full and going back through it again and again.

Like all good recipes, you may share with your family. Let them do and check off jobs from the Flipper. Working together, you can do it. I know you can!

Journaling—The Ultimate Memory

It is important to keep in mind that being a Messie does not mean just having a disordered house. A Messie has certain personal characteristics that lead her into a disordered way of life. These characteristics will never be eliminated nor should they be. Many of our personal characteristics are not bad, they are just misapplied or overdone. You do not need to change into another person to bring order and beauty into your home. You do, however, need to make some appropriate changes in your thinking and behavior in order to make changes in the house and make them permanently.

We take a threefold approach to changing.

1. In the first part of this book, and at points throughout, I have emphasized the intrinsic value of each person. A healthy respect for yourself will compel you to realign your environment to match with your inner beauty.

2. To strengthen that change, you need to use change-making techniques, such as goal setting, retraining of your thought habits, and support from self-help groups.

3. Some of your characteristics need to be rechanneled into neater ways of doing things. That brings me to a topic close to my heart—the journal.

Messies are sentimental people. Many also have poor memories. This makes a very unsettling combination for the Messie. When a Messie who is sentimental knows that the incidents of life which are important to her are apt to fade away, she makes certain adjustments in order to keep them alive in her memory. The most common ways are by keeping mementos, souvenirs, and pictures.

The pictures don't take up much room but the mementos do. Old jewelry, baby clothes, pressed flowers, and many other items that would not usually classify as typical remembrances are kept because they are a part of the past. Slowly our houses fill up with unpleasant heaps. We hate the clutter but we feel that if we let these things go, our past will go with them.

What are the alternatives to collecting all this clutter? The best alternative I have found is to keep a journal.

Journaling is enjoying a comeback in popularity. Before TV, when people had more time, it was a very widely practiced pastime. I remember finding an old journal a stranger had left in the attic of a house my grandparents bought. I wish I had kept it. Once you tune into the idea, you will be surprised at how many people, even today, you will meet or read about who keep journals. Most do not talk about it. It seems to be a secret pastime.

Maybe there is a reason for the secrecy. A journal is a place where one can bare one's soul. It can be an intimate activity in a world where we feel uncomfortable with intimacy. But for Messies, it is the perfect answer to the problem of preserving the past in memory.

Let's talk about how it's done. My journal is a 6″ × 9″, spiral-bound notebook. I bought it in a drugstore, I believe. It's not fancy at all. If you want something a bit nicer, most bookstores have selections of blank books that make wonderful journals. You can get books with lovely fabric bindings or even interesting journals imported from China or Italy. Art stores as well carry a selection of sketch books in a variety of sizes, bindings, and papers which serve as great journals. Use your imagination—after all, you are writing *your* book.

There are advantages to using a journal instead of one of those little five-year diaries with the lock on the front. If you have a predated diary, you feel compelled to write in it every day. If you don't, you feel guilty. In addition, those little diaries have minuscule spaces for writing. There are two final problems with the five-year, lock-on-the-front diary. One is that you might lose the key if you lock it and the other is that if you lose the diary, you have lost five years of memories.

Almost every day I write in my journal, but if I miss a day or two I don't panic. What do I write? Memories. Memories of the day past. Thoughts. Dreams. Hopes. Successes. Failures. Plans. And prayers. Journals are a wonderful place to sort out your priorities and needs. Some people get very creative, recording poetry and special quotations, even including drawings or gluing in special mementos. Consider your journal an empty canvas awaiting your own personal word paintings. The journal is the ultimate remembrance. Trinkets are only the shell of a memory; the journal contains the heart.

Personally, I write from front to back in the usual way for my regular entries. For special entries such as quotations, books I have read, songs or poems to remember, I write from back to front. When the front and back meet the journal is full and I start a new one.

Do people peek in my diary? I doubt it. My family is so used to seeing me writing, they pay no attention. I keep it beside my bed. If you are afraid people will intrude on yours, keep it hidden. If someone asks what you are doing, tell them that it is part of the Messies Anonymous program for household organization. That should be enough to dampen their curiosity.

You might find that your journal will help you to do the Mount Vernon method more easily. As you discard things, you may wish to record their passing in your journal. For instance, when you give away your maternity clothes (if you're finished with them), record that momentous occasion in the book. Write also, how important those births were to you. Include the significance of the great giveaway. An epoch of your life—the child-bearing years—has ended. It is so much more satisfying to do this than to keep a box of useless clothes in an already crowded spot.

We are Messies. We must learn to live in a satisfactory way with our own personalities. Keep your sentimentality. But keep those memories in a small book, not in piles and boxes which, in the end, muddy the memories you have of today.

Rugged Terrain—Special Problem Areas

PART THREE

13

Dollars & Sense

Caution: The following information is for Money Messies who are prepared to face the serious realities of putting their financial matters in order. Wimps need not apply.

Go directly to jail.
Do not pass GO.
Do not collect $200.
MONOPOLY

This chapter could be serious and minutely detailed, but it's not going to be. Many good books have been written on this subject alone and we could never hope to match their completeness in these matters. What we can do is set up some basic principles in money management, give you some personal tips, and direct you to those places where you will find more detail—when you're ready for it.

If you've read this far, I assume that you are serious about getting your money matters under control. At the same time, you're scared. After all, money is a very scary subject. Many psychologists believe that money is an even more volatile subject than sex. If you think about it, they're probably right. So you are probably right to be scared. But knowledge banishes fear.

Why Do Messies Avoid Setting Their Finances in Order?

There are several reasons.

Keeping money matters in order is not easy. This chapter will not give you effort-free methods of bookkeeping and accounting. But we didn't give you any effort-free methods of housekeeping either, and you conquered that, didn't you?

The fact is, this entire project is probably so complicated that no self-respecting Messie would dare attempt it *unless* she was truly convinced that she was worth it. And face it, when we muddle around trying to find a painless, unique way of avoiding a job, we generally spend more time doing the avoiding than it would take to do the job.

Picture yourself as John Wayne. Get that image in your head. Then hitch up your belt, wipe your brow, and plant your feet. It ain't an easy job, but it's yours. And you're gonna do it.

Keeping your finances in order is not glamorous. You can't invite the neighbors over and bask in their admiration as you can with a clean house. This job above all others is for your benefit alone. As such, it flows from a sense of dignity and self-worth. There are few comforts like the sense of having your finances in order and the knowledge that you and your family are reaching for some of your financial goals. And although the neighbors won't ooh and aah, your children shall arise and call you blessed; your husband also he shall praise thee. (Apologies to the author of Proverbs.)

Money matters are so messy, especially for Messies. Losing records, forgetting bills, avoiding detail work, forgetting that cash you need next week. The list goes on and on. Messies have their own special problems with money. But I'll let you in on a secret: *Cleanies have the same problems!* You'd be surprised at how many Cleanies are Money Messies. Okay, all their little pieces of paper are in one place instead of in the glove compartment, on the refrigerator, and in the drawer by the front door. But they still have trouble making order out of all the bits and pieces that make up life today. So be encouraged! Money Mess is not simply a matter of not caring or being untalented. Finances can be complicated and as such need special attention. So pay attention and prepare to win!

The final excuse for not keeping control is that *we are afraid that we might find out that we really are in trouble financially.*

In the early days of flying, pilots did not have accurate instruments to tell them what the plane was doing, so they learned to fly by the way their derrieres felt on the seats. If there was pressure, they were climbing; if there was little or no pressure, they were dropping. Sometimes their derrieres failed to give them enough information, and they crashed.

Some Messies are adept at using the seat-of-the-pants method of money management. They get a feel of whether the money is flowing in or out. And they hope that they are not about to get an unpleasant surprise and crash.

Pilots who fly by the seat of the pants and Messies who manage their finances by the seat of the pants are always under a certain amount of tension. There is stress in not knowing whether there's enough money to cover a check or whether you'll be able to afford that house. In business this is called "crisis management": you move from one crisis to the next, with no time for planning and no energy for life. When this happens you don't manage the money, it manages you.

It feels better for a pilot to be flying happily along in the clouds, feeling everything is all right, than to know that there's a mountain peak looming ahead. Messies are that way. An unfounded sense of well-being, even with an undercurrent of nervousness, is better than knowing for certain that we are in trouble. If we don't balance our checkbooks then it doesn't matter that we spend more than we make. This attitude is immature, foolish, and unworthy behavior. In kinder terms, you deserve better!

Money Management for Messies

When we start learning anything for the first time, we start with the basics. And in learning money management, Messies need to know the following basics:

There are four key words in money management:

1. *Income*—all the money that comes in, from whatever source. Income provides the means to pay

2. *Expenses*—daily, monthly, annually. The financial commitments that need to be met in order to . . . well, to live.

3. *Budget*—(considered a dirty word in most company). A process by which income and expenses are balanced against each other on a monthly or annual basis.

4. *Cashflow*—a semi-technical term for the movement of money in and out of our lives. Think of a *Budget* as a financial snapshot and *Cashflow* as a financial movie.

There are three Financial Realities:

1. You must meet your financial commitments (pay your bills).

2. You must keep records (because)

3. You must file your taxes.

There are two financial goals:

1. You should plan.

2. You should save.

What most concerns us is coping with Financial Realities. If we get these in order, then Financial Goals will begin to emerge as a natural outgrowth. So let's begin.

Reality #1. We must meet our financial commitments. In other words, pay our bills. Of course we must, you say. How utterly obvious. But for a Messie, paying bills can be a nightmare, for several reasons.

- *The bills are missing.* One of the first lessons a Messie learns is to find a *place* for things. As you've Mount Vernoned your house you've no doubt run across bills in every conceivable place. And by now you've probably herded them toward a central location: a drawer, a desk top, a shoe box. Now is the time to find a *place* for your finances. You need a place in which there is space to work, space to store records (more on this later), and a space for unpaid bills. Some people use a basket on top of the desk, some people post them on a bulletin board with the due date marked prominently, others simply use the first folder in their file. But you need a place. And you need to keep the Current Unpaid Bills together. When you get a bill, open it. Immediately throw away everything but the bill and the return envelope. Then put it with the rest of the Current Unpaid Bills.

  If you are a visual person—that is, if something is out of sight, then it is truly out of mind—then you must keep the bills in a place where you can see them. This helps avoid the second reason bills are not paid.

- *I forgot.* You may laugh, but to a Money Messie, this is a very real problem. That's why it's important that you have a place for these things, and important that you set aside a special time to do your financial chores: pay bills, do your filing, balance your checkbook, and so on. Pick the same time all the time. Some experts recommend once a month (for example, the first Tuesday of

271

every month), others recommend weekly (you probably will spend less time in the long run if you maintain it that regularly), others find it simply easier to do right after payday (that's when you have the money to pay the bills, right?). At that time you should review your finances, dole out allowances and living expenses, pay your bills, file the paid bills, and balance your checkbook. Which brings us to the third reason that bills are not paid.

- *The checkbook is a mess.* Now if there is only one piece of counsel that you take away from this chapter (assuming that you are still reading), make it this: MAKE FRIENDS WITH YOUR CHECKBOOK. And this is where courage, determination, and discipline come in. Remember John Wayne? "It's a dirty job, but someone's got to do it."

Why? Because your checkbook is the key to restoring order to your money mess. Your checkbook not only tracks the majority of your expense payments, but it also helps you determine what kind of expense it is (which helps in planning), whether the expense is tax deductible (which helps in preparing tax returns), and most importantly, gives you an up-to-the-minute report on your financial situation. There is probably nothing else in your life that gives you so much pertinent information in such a compact form.

"But I hate my checkbook! Things keep getting lost and I'm terrible at subtraction and my husband won't cooperate and I swear my hamster eats a minimum of one check a month. I can't do it!!" Okay—but you couldn't keep an orderly house when you started either, and now look at you! The key is to begin, then keep plugging away, and keep remembering—you deserve an orderly checking account.

CHECKBOOK RULES
Always record the check.
Always record the deposits.
Always reconcile your checkbook to your bank statement.

As following these rules becomes second nature, you can begin to use your checkbook to record what the payment was for and to mark off whether it is tax deductible. (Make a short list on the front cover of your checkbook record of those items that are tax deductible, then code those payments that apply.) But don't worry about that at the beginning. Just record the check and the amount.

Reconciling a checkbook to a bank statement is probably the key reason people (Messies and Cleanies) develop phobias about personal finance. I can't give you a step-by-step guide on how to reconcile your statement, but I can give you a few tips as you begin to puzzle out your own system.

1. Invest in a small printing calculator, one that uses a paper tape. Using a calculator makes the job of keeping a running balance much easier and the tape makes it possible to double check your work (yes, double check). You won't be as inclined to put off doing your arithmetic and you can easily take advantage of little minutes to catch up.

2. Don't forget to deduct fees. Many a balancer has been reduced to tears for spending the money that the bank already spent. Better yet, find a bank with free checking.

3. On the back of most check bank statements is a form to fill out to help you reconcile your account. Provided it isn't in finance-ese, this can often be a help in learning how it should be done.

4. If controlling one large checking account every month is too awesome, consider using two accounts, one for fixed expenses and one for flexible expenses. Into the fixed expenses account goes the money for the rent or mortgage, utilities, insurance, and car payments. These have been totaled for the year then divided by the number of paychecks that you receive in a year. The same amount of money comes out of every paycheck and goes into the fixed expense account. Then the funds are always there. If you get an interest-bearing account, you can even earn money while you're at it.

The flexible expense account covers living expenses and special purchases.

The point is this: Reconciling your checking account is very important in the fight to restore order. It is imperative. Unless you do, you can't hope to face *Reality #2: You must keep records*.

By records, I mean copies of paid bills, insurance policies, cancelled checks, deposit records, any piece of paper that has to do with finances. Obviously, some people keep *everything*, but most people are selective.

The reasons that records are necessary are:

1. Records make it possible to plan for the future. By knowing how we spent our money, we can plan for those expenses for the future, refining our spending habits so that we can achieve special goals, like vacations or college educations.

2. Records are necessary for preparing your taxes.

3. Records are to a certain extent required by law. Not the everyday receipts but certain records should be kept for five years. After that, you can't be audited, so then any record that does not relate to your future financial planning can be thrown out. Check with a local accountant to find out what records should be kept and for what length of time.

There are many systems for keeping records. Some are very complicated; some are not so complicated. A few basics include

For filing the monthly bills: An expanding 10×12 file. You will need to label the pockets yourself.

For cancelled checks, bank statements, deposit slips: A 5×11 paper file, with a flap.

For those items that you only deal with once or twice a year: Manila folders, suitably labeled.

To hold all of the above: A file drawer or cardboard file box.

By having a few simple tools and a special place to store them, you will manage to control the paperwork. Be certain that your file drawer or box is easily accessible. This means don't use the drawer in the bottom of the refrigerator or use the file as a base for a coffee table. Nothing discourages a system more than not being able to get to it. And be sure to clean out the files at the end of the year. Put all the papers together, first to be used for taxes, then to be bound, labeled, and stored.

Keeping records also means tracking cash expenditures. (This is advanced material, so read accordingly.) You will not be able to plan accurately unless you track how you already spend. This could mean marking purchases in your datebook or in a journal or on a wall calendar. The idea isn't to drive yourself crazy; the idea is to be free to use your money for the things you really want.

Let me tell you where I am in this money odyssey. Last year I hired a bookkeeper, Tina, to keep our personal records for our checking account. She divided the expenses into categories for each month. She balanced the checkbook, too. At the end of the year she summarized them for us. What a revelation that was! I never knew we spent our money like that! Do you know we spent—well, I'm not going to tell you exactly!—on our pets, and that didn't include dog and cat food. Of course our dog did break both his front legs (What an ordeal!) and our horse did develop colic (which can be fatal in horses) and needed the vet several times. Seeing how it added up in yearly terms was shocking. Several other categories were surprises, too.

Looking at our yearly totals, I discovered a large amount unaccounted for by any records. This was money we had taken out of the bank for miscellaneous expenses that we had no record for. To solve that problem, my husband and I are carrying around little books to record cash spending. I'll put those in a cash-only ledger book to see where the money goes and then with headings like Tina's check-ledger book, we'll really know where all the money goes. Each month I'll add the cash and the checks for each category for a record of total spending.

All of this record keeping is absolutely necessary. I could never have handled it five years ago. Back then my life and house were in such a jumble that even keeping up the little book would have been too much extra effort, and not losing the bank statement any month for a whole year would have been impossible, I am sure. It may be too much for you right now if you have trouble finding your shoes and keys on a regular basis. Just as soon as you begin to get your life under control, work on the money part, too. Maybe you are ready now. If so, get busy tracing the flow of that money.

And having faced Reality #1 and #2, you can face *Reality #3: You must file your taxes.* Some people enjoy the challenge of doing their own tax returns. Others really prefer to have someone else prepare them. This choice is entirely up to you. But either way, if you have been faithful in keeping up your checkbook and in keeping your records in order, preparing taxes will be a simple, nontraumatic experience. Unfortunately, the pain of paying the tax bill is something that no amount of organization can soften.

As these financial realities are faced, you will begin to have enough information and courage to face new challenges like the challenge of budgeting. In and of itself budgeting is no big thrill. But budgeting means that you will be able to

Save—Put away funds for the new living room furniture, a special trip, or the swimming pool.

Give—You will be able to regularly support those causes that are near to your heart.

Plan—You and your family will be able to achieve goals that until now you only dreamed about.

See, we got through this entire chapter without one chart or diagram. But remember, these are only the basics. So when you feel you're ready, you can expand and refine your financial savvy by reading (*see* Appendix) or attending classes.

And your rewards? In addition to the peace of mind that you've attained from knowing everything is in order, you will most certainly enjoy the bonus of extra dollars—money you've saved by not bouncing checks and by earning interest on your savings and investments. And if you catch yourself in the mirror with a smug, self-satisfied smile, remember ol' Duke Wayne. "Ya did good, little missy."

Photo Albums

SANDRA FELTON

If a picture is worth a thousand words, what's a negative worth?

When a reforming Messie begins the long and gratifying job of pulling the house into order by using the Mount Vernon method, frequently one of the things she finds is that there are packets of photographs to be found everywhere. They are in the desk drawer in the living room. They are in the bedroom drawer. They are on a closet shelf. Many times the industrious Messie also finds undeveloped cartridges of film.

Now the problem begins. We are forced to devise a plan to handle this avalanche of photos. This is an especially difficult job because what we are dealing with here are more than pieces of paper—they are memories, memories of our families. They are pieces of our lives and times, caught and frozen. These times and events will never come again. In short, our photos are personal, irreplaceable treasures. And we are the caretakers of these invaluable jewels.

So we come to the job of preserving and showing them weighted down with responsibility. And there are two tremendous obstacles in the way of our success.

1. The photos are not found in any order. Some are so old that we can't even remember the year or the people. Of course, the undeveloped cartridges must be developed before we can even begin to see what era they are from.

2. We are sticklers for order. When we finish putting in our photos we want to be assured that they are in perfect chronological order. Once we have gone around the entire house and gathered all of our photos into one box and spent our life savings on getting the film developed, we are still reluctant to begin. Why? Because we suspect that maybe, somewhere, undiscovered there is one package we overlooked. If we were to get our book all set up and then find that package, we would have to go back and try to rearrange all the pictures to fit that batch in. This would be a tremendous job. Would it not be better to wait to be sure that there are no other packages, we reason. AND PROCRASTINATION IS BORN. Its mother is perfectionism.

Take heart! There is hope! Here are the steps to follow to set up even the biggest challenge.

I will assume that you have collected up all of the pictures that you know about. (When I did the Mount Vernon method and thought I had them all, I found out that my husband had a cache stashed away in his desk, the one place I had not Mount Vernoned.) If you have overlooked one, don't worry. Begin anyway. I'll tell you how to solve that problem later.

First you need to go to the store and buy the photo album. Buy several at the same time if you think you'll need several. Buy the biggest ones you can find and make sure they have loose-leaf three-ring binder rings like a school notebook has. The pages that fit into the rings should have a clear plastic sheet which covers the photos once they are placed on the photo album page. They will usually adhere lightly when placed on the page under the clear plastic cover. Take along a couple of your snapshots when you go shopping: one vertical shot and one horizontal shot so that you can see how they would fit together on the page. The pages of some albums are just a little too short to take two vertical photos or a little too narrow to hold your horizontal ones. You would have nothing but frustration if you were to get home and find that the pages of your photo album did not quite jibe with your size snapshots.

The next step is to find some nice quiet time when you can go through your snapshots looking for clues as to when they were taken. DON'T take them out of the original packages because sometimes the date is stamped on the package, or you have a receipt in there that will help you guess the date. Too often the date doesn't include the year but look for it anyway.

Now the real work begins. Go through the packets of snapshots, putting them as best you can in chronological order out on a table. The size of the children, the size of the trees in your yard, the presence of people who have since moved away or died—these are all helpful clues. If you have moved and have different houses in the pictures, that is a BIG help, of course. Birthday cakes are helpful. Sometimes you can count the candles or you may have put the actual number of the birthday on the cake.

Once you have them somewhat in order, begin putting them in the book. Happily move along at an even pace. Put little tags with the dates and occasions as you go. I use pieces cut from three-by-five-inch cards for the information tags, since you can't write directly on the album page.

Don't let anybody know I said this, but sometimes you can actually cut a photo to the benefit of the album. The background or empty space to the side doesn't need to be included if the snapshot will fit better without it. Ignore your husband, children, or others in the background who are calling to you, "Are you sure you are putting those in the right order?" and "You are not *cutting* those snapshots, are you?" Smile and say, "I know what I'm doing. It's going to be great."

Now, what *does* happen if your worst fears are realized and you do find you have left out something from its proper space? *That's* what the loose-leaf pages are for. You simply take a blank page from the back of the album, put it in the spot where the left-out packet should have been, and you've got it back in order again. The *loose-leaf* pages are the key to the problem of keeping your photos in the proper order.

Try to get the whole job done in one swipe because you have all of the snapshots out and in certain spots on the table. You may have to do it in two sessions if you get worn out by all the decision making. (In which case, please put the things away so the house won't be cluttered. I know you're going to get right back to it tomorrow, but you don't really want the table all junky for that long, do you?)

One more word is necessary. There will be some snapshots that are not worth putting in the book. In that case, *don't.* Throw them away if you can or put them in a shoe box labeled *Discarded Snapshots.*

In order to avoid this problem in the future, try to keep shorter accounts with your photo album. Put your snapshots in shortly after they are taken. Now I always put the number of the birthday on the cake. (*Happy 16th Birthday, Doug.*) We also bought a camera that automatically records the date on each picture.

What to do with the negatives? Very big question. Some people rarely ever have prints made from a negative. Even so, throwing negatives away takes a hardier soul than most Messies have. In fact, such people are probably not Messies at all. The primary rule with negatives is "Handle with Care," which means handle as little as possible. Scratches come easily and cannot be repaired. To store negatives, get a supply of glassine envelopes at an art or photo supply store. Get the long size, designed to hold strips of negatives. Put the negatives for each roll in a sleeve (there will be more than one strip per sleeve), then label the sleeve with the date and event(s) of the pictures. If you're really ambitious, you can add the page numbers on which the photographs are mounted in the album. But the date and event should be enough to help you find the negative you want. The filled sleeves can in turn be organized, labeled, and bound with a rubber band to be stored with your "Discarded Snapshots" box. (Now labeled "Discarded Snapshots and Negatives.") Or you can buy one of those plastic pencil cases with a zipper that fit into a ring binder. Put the filled negative sleeves in the pencil case and put the pencil case in the binder after the last page of photographs.

You've done a big job. Why not reward yourself and include those you love in the celebration? Have a special cookout with the albums as the guests of honor to be shown off. You have done a very special thing. Congratulations.

15

Making Up The Bed

"When you make your bed you get a star."

RUTH KRAUSS
(A Hole Is to Dig)

An absolute *must* right from the beginning of the M.A. program is the daily making of the bed. If a person says that she does not see the need for making the bed daily, she will not succeed in changing her housekeeping ways.

The main reason given is this:

"I go to work early and I don't return until dinner time. I'm not home all day so why make the bed?"

This remark indicates several characteristics which will scuttle housekeeping success.

1. Lack of dedication to beauty and order for the sake of beauty and order. Any person, Messie or not, who doesn't care if they dress in a bedroom with an unmade bed, who can work away from home knowing the bed is unmade, and who can come home to an unmade bed, lacks enough of the spark of caring to get going in the right direction.

2. Poor planning and use of time. It takes one or two minutes to make up a bed. If a person feels she can't take one or two minutes to do a job as important and as rewarding as making up a bed, she won't have committed time for *any* housework. Oh, she may work on jobs that demand it, like washing the dishes so she can eat the next meal, but only emergencies will be done. Only the head will be out of the water.

3. Lack of willingness to change habits. If anything is true of Messies turning into Cleanies it is that there must be some definite habit changes. We may have to get up earlier or read the paper less or make the lunches at night or *something* to make things different, but we will have to change. Otherwise we remain the same frustrated Messies. The bed should be made as soon as it is empty. There are several problems with this approach. They usually involve the husband. Here are certain principles.

IF YOU SLEEP ALONE or get up last—begin to make the bed while you are still in it, straightening the sheets and corners from underneath with your arms and legs.

IF YOU TWO GET UP TOGETHER—make the bed together. He usually won't mind. It seems only fair.

IF YOU GET UP BEFORE HIM—either he can make it or you can, as soon as you reenter the room. Or, make up your side only. He can do his when he gets up.

IF YOU LEAVE BEFORE HE GETS OUT OF BED—in this case, he should make the bed. Do I hear you shouting, "But he will never do it!" Maybe he won't, but as the house becomes nicer and nicer, you'll be surprised at how enthusiastic the family—in this case, husband—will become about maintaining the "niceness."

There are other problems, like people who nap in the afternoon or who have different schedules where one sleeps at night and the other in the day. But let's make a general rule: When the bed is not occupied—no matter for how long—it will be made.

Now let's get down to the actual bed making.

Don't let bed making become a huge project. Every little wrinkle doesn't need to be absolutely smooth. Both sides don't need to be *exactly* even. *Just make it!*

Now as a further incentive, buy new sheets and a spread if you can. Beauty inspires enthusiasm. One further word: If the bedroom is a shambles, there is not as much incentive to make the bed because the beautiful effect is lost in the clutter. Plus, you and I know how hard it is to make the bed when we can't get close to the side of the bed because of all the books and papers cluttering the floor.

Now for commitment time. Check one below.

☐ I already make my bed each day. That's one thing I do right. Thank the Lord!

☐ Yes! Yes! I will start making the bed just as soon as it is empty each day. I can't wait to get up in the morning so I can begin!

☐ No. I don't believe I will make the bed up. It's not important to me. I like things the way they are.

16

To Work or Not to Work

The term "working mother" is redundant.
ERMA BOMBECK

Many women have already answered the question of whether to work or not in the affirmative. Single women, married women without children, single moms, and moms in two-career families make up a tremendous working force of women. Many of these working women are Messies who have added the time and effort of work outside the home to their already flustered lives.

Maria is a new member of the working force. Like many Messies, she was discouraged by the constant losing battle she fought with the house after she married. She finds it a relief to get up, get dressed, and get away from the clutter each day. Her job away from home is certainly more pleasant and fulfilling than the jumbled and harried existence she was leading. When she returns home at night, the Messie lifestyle is still stressful but at least it is short-lived. Maria is also thinking about getting a maid as soon as she gets things in good enough order for a maid to come, if she can find someone reliable and honest. It's too early to tell how her husband is going to adjust to this whole new way of life.

286

Maria is not a unique case. Fifty-three percent of all American women are in the work force today. An even higher number, 60 percent, of mothers with children under eighteen work outside the home.

Obviously, there are great variations in how women feel about their working. Twenty-five percent work primarily for personal satisfaction and 15 percent work for economic reasons. The majority of women feel their working has been beneficial to themselves and their families. But there are tremendous stresses along the way. By far the biggest stress for a working mom is lack of time to relate to her husband and, especially, to her children.

No one can have it all. Women today can have part of both a family life and professional life, but not all of the benefits of both. How well the trade-offs work between the two is important.

Sometimes, in the case of many single women who are their own and their children's sole support, the matter of trade-offs is beside the point. Survival is the top priority.

In cases where there is enough money being made by the husband or the husband-wife combination, women do have choices that can make working outside the home more satisfactory all around.

I have had to make those choices, as has every working woman. When I was first married, I had no job skills. It was a frightening thing to feel that I could not support myself or help my family if I needed to because I was not qualified to do anything. When my children were two and three and a baby was on the way (what timing!), I went back to school. I went to the local university only to inquire about taking some undergraduate courses. Through a wonderful set of surprising circumstances, I entered, instead, the master's program in education with a fellowship. This meant I didn't have to pay tuition. In addition, they paid me a stipend to attend school full-time. My husband was able to stay home with the children when I went to school in the afternoon and at night. We had a wonderful pediatrician who said she would make house calls if I was away at school with our only car when a child was ill. Sickness of a child is a big problem for moms who work or go to school.

By the way, there are two hospitals in Iowa where working parents can drop their sick children off for two dollars an hour. This is a lot better than the child staying home alone while sick or being sent to school sick. But I remember how much I appreciated my own mother's love and care as a sick child. It built a bond between us.

, When I graduated, I took a part-time job with a private educational clinic. My baby went to be with a close-by, long-established, grandmotherly church woman who had him as the only child she took care of.

My older children went to nursery school. I had a lot of time at home with the children since I worked only twenty-four hours a week. I held and enjoyed that job for about six years. I eventually felt I had to quit it, however, because it required that I work part of the summer. This meant my children were left at home part of the day without the supervision they needed. Too much time with too little guidance.

So I quit. I began teaching instead in a private school which my children also attended. This was just about ideal because we went to and came home from school together, and we had the same vacation off. I recommend teaching as one great career for moms.

My children are grown now. The "baby" is seventeen. The work of Messies Anonymous demands time, effort, and trips out of town. Even so, the family priorities are just that—*priorities*. I adjust my career for the family.

This adjusting of career for family is not just a feminine characteristic. Dr. James Dobson, the well-known psychologist, told me that he was so busy traveling and telling others how to run their families that he was neglecting his own. So he completely adjusted his type of outreach to stay in town for his family's sake.

As previously mentioned, Gordon McDonald, a minister with an erratic schedule, tells in his book, *Ordering Your Private World* (Thomas Nelson, 1983), that he schedules blocks of time for his family long before any other demands can be made on it.

In his book *Your Money Matters* (Bethany Fellowship, 1980), Malcolm MacGregor, a financial counselor, tells of canceling two appointments with important clients to attend a function important to one of his children. The clients were not pleased when he did, I might add.

Because I am not the sole support of my family, I have been able to make big adjustments for my children's sakes. I have also enjoyed working. It got me away from the house and provided interesting stimulation. For most of those years I lived as a Messie and our home was not pleasant from that standpoint. It would not have been any better if I had stayed home, however, because I didn't know how to make it different.

I don't know how women with families work a forty-hour week, and more, regularly.

From time to time I have a week of nine-to-five jury duty downtown. I find that during these weeks I cannot get much of anything done. We go on emergency alert at home. My husband buys TV Dinners, I (exhausted) go to bed early, the cleaning waits, and so on. I guess if I had a regular nine-to-five job, I would adjust. At this point, however, I don't see how I could do it. I don't see how any woman can keep a full-time job and do it satisfactorily. But many do. Many have jobs that require overtime work, as well. A full-time working woman with a family has the most stressful setup in our society today.

Let me add while we are talking about the children that finding a good place for them while Mom is at work is a major consideration.

How can we be sure that the baby-sitter doesn't spend much of her time on the phone with the kids planted in front of the TV? How can we be sure the sitter teaches our children the values we feel are important?

In my area, at this moment, a couple is in jail awaiting trial for abusing several young children in their baby-sitting service in one of the loveliest parts of town. This is an extreme case and certainly the exception. But when it comes to our children, can we be too careful?

Let us assume that the day-care arrangement we choose for our children is safe. How good is safe day-care for children? Opinions vary. "There is no hard evidence that day-care has a negative effect," says one expert. Another says, "If parents anticipate not providing enough time for one-to-one con-tact in the first three years, they should consider not having a child at all."

Brenda Hunter, author of *Where Have All the Mothers Gone?* (Zondervan), cites the only long-term study done on the effects of day-care. These findings were largely negative. Boys raised in substitute care were less interested in schoolwork, more aggressive, and more nonconforming. Girls in substitute care were less well-adjusted and less happy with their childhoods.

Most agree that there are differences between children raised in substitute care and those raised at home. Not all agree as to what these differences are. Those of us who have children need to be careful in assuming that substitute care will not adversely affect our children.

For the mother who absolutely must work, the only alternative is to find the best possible day-care she can afford.

For those who have a choice, the decision to work must be made carefully with the children's welfare in view. What greater priority or privilege can we have than the raising of our children?

There are other circumstances about working to consider as well. We need time to ourselves—time to think, time to read, to dream, and plan. Time to do our nails. Time to enjoy being alive and special.

We need time for our husbands. The majority of working women feel they don't have nearly enough time for their husbands.

We need time for chores and the house. This is a major consideration for a Messie, especially one who wants to reform. When women work, housekeeping becomes more of a conflict in the family than ever. Working women want their husbands to help more with home responsibilities than the husbands want to. Only about a third of working women consider that they have support from their husbands in running the house, marketing, and meal preparation, according to the book *Mothers Who Work* (Jeanne Bodin and Bonnie Mitelman, Ballantine, 1983). Twenty-seven percent of husbands help with cleaning. That means, of course, that 73 percent do not help with the cleaning. It is generally agreed that husbands today are thinking about helping more around the house than they have done in the past. They are approving in principle of men helping their wives in the house. Some younger men may actually be helping more around the house because *their* moms worked, leaving them to do household chores as kids. Men who marry later and have lived alone also tend to help more around the house. In general, however, the housework remains largely the domain and responsibility of the woman. Not much has really changed.

I know a young woman who wanted to go to work as a church secretary to bring in extra income for her family. Her husband said he would let her work on the condition she not let down in any way in her care of the children, house, and himself. Meticulously, she worked and did it all. No compromises or trade-offs for her. The last I heard, she was rushed to the hospital with a bleeding ulcer.

Because of the tremendous pressures, Messies, especially Messies who work outside the home, must put the principles of Messies Anonymous to work for them. We must set goals, dream dreams for the house, overcome procrastination, get control of our "collecting" tendencies, discipline ourselves in the use of time, and use the housekeeping skills that work for others. We must carefully set our priorities since we can't have it all.

There are many ways to approach the problem of working outside the home. Some women feel their primary job is to nurture. They are nurturers. Agatha Christie somehow sandwiched her writing into private little pockets of time when she didn't have anything else pressing from the family. Her family and friends apparently didn't realize she was writing at all because her work did not interfere with her homelife. Once she did take off from her volunteer hospital work to write day and night for three days and complete a book in one giant effort. She was basically a nurturer.

Other women base their work on being partners, not nurturers. Some take it to extremes. A couple, we'll call them the Thompsons, plan to live two thousand miles apart because she has been transferred to a new job location. One lives in Miami, Florida, the other in St. Paul, Minnesota. They plan to meet twice a month in cities and resorts easily accessible from Miami and St. Paul and to vacation together. They are long-distance partners.

Yet other women see themselves as providers. The provider places her job as a top priority as support for the family.

Most of us who work are a combination of these. We are nurturer/partner/providers. This can be rewarding but it must be done carefully to be sure that the partner/provider doesn't squeeze out the nurturer.

In the end the decision rests with you and your family. How do you see yourself? You can do it well *if* you keep it organized and set your priorities at the start.

17

Search and Destroy—Dejunking as the Ultimate Test

"Every day I'll throw something away, and I'll soon feel better and better."

Motto, Pack Rats Anonymous
PEG BRACKEN

In Messies Anonymous, we like to use kind and gentle words. We don't say *slobs*, we say *Messies*. We don't say *pack rat*, we say *collector*, and we don't say *junk*, we say *stuff*.

Maybe in the case of clutter we should vary our ways and use stronger language. Maybe we should tell it like it is and say *junk*. Let's get vicious on this subject. Clutter has brought more frustration, grief, embarrassment, and strain to people's lives than any other single aspect of Messiedom. No other single problem has so assaulted the dignity and self-esteem of its owners. While clutter is mauling our lives, we are loving it and dragging more of it into our homes. Are we masochists? Do we love to suffer? Why do we do this to ourselves? Is it really so bad? What can we do about it?

Why Do We Keep It?

There are some very good reasons for collecting junk—or so we tell ourselves. We have certain characteristics that make us want to save. We are—

Intellectual. Newspapers, books, college notes—who knows what these

293

might contain or when we might use them? We definitely *must* keep these items.

When doing the Mount Vernon method on my house, I decided reluctantly to let many of my college texts go. Proudly, I took them to a bookstore that bought used books. They were to be privileged to have them if they gave me a good enough price. What a disappointment I was in for. They didn't want them, even if I *gave* them away. Old college texts are pretty useless and, in many fields, quickly out of date. I ended up giving them to the Salvation Army. In the past, books were made to last both in binding and content. Now, however, many books are printed in bulk on inferior paper with paper covers. They are meant to be used and discarded, like Kleenex. Let the libraries do the storing. Magazines are the same.

Not long ago, a friend of mine told me that she had seen my picture in a magazine, which she had received the day before in the mail.

"Did you see the article on vacations in English castles in that same issue?" I asked her.

"No, I missed that. Too bad. I've already thrown the magazine away. I don't like things to pile up." Happily she walked away leaving me in shock. One day! And the magazine was gone. How could she? Messies think: *Cleanies must be mentally dull.*

Creative. Messies love to find unusual uses for clutter. Empty spools can be used to make a toy for baby to play with. Milk cartons can be used for planters. *Reader's Digest* pages can be folded down, sprayed, and made to look like a Christmas tree.

"Let's save our spools, milk cartons, and *Reader's Digests* just in case we have time to do any of these projects," we say to ourselves. Cleanies throw the junk out. Messies think: *Cleanies must be very unimaginative.*

Careful. One of the reasons Messies keep things is because they might need them in the future, "Just as soon as I throw anything out, I need it the next day," we often say.

That's what happens, too. The next day we do find a use for it and say to ourselves, *I knew I should have kept it.*

Sometimes we think this way deliberately. After it's gone, we decide to teach ourselves a lesson. So we find some use for the recently discarded item. We sort of punish ourselves for letting it go. That discourages us from throwing things out in the future.

Sometimes we need some lipstick fast and we find an old almost used-up tube that we can dip our little finger into to get some color. Sometimes we can supply the day-care center with egg cartons to make caterpillars with. We then confirm to ourselves, *I am right to keep things.* The truth is that the few times these things come in handy do not make up for the long-term distress of living with junk. Besides, if we lived in an orderly way, we'd know where the good lipsticks were to begin with.

It is inconvenient to need a discarded item, but it is much more inconvenient to live with scores of kept items that we might someday need. Messies think: *Cleanies do not adequately prepare for the future.*

Frugal. There is an old Greek story about a crippled man who begged a strong healthy man to carry him across the river. The healthy man agreed and the crippled man jumped on his back. When the two reached the other side, the crippled man would not get down. He clung so tightly, it was impossible to get him loose. For the rest of his life the healthy man paid for his kind decision to do the crippled man a favor. He carried him for life.

That's the way it is with our belongings. Once we buy them and let them into the house, they won't let go. They cling for life.

Those shoes that give us blisters (but cost so much), that vacuum that doesn't work but might someday if we ever do something about it, the home computer that no one knows how to use ("But they do say they are the thing of the future")— these all cost us money. We must keep them for life no matter how great a burden they are to us in order to justify the rightness of our purchase. Messies think: *Cleanies will throw away good stuff. They don't appreciate the value of things.*

Capable. Messies are very capable people in many ways. One reason clutter sneaks up on them is because they feel that they can handle it. At least that's what they think at first. Even when it is obvious to all others that the junk is out of control, Messies keep saying,

- "I can handle it just as soon as I get enough time."
- "I'll build another room."
- "We'll get a shed."
- "I'll rearrange the basement."

Messies think: *Cleanies don't have the ability to handle stuff like I do. They have to throw it away. I can handle it.*

Appreciative of good things. I gave away my family's cast-iron skillet. It is traditional for my family to use a cast-iron skillet to make corn bread. One skillet had been in the family for years. It *was* a great skillet. They don't make skillets that heavy anymore.

However, I really prefer to make corn bread in muffin pans, myself. I had no use for an iron skillet. Besides, iron skillets are a nuisance to clean. The one I gave away was a good skillet but not good for me. Messies think: *Cleanies don't appreciate good things.*

Helpful. "Someone may need these," we say, tucking the stocking with runs into our old stocking bag. "Perhaps to stuff a pillow. Stockings are hypoallergenic, you know."

"Someone may need these," we say, saving the attachments to the vacuum we are discarding because it is worn out.

So our house is full of old stockings, old vacuum attachments, and old everything else saved forever because we want to be helpful. Messies think: *Cleanies don't think of others enough.*

Sentimental. "Aunt Maude gave this to me on my tenth birthday."

"Oh, look, my bathing suit from the summer I was sixteen."

Or the hardest one of all—

"This was Mom's. She left all of her things to me."

Much clutter is the result of inheritance. It must be dealt with in the light of our present needs, not the past sentiment. Messies think: *Cleanies don't value the past.*

Hopeful. One thing that has shocked me into reality is that the things I have kept and valued are not wanted by other people. I always think that things are more valuable than they are. Some things *do* increase in value. Get the facts. *Know* that what you are gathering has a good chance of becoming valuable someday. Chances are that you are fooling yourself into thinking that upon your death, your family will be thrilled to come across some first-rate find. They will have it appraised and say, "What a smart person Mom was to keep this. It has become so valuable." Probably not. If you do decide to collect something for an investment, get some expert opinion now. Expert opinion certainly has opened my eyes. I have gone into a store with a box of treasures and walked out with that same box—the treasures now junk. I was sadder but wiser. All that saving for nothing. Messies think: *Cleanies don't realize how valuable things you save may become.*

So we go about rationalizing how right we are to gather junk and how wrong Cleanies are not to. Our lives are frazzled and frustrated. Theirs are orderly and peaceful, at least as far as the house is concerned.

For Messies, getting rid of our clutter is complicated by our tendency to mix ourselves with what we own. All these things are proof that we have lived a busy, full life. When Messies give things away, we feel as if we've lost a part of ourselves.

Those who surround themselves with clutter, frequently do so to show their worth. They collect the "in" things, even if they don't use them. If they are in the jogging crowd, they have jogging shoes, clothes, and gadgets even if they seldom jog. If they are in the sewing crowd, they have boxes of cloth and patterns, even if they haven't sewn in a long time. Some Messies keep a musical instrument they haven't played in years, or never even learned to play. These symbols show that the owners are joggers, seamstresses, or musicians, whether or not they jog, sew, or play music. This makes the Messies feel better about themselves. They feel more capable.

In another way, however, it makes the Messies feel worse. The unused jogging clothes, sewing material, or instruments put added pressure on the owners. They vow they will get to these things someday. In the meantime, their self-esteem drops lower because they are putting off one more thing.

I remember when I came to grips with the fact that I am not a seamstress. I have had two bouts of sewing fever in my life but recovered quickly from both. I think it is a nice thing for people to sew. It is an admirable activity, but I finally realized that it was not for me. When I came to grips with this sad truth about myself, I gave away two large boxes of material. I remember one beautiful piece of green wool with black flecks in it. Those boxes of material were like the crippled man who rode his benefactor's back. When they were gone (Salvation Army again) I was released. It was nice material, but it was nicer when it was gone.

What we need to do is know ourselves and set our own priorities. As long as we try to be everything we admire, we just muddle ourselves down in confusion. Streamline. Let's be willing to face our limitations. Better still, let's set limitations. Decide your priorities and pare down everything else. It may not all come at once. It took me a while before I could face the fact that I didn't really like to sew, even though I wanted to like it. Be comfortable with yourself as you are and live accordingly. And remember, once you begin to rid yourself of clutter, you are going to have to keep it up or it will gather itself back.

Where Does It Come From?

Where does all this clutter come from? Let's pinpoint the source areas so we can be on guard.

1. **Hobbies**—Equipment and papers such as magazines and instructions.

2. **Clubs and organizations**—Scouts, P.T.A., C.E.F., Right to Life, and so on.

3. **Vacations**—Maps, brochures, and souvenirs.

4. **Gifts**—What do I do with the hillbilly salt and pepper shakers my daughter brought back from Tennessee or the one ceramic tile with a picture of Brasília on it which a missionary from Brazil gave me?

5. **Inheritance.**

6. **Breakage and loss**—The cup with the handle broken

off but also saved in case we get to fixing it. Tupperware top with no bottom.

7. **"Worn out but still good"**—Old faded curtains (maybe we can dye them) and old slacks (for around the house).

8. **"Out of style"**—Ties, dress with a skirt too short but maybe we can put another skirt on it, and shoes hardly worn (they hurt).

9. **General paper**—Flyers, ads, work, receipts, magazines, etc.

10. **Kids**—School papers, hobbies, collections, toys, projects (rub-on letters, magazines to cut out, paper).

11. **Religion**—You *can't* throw away religious materials, can you! That's a sacrilege, isn't it?

12. **Home decorating**—Old fake fruit, old artificial flowers, old pictures stored away with or without cracked glass.

Don't confuse collecting with cluttering. Collectors generally show more restraint than clutterers. They are more selective and they don't keep just anything, especially if it is old, broken, or out of style. There are Cleanie collectors. A collection of any kind is tough to maintain, even for Cleanies, especially if it's a collection of trinkets. Joyce, a Cleanie mentioned in *The Messies Manual,* is a collector of all kinds of small animals made of wood, cork, shells, ceramics, and so on. Her husband built shelves in the windows to display them. They were on the mantel. A few were on tables. When they moved from their home of ten years into a smaller home, Joyce had four garage sales. She did not pack her treasures in boxes to be stored under the bed, in the utility room, or in a rented warehouse. She sold great gobs of her collection. When I asked her how she felt about parting with them, she said that to a large extent it was like lifting a burden. Some things she sold she misses now, like a large ceramic hippopotamus and dishes she used to use every day. When she told me that she missed them she sounded matter-of-fact, not distraught or regretful. As I was about to hang up she said that she had been stimulated by our conversation to begin to get rid of some more clothes. They had been given to her but she didn't like them.

"I believe I'll go right now and get those out of my closet," she said happily.

Not everyone can let go as successfully as Joyce. Just today a reforming Messie told me she had done the Mount Vernon method to her house. She had cleared the rooms and packed everything neatly and tightly into the closets. When she opened a closet, stuff fell out.

"I organized my things, but I didn't get rid of them. Should I?" she asked.

While she was talking, another Messie rushed up.

"Are many Messies pack rats?" she asked.

Yes, they are pack rats (we say *gatherers*). To all who ask the question, "Should I get rid of things?" the answer is, "Yes, get rid of a lot more. YES, YES, YES."

Cleanie collectors and Messie collectors vary in degree. Cleanie collectors can and do get rid of things even with regret. Messie collectors must learn to accept the pain of regretfully parting with stuff (shall we say *junk*) for the pleasure of order.

MEMORIES OR KEEPSAKES?

Why do we hold on to keepsakes,
which can rot, be lost, burn, be stolen,
or, get in the way?

Keepsakes are things.
Things become junk if they fail to have
tangible value.

Memories are better than keepsakes.
No one ever stole a memory;
nor lost one.

Keepsakes can occupy space
which may be needed for things of real
value.

Memories are stored in the heart and
mind—
there's always room for another good one.

Wouldn't it be awful if someone were to
deny himself memories
to make room for more keepsakes?

Wouldn't it be a tragedy if someone were
to deny memories
to others
in order to make room for his own keepsakes?

Keepsakes can be stolen, lost, burned.
We need less of them.

Memories are forever;
We can never have too many good ones.
Robert, Texas
Husband of a Messie

Peace Talks

PART FOUR

Cleanliness is not next to godliness. It isn't even in the same neighborhood. No one has ever gotten a religious experience out of removing burned-on cheese from the grill of the toaster oven.

ERMA BOMBECK

18 Life
(Without Guilt)

Guilt is a funny word. According to Webster's dictionary, it can mean, "responsible for a grave breach of conduct." This is judicial guilt. A person may commit a serious crime, say kill a person, and not feel bad about it at all. Some men on death row laugh about their crimes or say their victim deserved to die. They are judicially guilty but they don't feel guilty.

Another definition of *guilt* is, "a *feeling* of culpability, especially for imagined offenses or from a sense of inadequacy." In this case, a person feels as though he has done wrong, whether or not he actually has. This is psychological guilt.

So which is it with Messies? Scores of Messies have written to me saying that *The Messies Manual* lifted such a burden of guilt. Do Messies who feel guilty have real or imagined guilt?

In chapter 5, "Profile of a Messie: The Reasons" we discussed why some people have trouble with organization and others do not. It is generally because of a lack of one or several natural skills such as visual tune in, attention span, memory, and so on.

When these deficits combine to make a person feel inadequate, she reacts with protective devices such as procrastination, perfection, and guilt. All of this further diminishes her ability. After a while, some Messies say, "I don't care," and quit trying to bring beauty and order to the house. They say things like, "I don't care about the house. I have learned to live with it. I have other priorities." They are trying to escape from guilt.

Guilt can come from several sources: our own conscientious attitudes, the expectations of others, an objective standard we don't meet, or any combination of these three. Let's look at these.

1. Personal expectations. Sometimes guilt comes from ourselves. Messies generally feel guilty because things don't "work" right, not because they don't "look" right. When we lose things, don't have clean dishes for supper, or can't invite people over, we face our failure and that causes guilt. It is this frustration and guilt from living in such an unsatisfactory way that first drives most Messies to seek help. The desire for beauty follows after we have found order for our lives.

2. Others' expectations. Other people, like husbands, kids, and parents, expect us to keep a nice house. Some family members suffer silently, some complain, and others leave. It is true that overzealous Cleanies have run family members out of the house by their excessive neatness. But many have fled a house because of messiness, too. A university study found that the subject couples argue about most is not money, sex, or in-laws, but the condition of the house. Marriages have been ruined or greatly weakened by arguments over the mess the house is in. When one partner is a Messie and the other a Cleanie, there usually is a lot of emotional stress between them. However, the Cleanie helps to keep the Messie from going too far down the road to cluttered ruin. This is a plus for the Messie. Opposites do attract because each person seeks the other to balance his or her weaknesses. The Messie woman may be attracted to an orderly man. He may be attracted to her carefree attitude. As long as the differences are not too great and love prevails, it works for the benefit of the Messie's house. Sometimes, however, when the marriage is under stress or the husband is having a hard time at work and needs a peaceful home in which to recuperate, patience wears thin, tempers flare, people say things they don't mean, and the marriage is strained.

A man from Dallas called me to discuss his Messie problems: "I love to collect things. I have rooms full of stuff. I was divorced last year because of my collecting," he explained in a rather detached way. But I wonder how many emotional months or years he and his wife went through before the end. I wonder if he really felt as casual about it as he sounded.

3. Unmet standards. Sometimes we feel guilty because we have violated an important standard. Many suspect they have violated God's law. So then they face two problems. They feel that in addition to having to live in a messy house on earth, they also are under the cloud of heaven's displeasure. God *does* care about our houses, but not in a vengeful way. He cares because He sees us hurting. We are very special to God. Made in His image, we are people of worth. He has a special plan for our lives. It is not right that we should live frustrated, unhappy lives that demean and humiliate us and those who live with us. It is not right that we should be shackled with guilt and frustration which hinder us from being the people God wants us to be. It is precisely because we are made in God's image that messy houses bother us and those we live with. He is a God of order and beauty. We are not happy if we do not have some of that characteristic in our lives, too. So we strive for order. We feel guilt if we fall below whatever standard of orderliness we have set for ourselves.

I don't think we should feel any guilt about our housekeeping at all, not one twinge of guilt.

You do not have to punish yourself because the house is a mess. Frustrated? Yes, that's allowed. Guilty? No.

If you are one of the souls who has, in the past, convinced yourself that you *should* feel guilty about the house, you have a hard habit to break. People who feel guilty about the house, generally feel guilty about a lot of other things, as well. Please set about breaking the guilt habit as soon as possible.

Develop your feelings of worth. Seek out people who build up your self-esteem, who compliment you, who think there is something great about you even if it's not your housekeeping. You have worth whether you believe it or not. No one can give you dignity and worth; but people can take away your feeling of worth. It is your job to bring your feelings into line with reality. You are a person of supreme value. Recapture the joy of that fact.

Perhaps there are already people who value and esteem you, but when they compliment you, you reject the truth of their compliments. Write down all the good things people like about you and accept them even if you can hardly believe they are true.

As I have said in a previous chapter, avoid those who put you down. If you can't avoid them fully, void what they say as much as possible. You are a person of dignity. A person of dignity does not accept put-downs.

Face the area that is degrading your self-esteem. For Messies, the house is a big part of why we feel bad about ourselves. We need to do two things about that:

First, lower your standards of housekeeping. "WHAT!" I hear many screams coming across the nation to my house. "We are reading this book to get help and here this woman is destroying our motivations by telling us to lower our standards!"

Upon reading this, a man who bought this book for his Messie wife, hoping it will help her, is now deciding not to give it to her. *If the housekeeping gets any lower, we'll all have to move out,* he thinks.

Wait before you panic. I said lower your *standards*. Many Messies are paralyzed by unrealistically high standards. We know we can never reach the perfection we want, so we do all kinds of strange compensating that ends up producing a messy house. Overly high standards hinder success. Be more realistic in your goals and your housekeeping will improve.

Second, begin changing the house. Begin easy. Do the Mount Vernon method a little every day, taking one day a week off. Choose a few of the daily jobs on the Flipper to do each day while you are beginning the Mount Vernon method. Just do those two things—the Mount Vernon and the dailies—to get started. When you set up the Flipper System, be gentle on yourself. Don't set up jobs that would take two full-time maids all day to do. As you improve, you can raise your standards to a comfortable level.

Remember those dreams and goals we are keeping in our

minds. Thoughts will reproduce themselves in the physical world automatically. But it does not happen overnight. Your dreams don't have to come true right away to keep from fading. Have confidence in the strength of your dreams. Follow the techniques for keeping up your motivation. Do self-talks, listen to encouraging tapes, and read your goals frequently.

Relax. Don't feel guilty about the house. Begin the change. Don't pay attention if hubby says, "Boy, I bought you that book and I can't see that it's doing you any good!" Just keep going a little at a time. Be relaxed and happy. You don't have to prove your worth by having a spotless house. You are already a person of worth. When you really begin to believe you are a person of dignity, you will have the motivation to continue with the house until it reflects the wonderful person you are. People of dignity do not live in clutter. Therefore, the clutter will go— slowly but very surely. Perhaps then, compliments will come. If so, embrace them. Whether or not anyone compliments you, *you'll* know when success begins to come. Compliment yourself. Reward yourself.

You can relax because you know your determination is steady.

What will you do about the feelings of guilt because of the unchangeable past? Fight them. When punishing thoughts come to make you feel bad, make them go away. Say just the opposite out loud to yourself even if you don't believe it. Say it often and say it loud.

Why am I so strong against guilt? Because it is unnecessary and unproductive. Guilt saps our energy, discourages our efforts, clouds our goals, and lowers our self-esteem.

Acceptance of ourselves as we are, coupled with a feeling of our own dignity, will clear the path for change. When we see our failures to live up to our standards, we will not berate or accuse ourselves. We will begin, lovingly, to correct our faults. Trust me. Getting control of the house is a big job. We can't afford the time or energy to feel guilty. We've got work to do.

The final blow against guilt is that the closer our performance gets to our standards the less we'll struggle with the feeling of guilt.

As the house becomes more orderly and beautiful, positive feelings of joy and pride will replace it.

You do not need to leave your room. Remain sitting at your table and listen. Do not even listen, simply wait. Do not even wait, be quite still and solitary. The world will freely offer itself to you unmasked, it has no choice, it will roll in ecstasy at your feet.

FRANZ KAFKA

19 Liberty
(The Joy of Retreat)

An inability to stay quiet . . . is one of the most conspicuous failings of mankind.

WALTER BAGEHOT

The electricity went off today at the school where I teach part-time. The whole city was blacked out. It was time for me to go home but traffic spilling out of the city to escape the inconvenience clogged arteries in which there were no traffic lights working.

Unexpectedly, my life was stalled. Three hours to spend, or rather invest, in something. But what? Devoid of plans or of any way to generate elaborate efforts, I sat in the school library. The air conditioners were off, of course; there was no electricity to run them. We could hear the occasional voices of students at their lessons floating in the windows. We could feel the breeze and barely smell the smoke of the fire that had broken the electricity flow by burning a major cable.

In a library one reads. Without planning, I was alone with book, breeze, and quiet. The blackout was expected to be a long one. The news said it was extensive, covering the entire southern part of the state and involving over three million people. Could I drive home tonight without traffic lights working? Would the plans

Ivan and I had for dinner out and an infrequent movie be canceled? How could I cook tonight if I had to? I pitied people caught in elevators and was glad I was not one of them. The uncertainty of the future contrasted sharply with the serene reading I had been compelled to do in the library. Even the clocks stood still. We had two hours of powerless living.

Then suddenly and unexpectedly, life returned to normal as the power surged back. Students cheered as they turned on the air conditioners and closed the windows. They went back to normal. The library air conditioner, loud and mechanical, replaced the breeze and gentle voices of children outside. Life was indeed back to normal. But how nice it had been to be forced to delay my busy afternoon and float planlessly with nothing to do but what was at hand. Now the clocks and life had started again. What a shame.

Without electricity, I had seized the time with fervor. Lately I have begun to see the value of unpressured time. Time for me alone. Women today are parched for time alone. Not knowing the source of the thirst, we seek satisfaction in distractions. We feel the itch but can't place our hand on the place to scratch. We dissipate ourselves in many activities and can't find a source of renewal. The vague, unsatisfied need remains unsatisfied.

Women are givers. We give ourselves to our husbands and our children, to our obligations. In order to give in a satisfying way, we must have a source of replenishing. Anne Morrow Lindbergh, in her wonderfully insightful book for women, *Gift From the Sea*, reminds us that the more the nursing mother gives the more she has to give. Even she, however, must replenish herself with nourishment.

In pregnancy as well as nursing, we sustain life by the giving of our bodies. This is just a physical aspect of what women do emotionally and in many ways in the lives of those who depend on us. It is not that women resent giving. We resent giving purposelessly. We resent giving without our willingness being considered. We resent giving when we have been expended and our lives have not been replenished. This kind of exchange is not giving, it is just taking.

Modern lives are not geared for replenishing of soul and

spirit. We have gained conveniences but lost graciousness. To turn the tide requires a breaking of old patterns. We must seek a quiet room, a quiet place, a quiet time.

As a child, I was enchanted by a book called *The Secret Garden* by Frances Hodgson Burnett (Dell, 1962). The story is about a sour, lonely, orphaned English girl from India who is transported to a mansion on the moors of England to live. Left pretty much to herself by the servants and her absentee guardian, she finds the key to the hidden door of the secret and mysterious garden which had been locked untended for ten years.

> She was *inside* the wonderful garden and she could come through the door under the ivy anytime and she felt as if she had found a world all her own. Alone day after day, tending the neglected garden, it worked its magic on her and later through her on others.

Women today have chosen complicated lives involving food, clothing, activities for ourselves and our children. We have groceries to buy. We have the obligations of swimming lessons, dancing lessons, karate lessons, school functions, and doctor and dentist appointments. When necessary, we need to deal with plumbers and with repairmen who tend to our cars, refrigerators, and washing machines. Then there's the day-to-day maintenance—washing clothes, giving vitamins, fixing meals, buying clothes, sewing on buttons. If we ever have a moment to ourselves, say in the car while returning from dropping the kids off somewhere, we turn on the car radio to fill the void. When we pause to rest in the house, the TV mercifully distracts us from reflecting on the state of our lives. It is a chosen way of life for us. Women who have money enough to hire others to take the burdens of daily living, are just as busy in other kinds of activities as their less wealthy sisters.

America is a busy place.

"It's the American life-style," my friend says emphatically. "When we first returned to America from living in the Dominican Republic, we were so amazed at all that was available in the supermarket and other stores. There was so much. We weren't used to it."

315

"Did you like it?"

"Yes! At first it was fun. But after a while it was just so much clutter. We missed our more simple life-style."

Comparing the American life-style to the primitive cultures where there is much more leisure and the men maintain their comfortable life-styles with only a few hours of work a day, a sociologist commented, "In highly technical societies, we are sentenced to a life of hard labor."

One of the most thought-provoking statements I have ever read was a simple letter written by a member of our school faculty who had left the busy city life of Miami for a small college town in his native New York.

A marvelously talented mathematician and excellent musician, he had led our school to heights of musical achievement never reached before or since—the choir concerts, the madrigal dinners, the chamber singer! In addition, he sang in the local city opera chorus and gave voice lessons. All of this was in addition to his mathematics teaching schedule.

His wife, a graceful and very capable young woman, busied herself with working full-time as a personal secretary, carrying a crowded piano-teaching schedule in the late afternoons and on Saturday, and caring for two young children. I think she also typed term papers for others.

I cannot tell you how I admired their productivity and efficiency. How highly respected they were. What contributions they made. How we missed them when they left.

The letter they wrote to the school told a bit about their new life in New York State and added, "When we think of the busy lives we lived in Miami, looking back, we wonder why."

Activities, like barnacles on a ship's hull, crowd to fill in any vacant space. There are times, however, when we have a chance to stand back and reflect on our lives and wonder why.

My high school had a school prayer by John Greenleaf Whittier. At that time we prayed freely in public schools. The third verse of the prayer poem was meaningful to me then and speaks our present need so well.

Dear Lord and Father of Mankind

Drop Thy still dews of quietness,
    Till all our strivings cease;
Take from our souls the strain and stress,
    And let our ordered lives confess
The beauty of Thy peace.

JOHN G. WHITTIER

There will always be distractions. None of us, whether big-city-busy, or farm-busy or career-busy, are ever again going to have the responsibility-free life of a child who can spend unlimited time in a secret garden. However, to remain whole, we must find *some* time to spend alone in our secret garden. Perhaps it is a daily hour, a vacation alone, a day by ourselves. Eugene Peterson says it well: "The precedent to quit doing and simply *be* is divine." Time alone heals, strengthens, soothes, and refreshes.

Since I have a husband who works at home and children living at home, my house is seldom empty. I remember once when they had all left, probably to go visit Grandma at her house on the Florida Keys, and I had stayed home. Forced to be out on an errand, I was talking with a friend at her business. With a sense of urgency, I moved quickly, explaining to her, surprised at my own feelings, "I have to get home. There's nobody there and I have a chance to be alone."

When my children were smaller and more demanding of constant attention (I had three children in five years and the middle boy was hyperactive), occasionally I would fix the family dinner, serve it, and go out to dinner alone. It was not for the food. It was to be able to sit alone and reflect.

My schedule makes many demands on me and means I am with other people too much. Surely it is not this way with everyone. Perhaps it is with most. But do women who are alone more than I am really spend their time alone or do they spend it doing busy things with the TV on? When do we have time to slow down, to think, and to replenish the self?

When we understand the importance of solitude, we will find the time for it. Solitude is not valued by society however. We have to grab bits of it for ourselves if we are to have it. Gordon McDonald schedules time alone in his appointment book and consults his book when he is urged to do something. He says he has the slot scheduled. He does not say, "I need solitude." People wouldn't understand. In *Gift From the Sea*, Anne Lindbergh writes, "But if one says, I cannot come because that is my hour to be alone, one is considered rude, egotistical, or strange. . . . One has to apologize for it, make excuses, hide the fact that one practices it—like a secret vice!" Society admires much more the too-cluttered schedule, the unnecessary errand, the going life.

Too busy, we don't have time to bring order to our homes. Our checkbooks drift because we don't have time. We'll get to the folding of the clothes later—or better still, we'll just use them as we need them out of the basket. Worse than all of this is that our *inner* world is neglected, and that is so important. Plato once said that the unexamined life is not worth living. Our lives are too busy; plans are forgotten; memories are jumbled; joys are obscured. We are in such a hurry we hardly know who we are, much less how to develop and replenish ourselves.

Diane, a strapping pioneer woman nearing forty, suddenly found her challenges met and her life flat. For the first time, she was depressed and at ends. For Christmas, according to Gail Sheehy in *Pathfinders*, the woman's husband built her a very special gift: a tiny, round peak-roofed bonnet of a dwelling out back—an escape house. Her children's gift was a week for Mom in solitary; they brought her meals, tended the family house, and allowed no one to enter her hut. For seven whole days Diane simply "not did." When she came out, she knew she wanted to go back to school.

Her tomb of solitude became a womb in which she began to grow into a new life. We need solitude in order to grow.

We must stop, reflect, find solitude, take time just to be.

The story is told in the Talmud of a certain Rabbi Zusya. Reflecting on his reason for existence, he once said, "In the coming world, they will not ask me: 'Why were you not Moses?' they will ask me, 'Why were you not Zusya?' "

What about you? What about me? Are we the best Mary, John, or Sandra we can be? Or did we lose ourselves somewhere in the rush?

Whatever is true,
whatever is noble,
whatever is right,
whatever is pure,
whatever is lovely,
whatever is admirable—
if anything is excellent or
praiseworthy—
think about such things.

PHILIPPIANS 4:8 (NIV)

20 The Pursuit of Happiness

Less is More.
ROBERT BROWNING

How can we pursue the task of becoming the person we were intended to be?

How can we arrive at the point where we can look at our lives, including our houses, and say, "This is me and it is good." This was Rabbi Zusya's goal. We won't stumble across this. It will not come by accident. We must pursue it deliberately.

Seek Simplicity

Truly successful people are those who know how to seek and find simplicity in life. They seek it because simplicity acts as a unifying force which gives meaning to life.

The Messies Anonymous Mount Vernon method is a starting point for finding a more simple life because it helps us thin out the unnecessary clutter of "things." Some people try to reorganize their overabundance. Ladies' magazines encourage this by showing us how to store things in ever-expanding nooks and crannies. They urge storage of junk. Resist the temptation to pack more in tighter. Instead, take the opportunity to get rid of the clutter that complicates our living.

In addition, in order to simplify our lives, we must Mount Vernon our activities, throwing out or giving others some of the activities that jam our lives together into a mass of busyness. By cutting out unnecessary appointments, insignificant errands, and fruitless activities, we free ourselves from pettiness. Be careful not to use time-management techniques to organize your time so that you can crowd more activities in, to pack them tighter. We need to select only the most valuable activities. And these activities we keep can now take on a significance that they once lost in the hurry of our days. When life is rushed, life's activities then become mere "happenings." We must protect ourselves against this. Just as flowers left to grow in a jumble without being thinned out never reach their potential beauty, our lives left unthinned lose vitality and the ability to develop fully. We crowd our lives into mediocrity. We must thin our gardens for maximum beauty.

Seek Nature

Some of us live in beautiful, strengthening environments. Perhaps you only have to step foot on your porch to see the splendor of mountains and valleys below you. Perhaps if you glance out your window you look down on a panorama of azure and aqua ocean, blending in ever-changing, beautiful patterns. Or perhaps you see a placid lake reflecting like a mirror on still and quiet mornings. If so, you have the marvelous privilege of intertwining yourself with nature at a moment's notice. Most of us, however, are not so blessed. We must go out of our way to seek nature if we are to find it. It is imperative for us to do whatever necessary to seek nature's beauty. All people must regularly experience nature in order to develop into what God intended us to be. It was no mistake that Adam and Eve were put in a garden. We humans are made of the stuff of this earth and to it we return. We do not just walk on earth, we *are* earth. If we travel on too much concrete or stare at too many plaster walls without returning to our source of being periodically, we begin to lose the edge of who we are.

In South Florida, as in many other places, we have our problems with seeking out nature. The tropics, like a highstrung horse, are beautiful and exciting but difficult to live with. The heat, the brightness, the overgrowth of plants, the insects, all combine to drive us indoors, away from nature, into air conditioning and behind screens. Those who visit South Florida may feel that the ocean, palm trees, and sun offer a relaxing interlude, but those who live here long begin to feel the loss of the gentleness of the temperate zones.

In order to see and stay in touch with nature, our family has done several things. We bought a house with thirty feet of windows in the living room. Three of these six-foot windows are from ceiling to floor. Outside the windows, my husband has planted an abundance of tropical foliage. Through the windows we hear the birds, the neighborhood noises, and the splat of raindrops on the palm fronds. Strangely enough, as I write, I am being interrupted by a hailstorm as our rainy season begins. White ice marbles are jumping in the green grass as they hit. Nature is full of surprises.

In order to pull myself out into nature on a daily basis, I use a solar clothes dryer (known to some as a clothesline) instead of an automatic dryer. Because I dry my clothes in the outside air, I must go out regularly. I must feel the heat, the cool, the breeze; and I watch the sky for rain. Nature and I work together on drying clothes.

Our house has no built-in heat. For heat in winter, we use the sun and, occasionally, a small plug-in space heater. For coolness, we use fans and trees planted outside. Our bedroom has an air conditioner but it's seldom used.

We like being close to weather changes. In our house, we live *with* the changes, not against them. I am not, for a minute, suggesting that our way is the best for all people who live in the tropics and certainly not the way those in the temperate zones should live. I am only saying that if each of us is not careful in this technological society, we can seal ourselves so far away from nature that we only come out to use it for recreation. We need to enjoy it and live with it, not just use it, in order to develop ourselves fully. Wherever you are, make it a point to make contact with and seek out nature, preferably alone.

As a child, I walked on Arkansas mud. So firm was the consistency that I could actually walk on the mud without it sticking to my feet or squishing up between my toes. It was wonderful. I remember rowing in a Arkansas pond and looking into the mouths of hissing cottonmouth moccasins around the banks. I remember walking in the black, cool waters of a Florida stream.

I don't know why, but I am better today for these experiences; not because they were in the past, but because they are still a part of me today. We need to continue these healing touches.

Seek a Rhythm of Living

Nature has its rhythms of light and dark. It has its lunar month of twenty-eight days. Earth has its rhythm of seasons. We humans have divided our lives into weeks and calendar months and years in some loose cooperation with the rhythms of nature.

God works in rhythms. We see His rhythms in the nature around us. We also see it in creation where He worked six days and rested one. Following His example and injunction, orthodox Jews have strictly kept the sabbath rest one day out of seven. Life achieves a strong weekly rhythm in this way.

Rhythms give meaning to the movement of life. But for some of us the only rhythm kept is work until exhausted, sleep until awakened to work again until exhausted. We hit the floor running, grabbing coffee to stir us into action faster.

This is the pattern of a runaway life-style. Like music played too fast and without rhythm and pauses, we have a cacophony in our living. What we need to do is to set the metronome slower and follow a steady rhythm complete with significant pauses, called in music, rests.

To set up the rhythms of life requires planning. Gandhi planned to spin each day. Bernard Baruch planned to sit on a park bench each day. We must each plan a pattern to fit our temperament and schedule. I like to begin my day with a pause. Being a morning person, I usually awaken naturally about 5:30 A.M. Most often I arise immediately and go to my living room chair where I spend the next hour alone—no TV, no newspapers. I begin by writing in my journal. This starts my mind on a serene path. I read the Bible and occasionally other inspirational books. I think and pray. It is the fastest hour in the day. I keep no schedule for this hour. It is just my hour alone—but not altogether alone at all. As in Michelangelo's picture of the creation of Adam, I reach out my finger and touch that finger from whom all life flows and I am refreshed.

Too soon it ends. I get the family up, read the paper, make the bed, eat, dress, and leave for work. The tempo quickens, but the early-morning pause has given the day significance. Life rushes in clearer, fuller, more vivid than before.

I also observe Sunday as a day of pause. It gives the week rhythm. The Sunday-morning service is the high point of my week. We have a Sunday dinner as a family, when we get home. We rest in the afternoon and in the evening we go to a church function or watch television if no church function is planned. Once a month, our church family eats dinner together on the church grounds. Nothing special presses on Sunday. That's what's special about it.

The church hour has always been a time for a woman to be alone without distractions. An hour of prayer, meditation, instruction, and beauty. She, like each one at the service, stands solitarily before God. It is a time of significance, a time of re-creation. No bustle of children's demands or husband's needs should intrude because it is a special time.

A life with the metronome set too fast will not be able to fully enjoy this pause, however. Even such a significant aspect of life will become just another obligation—not a pause at all. If our lives are full of fruitless activities already, we will grudgingly awake on Sunday morning tired from a busy Saturday. If we awaken late, we will have to rush to the service after griping at the kids (and maybe husbands) to hurry. It takes half the service to unwind and settle down. When it is over, we rush on to more activities made all the more hectic because of the time we took to go to church.

I've lived this life so I know how fruitless it can become.

To make Sunday satisfying, Saturday has got to slow down. To slow Saturday down, we have to control the weekdays. We must force them to march more slowly, in a more stately manner. Only then are the pauses truly "rests."

Seek Beauty

Wherever they are to be found, seek moments of beauty. Many of these moments may be found alone in nature. Sometimes they surprise us as in sunrises and sunsets, sometimes on vacation trips or quiet walks. It is elsewhere, too.

We can make it a point to look for beauty in reading. I love biographies, autobiographies, or informative and inspirational books. Ordinarily biographies are written about people who have much to share. Much beauty is found there.

I wish I enjoyed fiction because exciting truths can be found in fiction. Each of us has his or her own reading interests. Keep reading, including poetry and informational reading which strengthens you. Paperbacks are great. Turn down their page corners. Mark them. Put notations in the margin or the flyleaf. State pages and their significance. One reason I mention so many books is in order to give some guidance in the shoreless sea of books from which to choose. Avoid mediocrity. It is in reading that we find the highlights and shadows that give depth to what would be an otherwise flat existence.

Another source of beauty is music. Perhaps no other area of life has reached such heights of glorious inspiration, and in contrast, such depths of ugliness. You are blessed if you have developed a taste for lovely, inspirational music. If not, try to develop a love for this kind of music. Attend concerts, buy records. Ask friends whose way of life you admire to tell you the music which is meaningful to them and go from there.

What shall we say about television and movies? There is much junk food of soul there. But there is good as well if we care to look for it. Selective viewing can help us find beauty on TV and in movies.

Finally, there is the house. Simplicity does not preclude beauty; it accentuates it. One reason we must get the house under control is in order to place beauty there. Imagine in your mind your house in order and beautifully appointed. How wonderful it is. Living in it, you are beautiful, too. The home reflects loveliness from within you. It reflects loveliness back to you. Seek that finishing beauty in your life, the beauty of your home.

Seek Quality

We can go through the motions of life without those motions being meaningful to others or ourselves. Only as we deliberately seek quality, will life awaken under the fingers of our activities. Rabbi Zusya felt it. Inside yourself you feel the need for quality as well. Then there will be a reason for housework. It will not just be motion. You are reading this book because you seek a quality life.

A student of Pablo Casals, the world-famous cellist, was bowing the cello notes under the master's supervision. Although she was technically accurate, something was missing from her performance, she knew, as she listened to Casals demonstrate those same notes to her. His notes pulsed and glowed from the bow in his hand.

"Bring it to the rainbow," he urged. "Always to the rainbow." Again and again she sought the rainbow and when she found it, joy and music flowed together from within her.

This is our task: to bring the notes of our lives to the rainbow of quality living through finding simplicity of life-style, relating to nature, establishing a satisfying rhythm of life, and enjoying beauty.

Once we feel the joy and pride of that glow, we can never be the same again. And the house? The house will begin to change naturally and surely from the force of the change within us.

Seek simplicity.
Seek nature.
Seek a rhythm of living.
Seek beauty.
Seek quality.

With regard to excellence,
it is not enough to know,
but we must try to have
and use it.

ARISTOTLE

APPENDIXES

MORE ABOUT THIS MESSIE

As I have told the story of how we can all gain control of our houses, I have frequently referred to my own experiences. Perhaps you would like to have a more orderly story of my life to fit things into.

But let me warn you that this story is rated R. The R stands for *Religious*. So if you don't like religious stuff, don't read any further. If you are curious and do read further, don't say I didn't warn you.

For the sake of the story, we will think of life as a trip of sorts. I think of childhood as preparation for the journey we will take—the journey of adulthood.

When we are packing in childhood for the life we will live, we will need to put as many good things in the suitcase of experience as we can. We must try to look ahead to see what we'll need. As on any long trip, we will need almost everything we pack—and more.

When I was young, I packed what I thought I would need. My tastes were rather classic. I took school seriously. I was also tutored in French and in art in addition to my school subjects. Learning was heady stuff for me and I dove in, packing a love of learning into my bag with relish.

Unknown to me, I was packing other things as well. Somewhere along the way, I packed a very strong-willed nature. I also packed a tendency to react poorly to serious problems. That is, I tended to overreact. If my children got sick, I thought they were dying. When anything bad happened, I thought it was disaster. As you can imagine, I had a difficult time coping.

During my childhood, I had a very religious nature. I went to a parochial school, attended church weekly, and tried to follow, seriously, a moral way of life. I supposed that these things would bring me peace with myself and with God. But it didn't work out that way. No matter how good I tried to be, I had no peace in my heart that things were right between God and me. I suspected they weren't. I felt that my sins were not paid for by my "good" behavior. In short, I carried around a lot of unresolved guilt.

About this time my uncle, who had been seeking his own kind of peace in drinking, gambling, success in business, and hobbies, had an experience with God which transformed his life. In sharing this experience with me, he put his finger directly on the problem. In the Bible, there is a verse that says, "Not by works of righteousness which we have done, but according to his mercy he saved us, by the washing of regeneration, and renewing of the Holy Ghost" (Titus 3:5). Another verse says, "For by grace are ye saved through faith; and that not of yourselves: it is the gift of God: Not of works, lest any man should boast" (Ephesians 2:8, 9). So *that* was the problem! God did not absolve our guilt by weighing our good works against our bad ones. I was going down the wrong road and wondering why I didn't arrive at the right place.

So, at the age of thirteen, in the midst of my packing other things in preparation for adulthood, I put into my bag a strong faith in the sufficiency of Christ's death on the cross to "regenerate" and "save" me. And sure enough, when I quit trying to persuade God to save me and just took the salvation He wanted to give, I found that peace I had been looking for. I packed that in, too, and moved on to a different path.

Year after year I packed, and when I got married at the age of twenty-one I started my independent journey. Of course, as we all do, I continued to pick up a few things as I traveled. But on the whole, I lived from the supplies I had already packed away during childhood.

Right away, I started to pull things from that large bag of stubbornness I mentioned earlier. Stubbornness is not a good commodity to bring into a new marriage when two people are trying to learn to live as one together. But there it was.

I also discovered that I had a large bottle of messiness. Its aura permeated the small apartment in which we lived. This was a surprise to me. Up until that time I had lived within my mother's organized and beautifully maintained home. I had assumed maintenance would come easily to me. It did not. Keeping the house under control was a struggle which was to continue for twenty-three years until I found a method that worked for me. Then I started to share it by founding Messies Anonymous. Now as Messies Anonymous continues to grow I am kept busy providing help for Messies through Messies Anonymous. In addition to helps through the mail, the number of seminars held for church and civic groups is increasing. Self-help support groups are catching on and I envision the day when help is available through these support groups whenever Messies seek encouragement in changing their lives.

However, in those early days, I found something else in my bag that I had not known was there. I had not put it in. It had been packed for me. I was born at a time when the medical profession and the world in general was just discovering the power of radiation. Doctors at that time decided it would add extra protection to the health of newborn babies if they gave a heavy dose of radiation to the thymus glands of those babies. I, like many other babies in more advanced hospitals, received this strong radiation exposure. In later years, this caused a serious problem to many of us.

One day as I was sitting on the couch beside my new minister husband, he said, "What's that lump on your neck?"

"You're kidding."

Sure enough there was a lump. The doctor I consulted said that there was no hurry to remove it. I could wait until my teaching was finished in a couple of months. There was no problem.

When the biopsy came back, however, there *was* a problem. It was thyroid cancer. At twenty-one, I was facing what I thought was certain death. My aunt had just died of cancer.

At this time all of the things I had packed were put to the test. The story is told that when a new ship is tested they take it out to sea, go full steam ahead and then shift it into reverse. Whatever is not tightly attached, falls off. That's what happened to me. A lot of things that were not attached fell off.

It was at that time I found in my bag that inability to handle problems which I mentioned earlier. I had not known it was there before. I also found that the strong desire to have my own way made me angry at the Lord, when I thought about the cancer. Why had He done this to me? I threw a tantrum to show Him how angry I was. But I didn't call it a tantrum; I called it depression. So for several years, the worst years of my life, I fought God over what I considered His mistreatment of me. I didn't realize at the time, that it was this anger at God that was causing my depression. When I realized it, I was ready to "forgive" God and to ask Him to forgive me. I was ready to yield my will to His.

It was a surprise to me that I did not die. The cancer did not recur. Time went by. I continued teaching. Children came. We celebrated our silver anniversary. One day I found another lump.

"No." The doctor was reassuring. "It's probably not a problem. It is a soft lump. I'm sure it's nothing. But we should do a mammogram just because it's good to have it done regularly. I'll make an appointment for you at the hospital."

It was cancer again. This time breast cancer. It resulted in a mastectomy. This time I found more good things in my suitcase to meet the crisis than I had found there before. I found more faith in God's will for my life and less desire to have my own way. I held fast to the verse in Genesis 18:25 which says, ". . . Shall not the Judge of all the earth do right?" I found God's peace in the midst of my problems. Maybe I was finally learning a little about how to travel in this life.

We got it early. There has been no recurrence. This incident reminds us of something very important. When we face death, which is what I do each time the doctor finds a life-threatening disease, it is very important to know which road we are on and where it will end. When I die, as we all do eventually, I am happy to know with certainty that my journey will end in my Father's home.

Jesus said: "In my Father's house are many mansions . . . I am the way, the truth, and the life: no man cometh unto the Father but by me" (John 14:2, 6).

I said earlier that this story was rated R. Perhaps it should be rated X for Xtra special and wonderful. Walking with God down the journey makes life so great—so wonderfully, specially, great.

God bless you as you walk this journey along with the rest of us. May your life be rated Xtra special and wonderful, too.

Appendix:
Ideas That Work—
Motivating Yourself

Inspire Enthusiasm—Have one or two things in your house that focus your interest and enthusiasm—like a shiny toaster, a sparkling bathroom, or whatever fuels your energy.

Do It for Others—Invite company over regularly. Nothing helps you to see what needs to be done better than knowing that guests will come and see your house from a fresh perspective. We tend to see the house from their standpoint when we know they are coming.

Get a Maid—Consider professional help. Wouldn't it be nice, *after* you have gotten organized, to have a maid come in and give the house a special cleaning? If you stay home while she is there, you can tackle some big job you haven't had time for and *really* have the house sparkling.

Switch Jobs—Mop the floor of a friend and have him/her clean your stove. Somehow it isn't as hard to do someone else's house.

Have a Cleaning Party—Have a friend over to sit with you and talk, or to help you, when you are cleaning or doing a special task like organizing a closet. The friend will help encourage you to throw things away. ("Will I need this, Jane? Naw, probably not, I'll throw it away.") Then stop long enough to put things away. Go out to lunch together or go eat the special lunch you fixed the night before to celebrate.

Work With a Time Limit—Do a job by time. Set the timer on your stove, or better still, put on a record. Plan to work for only two or three songs. You may find that once you start you'll go on for a while longer.

If you have a big job, put on a Marine Band album or the "1812 Overture." That will give you enough time and enthusiasm for a huge job.

Give Yourself Rewards—Reward yourself for a job well done. Food is a good reward if you're skinny. Even if you're not, there are some very good foods, like artichokes and crabmeat, that are real treats and not fattening. A piece of jewelry, a day with a friend, or an extravagant soap will do nicely.

Let One Success Lead to Another—Success is the biggest motivator. Once things are under control, beautiful, and convenient, you will not want to return to the old way again. The compliments of family and friends are the fuel that fires our minds, hearts, and bodies. And then there is that bottom line. We like the new way better ourselves.

Still More Tips for Organizing

Several sensible ideas will keep your house moving in the right direction:

Appliances—Beware of appliances. Even when they are "time-saving, easy-to-use," appliances (especially kitchen appliances) have many parts that need cleaning. Many parts also mean that there are more things to lose. The time that you save preparing food may be lost keeping the appliances clean and in order. Be tough: If all you need is a knife, use a knife, not a fancy motorized dicer-slicer-peeler-pulverizer.

Automate—If you know of any automatic products, use them. Some examples are fertilizer spikes that fertilize the plants so you don't have to do it so often. Some new cleaners that you can put in the toilet tank, not the old types that turn the water blue, clean the toilet automatically. Use anything that will lengthen the time between essential jobs.

Finally, START EARLY. For most people an ounce of morning is worth a pound of afternoon.

Also remember:

Early to bed, early to rise,
Makes your house neater than otherwise.

It's this attitude that gets most Cleanies off to such a good start in the morning. So get up, get dressed, and get going.

Bathroom Fixtures—Use liquid cleanser on bathroom fixtures because powdered cleansers dull the finish. If you have a very dirty sink or tub and feel you must use a powder, use Dutch Cleanser, Zud, or Bon Ami, since they have milder abrasives than most.

Books—If you have a large book collection, make the books work for you. Books make great insulation. Put bookshelves on walls that run between rooms to prevent sound from traveling through walls. Great for apartment dwellers. Put bookshelves on the outside walls to help keep the heat inside and the cold outside.

Closets, Cupboards, and Cabinets—Keep them closed. It's amazing how much cleaner a room will look.

Dirty Tub—Clean it right after using, before body oil has a chance to harden. You can even start the cleaning while you are in the tub. Don't use slippery cleanser while you are still in the tub, though. Don't use any harsh cleanser on any tub made before 1964. It will remove the finish. Believe me, I speak from experience.

Dusting—Always dust with a clean clothe. Better yet, make the *kids* use a clean cloth.

Elbow Grease—Something your mother said would clean everything. Origin unknown.

Fresh Air—Makes any room seem cleaner, somehow. An open window with a fresh breeze beats a commercial air freshener any day.

Gloves—Work gloves can make chores much easier and much more tolerable. They also protect your hands and nails from damage, and you won't get the smell of cleansers imbedded in your hands.

Hooks—Should be on the back of every bedroom door, inside every closet door, and inside the back door or wherever your family dumps their belongings. If you mount hooks at kid height, your children will be able to manage their own coats.

Ironing—Instead of ironing, try using a tailor's steamer on your clothes. Available in most department stores, these hand-held appliances work miracles on most wrinkles. Great for travel as well: lightweight, convenient, much better than a travel iron.

Junk—Be brutal when you have to be. Do you really need all those twist ties collecting in your kitchen drawer? If it's junk, name it and treat it accordingly.

Keeping Up With Things—Are you forgetful? Do you leave things lying around? Write your name, address, and phone number on all your small notebooks and other easy-to-lose possessions.

Keys—Keep a tray or small hook by the door to hold your keys. Then remember to put the keys there when you come in. And keep a spare set handy.

Lazy Susan—In addition to its traditional use in the refrigerator to hold condiments, a lazy Susan can make any cabinet or cupboard a place of order. For instance, in a spice cupboard or below a sink, or in a workshop or studio. Allows easy access to many things.

Leftovers—Put a list of leftovers on the refrigerator door. Cross them off as they are used.

Mount Vernon Method—Your personal Declaration of Independence.

Neglect, Don't—Places most often neglected (because you're usually thinking about something else): the bathroom mirror, the telephone, light switch plates, lampshades, the underside of the lid of a step-on garbage can.

One Room, One Purpose—Make it a point to use each room for the function for which it was designed. This means don't take off your shoes in the living room and don't eat in the bedroom. Plan to eat in the dining room or kitchen and undress in the bedroom.

Organizers—Believe it or not, there are people who are professional organizers. They'll organize your closets, your kitchen, your garage—anything. Check the Yellow Pages under "Organizers."

Plastic Ice Trays—Don't wash these in warm water. You will remove something that keeps the ice from sticking. If you already have washed them in hot water, spray lightly with Pam to restore the slick surface.

Pot Holders—Nothing makes a kitchen seem cleaner than spotless pot holders. Unfortunately, they don't stay spotless. Wash them often, and know when to give up and buy new ones (toss out the old ones!).

Questions, Ask—If you know a Cleanie (and who doesn't?), ask her how she solved certain housekeeping and organizing problems. Even if it's your mother. Don't ask general questions—be specific: "How do you keep the cabinet under the sink in such good order?

Refrigeration—The reason they tell you not to use sharp objects to de-ice the refrigerator is because a sharp object could easily puncture the wall and a gas line inside the wall. When you puncture a gas line, you have dealt a death blow to your refrigerator. So now you know.

Ring-Around-the-Collar—Use shampoo on collar and cuff rings. Shampoo is meant to clean body oil, which is what that ring is.

Sheets—Get a different color set for every bed in the house. One set/one bed. When you change the sheets, don't put on a new set and throw the old set in the basement for washing. Wash the set you took off immediately and put it back on the bed it came off of. No folding, no laundry buildup.

Shelf Lining—Use sheet linoleum (you can buy it in smaller pieces at places like K-Mart) to line your shelves. If you have a kitchen cabinet that has an open space above the top cabinet, be sure to cover this or it will get REALLY dirty and greasy.

Stand It Up—There is more air space than surface space, so it is a good idea to stand up anything that can stand up rather than lay it on a table, desk, chair, or sofa.

This is particularly true of magazines. If you have several special issues, make a magazine holder from a cereal box. Cover the cereal box with wood grain Con-Tact paper. It will look like a library box. Then place the magazines in it and put it on a bookshelf so that magazines are standing up instead of laying down.

If your drawers are crowded, consider hanging up your nightgowns or anything that can be hung up. This is the same principle in a different form.

Storing Sheets—When you fold your sheets, fold the sheets and the pillowcases in one bundle, with the flat sheet covering them all. Then you can grab the whole set to be put on the bed with one hand.

Teenagers—Great source of energy. You can hire teens to help you with your yard work and general cleaning for very little money. There are often places you can post cards at local high schools or colleges, if you are looking for help. Be sure you know what you want done, listing specific jobs and the realistic time involved.

Umbrellas—Most Messies despair of ever having umbrellas when they need them. Buy cheap ones. Keep one in the car, one in the office, one in the house. Periodically look around and see if two are in one place. If so, carry one back to its own home.

Vacuum Easier—Use an upright vacuum like Regina, Hoover, or Eureka. The uprights are so much easier to put away and get out that you will be inclined to vacuum more often because it's not "too much trouble" to get this kind of vacuum out for a little job. If you have an upstairs, keep one of the lightweight upright vacuums that can be hung from the wall in an upstairs closet on the second floor for easy access.

Vinyl—Don't put oil on vinyl to make it soft and shiny. It will eventually harden it and cause it to split. There are good vinyl protectors on the market. Grocery stores, drug stores, and auto supply stores carry them.

Volunteer—Not yet. Postpone your volunteer activities until you have your own house in order. Then be selective in your volunteering.

Waxing the Bathroom—You can use wax like Turtle Wax to polish and wax bathroom fixtures (not the inside of the tub, please). You can also use Pledge or other furniture polish to wax the ceramic tile if you wish. Just be sure that wax does not make any area in the bathroom slippery.

Window Cleaning—Use a squeegee and water spray. This is the easiest way. Also use a squeegee on the walls of your shower. It will keep water spots and soap deposits from building up.

Windows—Washing windows on a dreary winter's day gives you a new outlook on life. There's nothing like getting the dog's nose prints off a big window to make you feel the whole room is clean.

Xerox—Type up a basic grocery list containing all those products you consider absolutely essential to your pantry. Put it in the same order that the store you shop is in. Leave blanks for additional things you will need from time to time. Then Xerox the list. You can check off the things you need, writing your additions in—and off you go.

Yard Sale—Yard sales are to Messies what bakeries are to dieters. Dangerous? Irresistible! So don't go. Or if you must, don't take any money with you.

Zipper-top bags—Great for organizing children's toys that have a million pieces. Also for safekeeping of valuable pieces of hardware your husband has entrusted you with, spare buttons, and so forth.

Books are no substitute for living but they can add immeasurably to its richness.

MAY HILL ARBUTHNOT

Books on Housekeeping

Aslett, Don. *Is There Life after Housework?* Cincinnati: Writer's Digest Books, 1981.

An absolute must as a "how to" book on cleaning. Not to be used until you have become organized enough to get around to these jobs he tells us how to do so quickly and so well.

Brace, Pam, and Jones, Peggy. *Sidetracked Home Executives, from Pigpen to Paradise.* Vancouver: Binford and Mort, 1979.

This is a funny, helpful approach that works for people who have a housekeeping problem. Furthermore, the writers speak from experience.

Conran, Shirley. *Superwoman, For Every Woman Who Hates Housework.* New York: Crown Publishers, Inc., 1978.

This is a big, expensive book that ends up sounding as if it was written for women who love housework. It has some helpful items, however, and covers many topics.

Editors of Consumer Guide. *The Fastest, Cheapest, Best Way to Clean Everything.* New York, Fireside, Simon & Schuster, 1982.

If I could buy only three books on housekeeping, this would be one of them. It names brands and tells how to use them. By the way, the other two books I'd buy would be *The Messies Manual* and *Is There Life after Housework?*

McBride, Pat. *How to Get Your Act Together when Nobody Gave You the Script.* Nashville, TN: Thomas Nelson Publishers, 1982.

A clearly written book dealing with time management as it applies to the home. A good supplement to reading on this subject.

McCullough, Bonnie Runyan. *Bonnie's Household Organizer.* New York: St. Martin's Press, 1980.

This work is especially valuable because it has four chapters on training children and it is strong in the areas of creating storage space and organizing cupboards.

McCullough, Bonnie Runyan, and Monson, Susan Walker. *401 Ways to Get your Kids to Work at Home.* New York: St. Martin's Press, 1981.

This book touches on and explains further many of the ideas mentioned in *The Messies Manual.* It's good.

Pinkham, Mary Ellen. *Mary Ellen's Best of Helpful Hints.* New York: Warner Books, 1980.

Lots of hints about lots of things, helpfully indexed. There will be many ideas you can use.

Winston, Stephanie. *Getting Organized.* New York: Warner Books, 1978.

One of the best books I have found on the subject, it is widely know and frequently mentioned in the paper. A strong and valuable section is the one called *Time and Paperwork* since it deals with how to handle the various paper items that come into the house and group themselves in little piles.

More Reading

Aslett, Don.
Do I Dust or Vacuum First? Cincinnati: Writer's Digest Books, 1982.

Aslett, Don.
    Clutter's Last Stand. Cincinnati: Writer's Digest Books, 1983.

Casewit, Curtis W. *Diary: A Complete Guide To Journal Writing.* Allen, TX: Argus Communications, 1981.

MacDonald, Gordon. *Ordering Your Private World.* Nashville, TN: Thomas Nelson Publishers, 1985.

Peterson, Jean Ross. *Organize Your Personal Finances: Turn Chaos into Cash.* Whitehall, VA: Betterway Publications, Inc.

Pinkham, Mary Ellen.
    Mary Ellen's Best of Helpful Hints, Book 2. New York: Warner Books, 1981.
    Mary Ellen's Best of Helpful Kitchen Hints. New York: Warner Books, 1980.
    Mary Ellen's One Thousand New Helpful Hints. New York: Doubleday & Company, 1983.

Rushford, Patricia H. *From Money Mess to Money Management.* Old Tappan, NJ: Fleming H. Revell Publishers, 1984.

Waitley, Denis E. *Seeds of Greatness: The 10 Best-Kept Secrets of Total Success.* Old Tappan, NJ: Fleming H. Revell Publishers, 1983.

Young, Pam, and Jones, Peggy.
    Sidetracked Home Executives. New York: Warner Books, 1981.
    Sidetracked Sisters Catch-Up on the Kitchen. New York: Warner Books, 1983.

Winston, Stephanie.
    Getting Organized. New York: Warner Books, 1980.
    Getting Organized: Storage. New York: Warner Books, 1981.

To obtain further help from Messies Anonymous, write to:

Messies Anonymous
5025 S. W. 114th Avenue
Miami, FL 33165